Qualitative Research for Physical Culture

D1593439

Also by Pirkko Markula

WOMEN AND EXERCISE: The body, Health and Consumerism (*co-edited*)

OLYMPIC WOMEN AND THE MEDIA: International Perspectives (*edited*)

CRITICAL BODIES: Representations, Identities and Practices of Weight and Body Management (*co-edited*)

FEMINIST SPORT STUDIES: Sharing Joy, Sharing Pain (*edited*)

FOUCAULT, SPORT AND EXERCISE:
Power, Knowledge and Transforming the Self (*co-authored*)

MOVING WRITING: Crafting Movement for Sport Research (*co-edited*)

Also by Michael Silk

SPORT AND NEOLIBERALISM (*co-authored*)

CORPORATE NATIONALISM: Sport, Cultural Identity and Transnational Marketing (*co-edited*)

QUALITATIVE METHODS FOR SPORTS STUDIES (*co-edited*)

Qualitative Research for Physical Culture

Pirkko Markula
University of Alberta, Canada

Michael Silk
University of Bath, UK

First published 2011 by
PALGRAVE MACMILLAN

Palgrave Macmillan in the UK is an imprint of Macmillan Publishers Limited, registered in England, company number 785998, of Houndmills, Basingstoke, Hampshire RG21 6XS.

Palgrave Macmillan in the US is a division of St Martin's Press LLC, 175 Fifth Avenue, New York, NY 10010.

Palgrave Macmillan is the global academic imprint of the above companies and has companies and representatives throughout the world.

Palgrave® and Macmillan® are registered trademarks in the United States, the United Kingdom, Europe and other countries

ISBN 978–0–230–23023–1   hardback
ISBN 978–0–230–23024–8   paperback

A catalogue record for this book is available from the British Library.

A catalog record for this book is available from the Library of Congress.

10   9   8   7   6   5   4   3   2   1
20 19 18 17 16 15 14 13 12 11

Transferred to Digital Printing in 2014

Contents

List of Tables

List of Figures

List of Boxes

Preface: The 7Ps of Qualitative Research

Purpose of the book

Physical culture as a field includes several scholarly disciplines, such as adaptive physical activity, dance studies, leisure studies, outdoor education, physical cultural studies, physical education, recreation, sport development, sport history, sport management, sport pedagogy, sport philosophy, sport policy, sport and exercise psychology, and the sociology of sport. All of these disciplines have utilised qualitative methods to examine various expressions, experiences and structures of the physical. Like the field of physical culture, qualitative research includes multiple research designs, methods and ways of presenting this type of research. These different, sometimes contradictory and messy, understandings of what counts as good qualitative research can be extremely confusing for students and scholars. This book is designed to aid qualitative researchers in negotiating some of these meanings as they take their journeys through the research process. To make sense of this multiplicity and to offer guidance for researchers and students across the interdisciplinary field of physical culture, we have structured the book based on our experiences as teachers and researchers of **designing**, **doing**, and **disseminating** qualitative research. To make further sense of the qualitative research process, we have divided it into **7Ps: Purpose, Paradigms, Process, Practice, Politics of Interpretation, Presentation** and **the Promise** of qualitative research. Below we explain the structure of the book in more detail.

The first 3 Ps – **Purpose**, **Paradigms** and **Process** – relate to the design of the research process. By this, we mean the plan and structure of the qualitative research project.

Purpose: Why should a researcher engage in qualitative research? To map, to critique or to create social change? What are the ethical considerations? What kinds of qualitative research are meaningful?
Paradigms: What specific parameters does the qualitative researcher choose for the research project? Post-positivist, humanist, poststructuralist/modern?
Process: How does a qualitative research project look? Each project should include some form of to include an introduction, literature review, method section, analysis/discussion and conclusion.

Because the collection of empirical material and its interpretation are difficult to separate, we have combined the next 2 Ps – **Practices** and **Politics of Interpretation** – together in a set of chapters that outline common methodological practices and ways in which to interpret empirical material in qualitative physical culture studies.

> **Practice and the Politics of Interpretation: Interviewing**: What are different types of interviews? How are they used? How are they analysed?
> **Practice and the Politics of Interpretation: Textual Analysis**: What are the different types of textual analyses? How are they used? How are they analysed?
> **Practice and the Politics of Interpretation: Narrative Analysis**: What is narrative analysis? How is it practised? How is empirical material from narratives analysed?
> **Practice and the Politics of Interpretation: Field Methods**: What are the different types of field methods? How are they used? How is empirical material from field methods analysed?

The final 2Ps – **Presentation and The Promise** – consider the process of writing and disseminating qualitative research. Further, we consider how to judge qualitative research and to what standards the work should be held.

> **Presentation**: What are the different ways of writing-up qualitative research results? What are the various ways in which qualitative research can be **presented** to diverse audiences – dissertation committee, grant bodies, journal editorial board, established conventions of academic research, communities outside of academia.
> **The Promise**: What is good quality qualitative research? Given that qualitative research includes multiple ways of approaching, understanding and conducting research, what are the multiple criteria by which to judge the quality of such research and how to choose between such criteria.

How to use this book

While the 7Ps offer a general pathway through the journey of qualitative research, researchers with different levels of experience engage in qualitative research for multiple reasons. Consequently, while the 7Ps approach aims to map out an entire research project in a comprehensive manner, certain components of the text will be more valuable for some readers, while other sections more useful for others. It is important to note that all the 7Ps are interrelated, but some might take precedence over others during certain qualitative projects. In addition, researchers at different points of their research careers might find different Ps more relevant.

The undergraduate researcher who embarks on a qualitative research project for the very first time, may find it relevant to start with the process (Chapter 3) of doing research to gain an overarching picture of what a research project may look like and how it could be constructed. In addition, these researchers might focus on learning how to practise the different qualitative methods (or practices) (Chapters 4–7) before engaging in a discussion of the different paradigmatic approaches.

The more experienced graduate researchers will need to have a greater understanding of how their research is philosophically grounded within the parameters of certain paradigmatic approaches. They could, thus, attend more closely to the discussion in Chapter 2 and consider how the methodological practices, the interpretation of the empirical material and the judgement of their work are underpinned by the paradigmatic considerations.

Given that the field of physical culture is informed by many different academic disciplines, a researcher wishing to be introduced to the logic of qualitative methodologies may well focus on the discussion of paradigms in Chapter 2 and their connections to various methodological practices (Chapters 4–7). Seasoned academics already familiar with the structure of qualitative research might consider such aspects of qualitative research as employing previously unfamiliar forms of qualitative methods or using alternative forms of writing style (Chapter 8). Meanwhile, researchers interested in the political purpose (see Chapter 1) of their project would likely address the various links between the purpose and the promise to which their work might be held (Chapter 9). Finally, as this book is offered as a teaching tool for various research methods courses, it should provide an invaluable tool for researchers to guide their students.

Acknowledgements

Pirkko Markula: I would like to thank the students in PERLS 581 course for providing the initial inspiration for this book. I am particularly thankful for Nike Ayo, Marianne Clark, Jennifer Hardes and Judy Liao, who provided extremely valuable feedback during the writing process. In addition, I would like to acknowledge the Faculty of Physical Education and Recreation at the University of Alberta for providing the necessary academic support for me to complete this book. I am also deeply indebted to my previous fellow graduate students at the Department of Kinesiology at the University of Illinois at Urbana-Champaign, my advisor Synthia Sydnor, and Norman Denzin, whose initial belief and support for qualitative work in physical culture has been my continual inspiration. Finally, I would like to extend personal thanks to Jim Denison, whose reflections on qualitative research and alternative ways of writing and whose personal support have made writing this book possible.

Michael Silk: There are a number of colleagues and students with whom I have had healthy debate concerning research methodology. Professor Ann Hall stimulated this interest seventeen years ago when I took her 'research methods' class at the University of Alberta. Since then, colleagues, especially, John Amis, David Andrews and Anthony Bush, and former and current graduate students such as Perry Cohen, Jess Francombe, Andrew Grainger and Josh Newman have ensured that continued discussion about the philosophy of research is kept alive. I owe a considerable debt to those who have produced the numerous research texts and articles that provide the basis for this book; the work of Norman Denzin continues to inspire. There are a number of groups of students who have endured previous drafts of this text and provided invaluable feedback. In part, the text of this book comes out of the final year 'Undergraduate Research Seminar' students in the Department of Education at the University of Bath. Finally, and as ever, my wife Jennie and my daughter Nancy put up with me during the inspiring (and not so inspiring!) moments involved in producing this text.

Part I
Design

In this section, we address three of the 7 Ps of qualitative research: **Purpose, Paradigms and Process**. Chapter 1 focuses on the *purpose* of research. For example, we ask readers to consider why they are planning to engage in qualitative research. Who will be influenced by the results? What kind of qualitative research is meaningful? We also consider the ethics of conducting qualitative research. In Chapter 2, we consider the role of *paradigmatic approaches* to qualitative research in physical culture and what the paradigmatic parameters mean for the research process. It is likely that qualitative researchers will find themselves carefully negotiating paradigmatic boundaries when defining the purpose and practice for their research. We then introduce the actual *process* of doing physical cultural research in Chapter 3.

1
The Purpose of Research in Physical Culture

In this chapter, we will

- Introduce the term qualitative research;
- Introduce the term physical culture;
- Discuss the possible purposes for qualitative research in physical culture;
- Discuss the ethical conduct of qualitative research in physical culture.

Within this chapter we offer an entry point into the conduct of qualitative research by focusing on the *purpose* of qualitative research. Why is this work important? What will it say that has any value? Is this project meaningful, and if so, to whom? The purpose of research will frame its design, practice and presentation. Qualitative researchers may undertake a piece of research to convince policy makers, to alter public opinion, to drive consumption of a product, to provide evidence on an issue, to expose instances of injustice, to offer competing voices or points of view, to interrogate taken-for-granted ideas or assumptions, to save lives, to make people 'better' (physically, socially), or to advance understanding of a particular phenomenon. While we do not value one purpose over another, it is important to have a clear purpose that will guide the researcher through the entire conduct of the research. Before it is possible to define a purpose, it is important to understand the terms 'qualitative research' and 'physical culture'.

Understanding qualitative research

Qualitative research has evolved over several decades across several scholarly disciplines. Norman Denzin and Yvonna Lincoln observe that while qualitative research can be understood as a field of its own right, complex assumptions surround the term as it 'crosscuts disciplines, fields, and subject matters' (2005, p. 2). It is obvious that with such diversity, qualitative research must be understood against the historical context of each discipline and/or field. However, Denzin and Lincoln offer a definition of qualitative research which includes the following components:

- The 'situated' qualitative researcher;
- Multiple material practices;
- Interpretation of meanings.

We will now discuss each of these characteristics in more detail.

The qualitative researcher

A qualitative researcher is understood as an observer in the world, but always as a 'situated' observer. It is openly acknowledged that the researcher's background and situation influence the research process and shape the research results. Nevertheless, researchers should be aware of their impact through carefully reflecting on the meaning of their part in the process: how do they construct their projects and why do they choose to act in certain ways? Therefore, while qualitative researchers might have multiple aims and purposes, they need to be open about their subjective influences and their reasons for engaging in research. Such a researcher needs to be well immersed in both theoretical and methodological concerns. Denzin and Lincoln note that a qualitative researcher 'works between and within competing and overlapping perspectives and paradigms' (2005, p. 6). Therefore, it is important to be familiar with several different qualitative approaches. We discuss qualitative research paradigms in Chapter 2 to help researchers of physical culture to negotiate the jungle of competing approaches in an informed manner. Denzin and Lincoln summarise that 'qualitative researchers stress the socially constructed nature of reality, the intimate relationship between the researcher and what is studied, and the situational constraints that shape the inquiry' (ibid., p. 10). We elaborate on the role of the researcher in qualitative research in physical culture in Chapter 3.

Multiple qualitative practices

Qualitative research is characterised by multiple methodological approaches and practices. As Denzin and Lincoln note: 'Qualitative research, as a set of interpretive activities, privileges no single methodological practice over another' (2005, p. 6). For example, qualitative researchers can employ such methods as interviews, textual analysis or narrative, or engage in a 'field' of physical culture more directly by using such methods as case study or ethnography. Often qualitative researchers combine more than one qualitative method to 'situate' better the activity under interest within its context. In any case, the meaning of collecting empirical material is to 'make the world visible' as qualitative researchers 'turn the world into a series of representations' (Denzin & Lincoln, 2005, p. 3). We discuss these multiple qualitative methods in Chapters 4–7 and the ways of representing qualitative research in Chapter 8. While qualitative researchers might use multiple methods simultaneously, they adopt one paradigmatic stance at a time.

Qualitative interpretation

Qualitative research practices are designed for an 'interpretive, naturalistic approach to the world' (Denzin & Lincoln, 2005, p. 3). This means that qualitative researchers seek information 'directly' from the phenomenon in question by asking people, observing actual situations or interpreting what people have written. Unlike quantitative researchers, who often focus on artificially controlled laboratory situations or mail out pre-validated questionnaires, qualitative researchers have to often venture 'out to the world' to interact directly with people and events to obtain empirical material for their studies. They 'make sense of, or interpret, phenomena in terms of the meanings people bring to them' (ibid.). In qualitative research, the emphasis is placed on 'the qualities of entities and on processes and meanings that are not experimentally examined or measured' (ibid.).

In summary, in this book we understand qualitative research as an interdisciplinary field that cuts across several disciplines and fields of research. In addition, qualitative research is multiparadigmatic in nature and is sensitive to multiple practices for collecting empirical material to make the world visible. Qualitative researchers see the world as socially constructed and understand their research as an interaction between researchers, participants and what is studied. Qualitative research is historically and contextually situated within the fields of research. Consequently, throughout this text, we will highlight a variety of qualitative research practices for physical culture, but emphasise the need for a theoretical vocabulary for interpreting any particular aspect of physical culture under scrutiny.

Understanding qualitative research in physical culture

As Denzin and Lincoln (2005) have asserted, qualitative research cuts across several disciplines and several subject matters. The subject matter that crosscuts this book is physical culture. We understand *physical culture* to include multiple forms of *being physically (in)active*. Such practices as exercise, dance, fitness, health, movement, recreation, work, elite sport, recreational sport or coaching sport can engage the physically active body. Researchers in different disciplines are interested in researching physical culture.

Exercise physiology and biomechanics, for example, are disciplines that specialise in the physiological ability and the mechanics of the physical body. Sport medicine and sport nutrition examine how the performance of the human body can be enhanced through preventing injuries or providing optimal nutrition to athletes or other physically (in)active people. They favour laboratory techniques with small samples or large scale, quantitative surveys to collect their information. The disciplines that provide laboratory results related to the physical functioning of the human body are generally classified as **natural sciences** (for further discussion of the principles of this type of research see Chapter 2). There are also a number of **social sciences** that examine physical culture. The social sciences are interested in how physically active 'bodies' act in particular social and cultural environments. Traditionally, disciplines such as physical education, sport history, sport philosophy, sport and exercise psychology, sport management, sport sociology, and adapted physical activity are included in the social science of physical activity. In addition, other areas such as leisure studies, recreation, health and physical activity, sport policy studies, sport coaching, and sport media and journalism have emerged around the topic of physical activity.

Most practitioners of physical culture need information from more than one discipline. For example, physical education teachers, fitness leaders and coaches need to understand the functioning of the physical body as well as how the individual becomes motivated and learns to practice movements. In addition, they need to be aware of funding, marketing, media relations, the social and cultural standing of their profession and the physical culture they represent. For example, to create a training programme coaches need to understand the physiology of stress, work and recovery as well as the dynamics of effective leadership and how to manage different types of people with whom they need to interact. For example, coaching an unfit beginner with low self-esteem would be very different from coaching an elite athlete.

Furthermore, coaches need to understand the institution that employs them, the human relationships within it and how it is located within a particular social or organisational context that will determine funding possibilities. For example, working for a 'minor' sport will not provide the same sponsorship possibilities, spectators and television deals as a 'major' sport provides. Most researchers of physical culture specialise, however, in one aspect of physical culture and tend to choose between natural sciences and social sciences, and further between the different disciplines within each. In this book, we focus on the social sciences. Social science researchers of physical culture can use quantitative methods (see Chapters 2 and 3 for a more detailed discussion of quantitative social science research) or qualitative methods.

It is important to note that qualitative research is a more recent development than its more established quantitative sibling. Therefore, in some physical culture disciplines quantitative research is perceived as the predominant way of conducting research and, thus, some researchers have only been educated in quantitative methods. In addition, quantitative research might be 'valued' in a particular department or among one's peers. Governmental policy makers often prefer quantitative, 'evidence based' research to support their actions and often governmental grant agencies prefer to fund quantitative research that they define as most useful. Despite the dominance of quantitative research in certain disciplines of physical culture, qualitative research has become increasingly popular in sport and exercise psychology, sport history, sport management and adaptive physical activity, whereas physical education and sport sociology already have a strong tradition of qualitative research.

As detailed by Denzin and Lincoln (2005), qualitative researchers of physical culture also openly acknowledge their subjective influence on the research project and embrace multiple qualitative methods to interpret the meanings embodied in physically active bodies in various social, historical and political contexts. They focus on identifying how experiences become meaningful within certain social and historical contexts. These qualitative social scientists are interested in *how bodies matter* at certain points in time and in certain situations. In other words, qualitative social scientists of the physically active body often aim to understand how individual moments of physicality (e.g., sport, dance, movement, the coaching moment, physical education) are shaped within the social context.

While qualitative social scientists of physical culture embrace multiple movement forms, contexts and meanings, they also need to engage in *meaningful* research that has a clear purpose. The articulation of a purpose can take different forms depending often on the researcher's paradigmatic stance (see Chapter 2 for further explanation of the paradigms). However, each research project should be, in one way or another, meaningful: it should matter to someone.

The purpose of qualitative research of physical culture: Mapping, critique and social change

To further encourage research 'that matters' and the development of a strong purpose, we provide three possible purposes for a good qualitative research project: mapping, critique and/or social change. These purposes can overlap. For example, one research project might achieve more than one purpose. In addition, there might be other reasons why a researcher takes up an investigation. Nevertheless, these three guides are intended to aid a researcher to produce a purposeful, qualitative social science research project.

Mapping refers to a research project that aims to provide a general overview or 'topography' of a behaviour, phenomenon, practice or 'field' of physical culture. This is particularly meaningful when not much is previously known about the topic. To create a map of this 'landscape', the researcher needs to draw the relationships between the different facets of the phenomenon under investigation, highlight the differences and impact of each relationship and then link the map with those previously drawn. For example, one might be interested in describing such less examined, rare or niche sports as orienteering, ultimate Frisbee or women's ski jumping, or such exercise forms as Zumba, for which there is not much research information. To provide a map of any of these physical activities, the researcher needs to look at the different relationships that enabled the activity to be born, map who is currently involved, why these particular types of people have chosen to participate, and draw lines that connect the 'new' activity with the landscape of related 'old' sports, and, indeed, with the social forces that allowed an emergence of a new form of activity at this particular point of time. For example, a researcher may well want to think through how a 'sport' such as Red Bull Air Racing has been created and the social forces (e.g., commercialism, sponsorship, a consumer economy, tourism) that have impacted upon this. Or the researcher might want to map why obese children do not want to participate in physical activity. In such a project, the researcher needs to draw a map that connects the social meanings about 'fat', physical activity and children's desire to move, into one picture or map. The researcher would first need to trace how (children's) obesity has been defined (and by whom) and how it has become a 'problem' worthy of investigation in the current culture. In addition, the researcher needs to describe who the obese children are, why they are physically inactive and what do they like to do in their everyday lives. To examine the relationship between these issues, the researcher would need to examine how physical (in)activity is defined (and by whom), how it is connected to obesity, and why children dislike physical inactivity. These projects that map the general features of a practice of physical culture, are often necessary before the researcher is able to critique or illustrate a need for change.

Critique refers to projects that provide a social critique of a behaviour, phenomenon, practice or 'field' of physical culture. In these cases, the researcher has identified a 'problem' beforehand, for example, through previous research literature that has provided a map of the topic at hand. For example, a researcher has identified that certain sports are only accessible to certain populations, which, the researcher determines, is a problem because everyone should have a right to participate in a sport of their choice. The researcher might determine that, for example, youth soccer is available only for highly skilled boys from upper-class areas where there is a well funded, competitive youth coach to maintain a programme. The researcher can then provide a critique of such limited access because it excludes girls, disabled, low-income players and participants who do not want to play competitively. Or the researcher might critique, based on a research project, the ways different elite sports are funded. Or a researcher may want to examine why women athletes, despite their growing numbers, are seldom a part of sport reporting, and the ones that appear in the sport news are selected more for their appearance than their athletic prowess or sporting experience. The researcher can then provide a critique that explains such a practice of exclusion. It is important to note, however, that critique does not necessary lead to change in the situation that was examined.

Social change refers to research projects that provide clear suggestions or praxis for creating social change. To engage in such a project, the researcher would usually have to have knowledge of previous research that mapped the behaviour, phenomenon, practice or 'field' of physical culture as well as how this has been critiqued. Again, this could be through understanding previous research, through knowledge gained by doing the project or through the ways physical activity is currently practised in the social context that the researcher aims to change. Against such a background, the suggestions for social change become more meaningful. For example, a researcher interested in women's fitness can find enough previous research that maps how exercise works as a practice to promote a type of 'ideal' 'feminine' body that characterises the field of fitness. There are also several published academic critiques of the impossible, thin, toned and young feminine body ideal that is often the goal of women's exercise practices. Therefore, it is meaningful to engage in a research project that aims to provide alternative exercise purposes and thus, change the ways in which fitness is socially constructed primarily as a 'workout' for sculpting a culturally defined body 'ideal' or 'norm'.

Purposeful qualitative research projects, whether they map, critique and/ or create social change, do not exist in isolation. As they are related to previous academic literatures, they also exist within an array of (fluid) disciplinary boundaries that might prefer particular types of methodological practices. As mentioned earlier, some researchers are opposed to qualitative research because they do not have sufficient knowledge of qualitative methods, they find qualitative research a 'threat' to their research, they do not want to reflect on the purpose of their own research or they simply do not want to know about or accept any other way of doing research from their own. While these are not very sound grounds for rejecting qualitative research, they are, nevertheless, real. We refer to such resistance as the 'politics' of qualitative research. Consequently, all research is always *political*, whether the researcher likes to admit it or not, in a sense that it will have an impact either on the researcher's academic discipline, a broader field of physical culture, or on individual's (including the researcher's) lives. These politics manifest in qualitative researchers' everyday working environment in multiple ways.

In case one faces strong resistance to conducting qualitative research, there are several possible ways to react to the situation. Sometimes it might be best to yield. For example, if one's research supervisor has strong objections, prejudice and no qualifications in qualitative research, it might be best to conduct a good quality, quantitative study instead. Alternatively, one could look for a new, more like-minded research supervisor, department or institution (perhaps more apt at the graduate level). However, in some of the more traditional disciplines of physical culture, it is more difficult to get qualitative research accepted. In a safe case, one should go with the 'flow', but one can also switch to a discipline with a more developed understanding of current trends in social science where it is possible to conduct good qualitative research within a positive environment. If a researcher is located within a quantitative discipline and has little knowledge of but a desire to know more about qualitative research, one can also proceed carefully by first experimenting with combining quantitative and qualitative research and progressing gradually towards qualitative research. This is often called the 'mixed-methods' approach (see Denscombe, 2007). It is important to emphasise, however, that different types of research should be judged on criteria developed specifically for their type (see Chapter 9). Consequently, there exists 'good' and 'bad' quantitative research, similar to 'good' and 'bad' qualitative research, and the merit of each needs to be determined based on the purpose of the research rather than through mutual comparisons.

We do not promote one, universally acceptable, privileged way of conducting (qualitative) research on physical culture. We are far more interested in – and feel that there is greater progressive potential in – a field that is in tension, in healthy contestation and in debates surrounding the purpose of research and its subsequent impact on method, interpretation and (re)presentation of research. Nevertheless, we want to promote self-reflexive researchers who engage in research that matters. This requires sound knowledge of both quantitative and qualitative research logics and an ability to make informed choices within the institutional constraints of academia. We do hope that qualitative researchers are able to think about purposeful research that is *meaningful* to a range of communities. We suggest that qualitative research into physical culture is characterised by a plurality of research purposes within an environment in which diverse positions exist alongside one another and foster multiple methodological approaches. Meaningful qualitative research should also be meaningful for its participants: it should be conducted in a manner that is sensitive to the needs of its participants. This sensitivity refers to research ethics.

Ethical approaches to qualitative research in physical culture

Everyone conducting social science research on 'human subjects' will be involved in research ethics. While the term 'research ethics' has evoked varying responses from the large and diverse community of social sciences researchers, research ethics refers to guidelines that are developed to ensure that all research participants are treated with dignity and respect. These guidelines suggest that all research should be conducted in a manner that is not harmful for the participants or the researcher.

The current thinking on ethics regarding research that involves human subjects (or participants) stems from the Nuremberg trials after World War II. In these trials, some Nazi scientists were examined with regard to their experiments involving Jewish prisoners. These prisoners were not informed about the procedures of the experiments; neither were they asked if they wanted to participate and the participants certainly did not benefit from the research. Some died. Based on these trials, the so-called Nuremberg code for ethical standards for biomedical research was developed. To further clarify the ethics of biomedical research, The World Medical Association verified the Declaration of Helsinki in 1964.

Box 1.1 The Nuremberg code

- Voluntary consent is essential
  - o Capacity, opportunity, power of participant
  - o Extent, possible outcomes of research must be identified
- The research must yield results that are 'good' for society or at least a subset of society
- The research must be justified on the basis of previous research
- The research must avoid all necessary suffering or injury
- Death or disability can not be expected at all
- Risk should never exceed humanitarian benefit
- Any risk should be avoided through facilities and preparation
- Research should only conducted by scientifically qualified persons
- The participants have the right to withdraw or end the study at any time
- The researcher has the responsibility to end the study if it appears that death, injury or disability might be outcomes of further participation

Modified from McNamee, Olivier & Wainwright (2007).

The current understanding of research ethics therefore stems from ethical abuses by scientists and is thus designed to combat such misconduct, particularly in biomedical research (McNamee, Olivier & Wainwright, 2007). To ensure ethical conduct that is more appropriate for social science research, many disciplinary organisations have developed their own 'ethical standards' and many social science researchers are expected to refer to the ethical requirements of their professional body (e.g., the British Sociological Association standards of ethical research or the British Psychological Association standards of ethical research). The established guidelines provided by a professional association, however, have not always ensured the ethical conduct of the research, as often the ethical principles do not translate into actual practices that would ensure dignity and respect for the participants. For example, the mere mention of having read the ethical standards recommended by one's disciplinary association does not mean that the researchers actually take any action to treat their participants ethically. Consequently, many universities, faculties or departments have established research ethics boards. For example, Institutional Research Boards (IRB) in the USA, and Research Ethics Boards (REB) in Canada provide ethical approval for research. Although it is difficult to offer any form of standardised structure, often REBs and IRBs are multidisciplinary and their academic members represent different research paradigms. In Canada, the REBs are usually constituted of academic staff, community representatives and student representatives (for the structure of IRBs, see McNamee, Olivier & Wainwright, 2007). The members of the board might or might not have expertise in each researcher's particular research topic or methodology. Consequently, some qualitative researchers are critical of these boards.

These critics argue that the boards link 'the philosophy' behind ethical concerns with a need to preserve the values of quantitative research as universally accepted criteria for good social science (e.g., Christians, 2000; 2005). Lincoln (2005) claims that the IRBs in the USA base their conduct primarily on ethics for biomedical research, which provides unsuitable criteria for qualitative research and promotes politically correct research aligned with neo-liberal, conservative agendas. McNamee, Olivier and Wainwright (2007) also acknowledge that qualitative researchers might be disadvantaged if the boards assess whether the researchers have asked 'right' quantitative research questions, whether the study can answer these questions, whether the study will provide valuable knowledge and whether there are enough participants for statistical analysis (McNamee, Olivier & Wainwright, 2007). Nevertheless, the quality of qualitative research cannot be judged by quantitative standards (see Chapter 9 for judgement criteria for qualitative research) and as judgements of quality do not concern research ethics per se, the ethics board should not provide judgement criteria for any research. Therefore, **the role of an ethics board** should be to assess the **ethical conduct** in the research, **not the quality** of each research project. While bad quality research might also be unethical research, the primary task of the ethics boards is to help the researcher ensure that the project will be conducted in an ethical manner that is sensitive to the participants' and the researchers' rights. Sometimes a research project might be designed up to the best research standards, but nevertheless would not be deemed ethically acceptable. For example, the Nazi medical experiments in concentration camps were conducted with the best validity and reliability for logical empirical research, yet would hardly be considered ethical, not least given that the participants did not consent and were not treated with dignity and respect (McNamee, Olivier & Wainwright, 2007). Indeed, if qualitative researchers believed that their research was assessed based on its methodological stance (e.g., using qualitative methods and subjective epistemology) instead of its ethical conduct, they would have the right to point out this misperception to the board and ask for a re-review. For example, in Canada the research tri-councils (the three main research funding councils) have published ethical guidelines for research that state how ethical standards should be assessed. Each researcher would refer to these guidelines to ensure that their application is treated fairly by the ethics board.

The most important aspect of research ethics (i.e., to treat participants with dignity and respect) is to engage explicitly in the practice of ethical conduct (not only to refer to it) and, in the resulting publications (whether student work, thesis, published article, book chapter or book) be able to articulate clearly how one practised ethical research. Consequently, ethical research conduct, while not necessarily similar to quantitative research, is also vital for qualitative researchers who use human subjects. It is imperative that these researchers find out what the ethical approval process is at their university. The ethical guidelines will differ in different cultural contexts, but most of the westernised universities adhere to similar ethical principles. We use the Canadian tri-council ethical guidelines for qualitative research as an example to highlight the main principles of ethical research conduct.

In Canada, ethical research conduct refers to procedures that are to ensure that all research participants are treated with dignity and respect. Respect for human dignity is seen to be accomplished through adherence to the following principles:

- Respect for dignity;
- Free and informed consent;
- Vulnerable persons;
- Privacy and confidentiality;
- Justice and inclusiveness.

We discuss each of the principle in turn, explaining what they mean in the practice of qualitative research: what are the actual 'measures' that each researcher needs to take to ensure that the project is ethical?

Respect for dignity

As already stated, respect for human dignity is the base for all other principles of ethical research conduct. The actual definitions of respect can differ in different cultures, but in most westernised cultures this principle is based on the ideal of individual autonomy: a right to individual self-governance. McNamee, Olivier and Wainwright (2007) further define such aspects as freedom from controlling influences and a capacity for intentional actions as parts of individual autonomy. This concept of individual autonomy further translates into a principle of respect: a researcher must respect a participant's individual autonomy. This concept has good and bad points, but it is, nevertheless, a defining principle in many western countries and not only for research ethics. Not all cultures have individual autonomy as a defining principle for respect. Therefore, if one is planning a research project within a culture with a definition of respect that differs from the principles listed here, one needs to find out an alternative, culture-specific definition and the principles that follow it. The absence of westernised ethical principles does not mean that the researcher can now ignore all ethical concerns and simply embark on the project. On the contrary, it means extra work and time spent familiarising oneself with the cultural context and a careful development of an ethics procedure that respects the dignity of the participants as they define it.

Some critics connect the principle of individual autonomy to a neo-liberal ideology of individualism and thus believe that adhering to research ethics based on such a concept further preserves conservative research practices (e.g., Christians, 2005; Denzin, 2003). They favour a so-called communitarian model that stresses the benefit of the group instead of an individual. In this model, 'the community is ontologically and axiologically prior to persons' (Christians, 2005, p. 150). In addition, a communitarian model aligns with the benefits of research to the community instead of the avoidance of harm or misconduct as the starting point for research ethics. As Christians explains: 'In communitarianism, conceptions of the good are shared by the research subjects, and researchers collaborate in bringing these definitions into their own' (2005, p. 157). This approach is particularly suitable for research projects employing participatory action research that focuses on the entire community (see Chapter 7). However, most qualitative research projects do not necessarily focus on a clearly defined 'community'. Even if they did, it is often difficult to find a consensus on what exactly benefits the entire group. Because it is possible to emphasise the benefits of qualitative research by slightly modifying the 'traditional' ethics process, it is often the most suitable for most qualitative research projects that have diverse participants. In any case, a qualitative research project following the ethical principles based on individual autonomy is more respectful for the participants than a research project with no concern for ethics at all. In addition, participants in westernised countries most likely expect a certain degree of respect for their autonomy since it is a defining principle in most of these societies. We will, therefore, detail the most common ethical principles based on the respect for individual dignity. Again, we have aimed to discuss these as specific to qualitative research projects.

Free and informed consent

This principle refers to the Nuremberg code's principle of participants having to agree knowingly to take part in the research project. They should not be forced and should have received sufficient information of the research project to be able to make an informed choice regarding their participation. Therefore, the researcher must be able to demonstrate that each participant has voluntarily decided to become involved in the study. To ensure that this principle is adhered to, the ethics board usually first wants to know how the researcher plans to **contact the participants**. While the initial contact can take place in many ways (e.g., an informal verbal contact, an email contact, a formal information letter, through an informant or a contact person), it is important to be able to explain explicitly how the first contact will take place and what the initial message will contain. To ensure that each participant has been fully informed about the project, the researcher should prepare a written **information sheet** or provide evidence of verbal information given to the participants. It is a good idea to seek feedback from the ethics board regarding the suitability of the information letter and many ethics boards request to see such letters with the ethics application. It is therefore obvious that one needs to prepare one's research ethics before conducting the actual project.

It is common that academic researchers, immersed in their own context, use theoretical language that is incomprehensible to the intended participants unless they are other academics. Therefore, to obtain a 'truly' informed consent, it is very important to be able to explain the project in the language of the participants, not simply to repeat one's research proposal, thesis proposal or grant application text in this letter. In addition, the information letter should be short enough (usually no more than 1 page) for the participants to read in a convenient amount of time. In the information letter or sheet, the researcher should explain the purpose of the research; what is required from the participants (e.g., an interview that takes about one hour) and how the researcher intends to follow the ethical guidelines (e.g., voluntariness of participation, benefits of participation, privacy and confidentiality, and inclusiveness – we explain these principles further below) in a comprehensible manner. In addition, the researcher should explain how and when the participants obtain this information and how they provide their consent to participate. Again, it is important to understand that the purpose of preparing an information letter in advance is not to bother the researcher with unnecessary and time consuming procedures that only complicate their already busy schedule, but to think how the participants can be treated in an ethical manner. The idea is not to question the researcher's integrity or the meaningfulness of the research topic at hand, but to ponder why anyone should participate in the researcher's project and how this participation is beneficial and safe to the participants.

To demonstrate that the participants have indeed voluntarily, knowingly and freely decided to participate in a research project, the researcher should obtain their 'consent'. This consent can be implied, obtained verbally or it can be in a written, signed form. In any case, the researcher should retain evidence that such consent was obtained from each participant. An implied consent can be used, for example, in questionnaire research where the participants consent by filling out the survey form. If they decline their consent, they simply do not return the form. Verbal consent can be used in situations (e.g., during field work) where signing a written consent would be awkward or unsuitable or when the participants are not comfortable reading or signing a written consent form. However, the researcher needs to retain some evidence that this actually happened (e.g., by audio-taping the consent 'situation'). However, the most common form of obtaining consent is through signing a written consent form. Through this form, the researcher needs to obtain consent for the participation and it thus needs to contain all the information that the participant has agreed to (e.g., to audio-tape an interview, to use a pseudonym to ensure privacy) and also to ensure that the participant has been well informed about the project and indeed is taking part voluntarily in it. Many ethics boards provide model 'consent forms' that researchers can modify for their own use. However, it is important to have a consent procedure prepared with one's ethics application to ensure that the actual research situation is ethically handled. In some research projects (e.g., participatory action research) where community based rights (rather than individual autonomy) are appropriate premise for research ethnics, the researcher needs to seek other ways of ensuring that the community's rights, rather than individual's rights, are respected (see Christians, 2005).

The participant also has a right to **withdraw** from the study or withdraw from providing certain information for the study. How the researcher intends to observe this right needs to be clearly indicated in the information letter and the consent form.

Vulnerable persons

Research ethics should particularly ensure the dignity and respect of persons who have diminished competence to make decisions. These are research participants that are particularly vulnerable for misuse. Children, the disabled, the elderly, the poor or other individuals who do not have the means, education or ability fully to comprehend the research purpose can be understood as vulnerable participants. Research among these participants usually requires special procedures that protect their interests. Consequently studying, for example, children in physical education classes, requires a rather elaborate ethical process that in many countries includes obtaining consent from the university, school board, parents, children, and increasingly in the British context, from authorities such as the police who will provide a criminal records search on the researcher. Sometimes, a guardian can provide consent for vulnerable persons. Again, having to be extra careful with making sure that the dignity of these persons is respected should not prevent one from conducting such research, but should make the researcher think carefully how their research project can be meaningful for these people as well as the research community.

Privacy and confidentiality

This principle refers to the participants' right not to be identified in the research project. McNamee, Olivier and Wainwright (2007) note that there is often confusion between the principles of confidentiality and anonymity. In the strictest sense, assuring complete confidentiality would mean that the researcher never shares any of the empirical material obtained in the research project with anyone. This is, of course, impossible, because the researcher could never publish any findings from the project. Therefore, McNamee, Olivier and Wainwright (2007) emphasise that it is important to be clear that what is actually assured is anonymity. Qualitative research that often focuses on personal issues, feelings, life events, problems, crises or ideas, participants are particularly vulnerable to 'invasion of privacy, unwanted identification, breach of confidentiality and trust, misrepresentation and exploitation' (McNamee, Olivier & Wainwright, 2007, p. 145). While not all participants want to be anonymous, most prefer not have their names or anything else that identifies them included in the final, written research project. Neither is the researcher, most of time, interested in a particular participant's experiences or thoughts, but is looking to map themes or critique or change an issue about which the participant can provide nuances, information or opinions. Naturally, life history research or autobiographically based research are exceptions where the participant(s) might need to be named. The most common way of providing privacy is to use a pseudonym (a false name) for each participant and the research setting (e.g., the school, sport club, university, fitness club). Usually, the cultural setting (e.g., the country where the research was conducted) is provided to account for the cultural diversity of the results. Sometimes it is not possible to 'mask' the participants' identities due to their very public standing (e.g., famous sportspeople), but then the researcher must negotiate this with the participants to clearly explain how the risk of being identified is handled in the project.

To ensure the privacy of the research further, the research information must be kept confidential. This means that the researcher must clearly stipulate who has access to empirical material that is attributed to the participants. For example, it should be made clear who can listen to the original audio-taped interviews from which the participants might be recognisable. Usually researchers limit this access to just themselves (and a possible transcriber) to limit the risk of loss of confidentiality. In addition, the participants need to know where the empirical material is kept and how it is to be used in order to be assured that what they say or write is used for the purpose that the researcher has identified in the information letter/sheet and not for any other purpose without their knowledge and consent. All this information should be included in the consent obtained from the participants.

Justice and inclusiveness

This principle refers to the 'beneficence' of the research project: a qualitative research project should provide some benefits for the participants. A key ethical principle concerns the distribution of benefits and costs of research in such a manner that no segment of the population is unfairly burdened by the research. Occasionally, some groups, usually minority groups, attract such a quantity of research interest that it becomes a burden to their lives. For example, in Canada some of the small Northern aboriginal tribes have researchers continually investigating their lives. In other contexts, some schools might become over-burdened by constant requests for all types of research, ranging from student projects to large-scale research projects, so that their 'normal' functioning is interrupted by the constant presence of one or more researchers. In this sense, it is important to consider in advance what benefits one's study provides to the participants, particularly to vulnerable individuals.

In general, it is ethical to consider the benefits and harms of the research for its participants. This parallels our research approach that urges the researcher, before embarking to the actual project, to provide a clear purpose for the project: to whom is this research meaningful. Sometimes, one's research project might not immediately provide tangible benefits for its participants as it is designed to challenge theoretical thinking in one's discipline. Nevertheless, a meaningful research project, if it uses human participants, should provide some benefit for its participants. The researcher should be able to articulate clearly the benefits in the information letter/sheet to the participants.

In addition, the researcher should clearly indicate any possible harmful effects of the research project. These can range from physical (e.g., risks of taking blood for research purposes) to psychological or other harms. A risk of psychological harm can refer, for example, to an interview in which the participant is asked about 'sensitive' issues, such as sexual harassment or abuse, sexual orientation, suffering from illness, grief or another troubled period of life, participation in crime or illegal behaviour, or any other aspect that might cause mental distress. Other harms can refer to the distress, disorientation or disturbance that the research can create in participants' lives or in their community. For example, a researcher might consider whether participant observation is destructive to a sport team that is trying to prepare for an important competition. Naturally, any research project should minimise the harm and maximise the benefits to its participants (and the researcher). Nevertheless, the researcher needs to detail the possible harms to the participants and also provide measures to deal with the risks of the research. For example, an interview research with eating disordered athletes might exacerbate the symptoms (but might also have therapeutic effects) and an inexperienced researcher should not engage in such a project. In case of a relapse due to participation in research, the researcher needs to be able to provide access to counselling to offset the harms of the interview. The interviewees need to be clearly informed by the risks, but also the counselling service to make an informed choice of their participation.

In summary, a meaningful research project is also an ethically conducted research project. While adhering to ethics requires thinking of the participants' best interests in addition to one's own research interests, it will also result in a better project because it dismantles the binary between the researcher as an arrogant, superior expert who has the right to any 'data' and the passive, 'brainless' participant whose sole task to give the researcher what they want. Therefore, it is important to prepare one's ethical procedures carefully even if it requires extra time. As with all aspects of research, doing it the first time is the most difficult, but understanding the principles – why one should go through all those procedures – should help justify the need for ethically conducted research. At the same time, the purpose of ethics is not to prevent research. Instead, ethical conduct is a matter of thinking creatively about how the researcher's interest might match respect for the participants' dignity. With proper ethical conduct, research in physical culture becomes a more democratic practice that is pedagogically, politically, theoretically and ethically informative for the researcher and the participants alike.

Box 1.2 Ethical dilemmas for qualitative researchers

Case 1

You are writing a life history of a successful long distance runner for your dissertation. She has agreed to be interviewed. During the interviews you develop a good rapport and your interest and enthusiasm in her running career really impresses the runner. However, after transcribing the interviews, you feel that you would like to supplement your interview data with some participant observation. Your participant has no problem as you got along really well previously and she invites you to follow her to one of her competition trips. During the trip, you cannot help but notice that she only drinks coffee in the morning, skips lunch and has only salad for dinner. In the interview, however, she told you that she meticulously fills in a food diary. You start suspecting that she suffers from anorexia nervosa. What should you do?

Case 2

You are interested in examining how sport can create long-lasting friendships. You have decided to interview some of your teammates from college with whom you still keep in touch regularly. During the interviews, the participants also begin to talk about you and how they were afraid of you as the captain, how you publicly embarrassed them if they made mistakes and were very angry with them if they didn't perform well. They talk about how they found you a very controlling personality. How should you react?

Case 3

You have conducted participant observation and interviews in a yoga class. In the informed consent form you state that you will let the interviewees read the results section of your dissertation before you hand it in. You have decided to represent your findings through a piece of fiction in which you have constructed a character who exemplifies some of the most important aspects of your findings. One participant reads it and, claiming that it does not represent him and what he has said, now wants to withdraw from the study. What should you do now?

Case 4

You are conducting participant observation in a sport team. Initially you have found it difficult to blend in and get the athletes to talk to you. You are, however, finally getting to be included in their conversations. One day you are talking with a group of athletes and one of them tells a homophobic joke and everyone laughs. You laugh along, like everybody else. The manager, however, has overheard the conversation, thinks it is inappropriate and demands that you leave the setting because you seem to solicit such talk within the team. What should you do?

Case 5

You interview a fellow athlete to talk about the process of drug testing in your sport. Turns out that the athlete uses drugs, because, as he says, everyone does and what he uses aren't really drugs anyway. You are really against any kind of doping. How should you deal with this information?

Case 6

You have been granted permission to interview a coach and a set of young talented athletes with whom he works. Initially, the purpose of the project was to find out participants' views about the training programme and how these can be fed into producing a better programme. However, as you talked to the young athletes, you begin to build up a picture of disenchantment and emotional and physical abuse. The coach has asked to meet you to discuss what his athletes have told you. What should you do to safeguard the participants? If you inform the coach, how may he react? Who will benefit? What will happen to the research project?

Summary

In this chapter, we have introduced the terms qualitative research and physical culture to highlight how qualitative methodological practices can be meaningfully combined with the subject matter of physicalculture. Qualitative researchers of physical culture embrace the characteristics of qualitative research – the situated researcher using multiple methods to analyse multiple context specific experiences and meanings – to look into the ways individuals make sense of different physical activities in different social contexts. A meaningful qualitative research project nevertheless requires researchers to determine a clear purpose for conducting a particular type of research on a particular topic. We identified three broad ways of thinking about a purpose – mapping, critiquing and/or creating social change – for qualitative research projects. These are provided as general guides for identifying a meaningful qualitative research project, not as categories within which each research project must fit. Finally, we discussed the ethical conduct of qualitative research, which is an integral aspect of purposeful qualitative research that is likely to 'make a difference'. In short, purposeful qualitative research aims to produce ethical and meaningful work on physical culture. At the same time, meaningful qualitative research is characterised by diversity and the challenges that arise from the politics of research in the multidisciplinary field of physical culture. These challenges continue to shape, refine and create qualitative research practice. Because qualitative research is somewhat of a contested term, there are multiple varieties and definitions that depend on the purpose and paradigmatic orientation of the researcher. In the next chapter, we detail the notion of 'paradigm' and explain how qualitative researchers might locate themselves within these logics.

2
Paradigmatic Approaches to Physical Culture

In this chapter, we will

- Introduce the term paradigm;
- Discuss post-positivism as a paradigmatic approach to qualitative social science;
- Discuss anti-positivist approaches – humanism and poststructuralism/ postmodernism – as paradigmatic approaches to qualitative social science.

> The practice of social inquiry cannot be adequately defined as an atheoretical making that requires only methodological prowess.
>
> (Schwandt, 2000, p. 190).

As Schwandt indicates, there is more to the design of a study than just choosing a method or tool. The actual practices used by qualitative researchers in the field are underscored by our second P: *paradigms*. Paradigms provide the orientations towards how researchers see the world (ontology), and the various judgements about knowledge and how to gain it (epistemology). Together ontological and epistemological assumptions form the philosophical parameters that guide decisions on appropriate methodological practices that will allow the investigation of particular instances of physical culture. In this regard, paradigms guide all aspects of undertaking research (questions asked, ethical stances, research actions, methods choices, writing choices, relationships to the participants, judgement of the quality of research). In this chapter, we turn to the paradigmatic frameworks that make up the world of research design.

The research paradigms: Ontological, epistemological and methodological approaches

The history of 'science' has been replete with tension over the 'correct' or 'valid' ways through which to approach a research enquiry. This recognition speaks to a deeply entrenched, and at times quite bitter, battle within the field of research design: the debate over legitimate research designs and methodologies.

It was the work of Thomas Kuhn that brought the concept of the paradigm into the popular lexicon of research design. Kuhn (1970) suggests that a paradigm is the entire constellation of beliefs, values and techniques shared by the members of a given scholastic community. Denzin and Lincoln (2005) further propose that a paradigm encompasses axiology (questions of ethics within the social world), ontology (the nature of reality and the nature of the human being in the world), epistemology (how one knows the world and the relationship between the knower and the known) and methodology (the best means or practices for gaining knowledge about the world).

Box 2.1 Paradigm definition

A paradigm is an overarching set of beliefs that provides the parameters – how researchers understand reality and the nature of truth, how they understand what is knowledge, how they act and the role they undertake, how they understand participants and how they disseminate knowledge – of a given research project.

Paradigms are important because they provide the boundaries for the researcher's ethics and values, actions in the social world, the control of the study (who initiates the work, and asks questions), the voices deployed in the accounts of the research and, indeed, the very basic and fundamental understanding of the world the researcher is investigating. This means that researchers of physical culture also need to be clear about what they believe is the 'real' world where physical culture exists (ontology), how they can know or understand this world (epistemology) and how they can obtain knowledge about it (methodological practices). However, not all researchers of physical culture will share the same paradigmatic approach and certain paradigmatic approaches tend to dominate a given field of study, thus providing the set of beliefs guiding the researchers' actions (Denzin & Lincoln, 2005).

Paradigmatic approaches to studying social science

As we have already indicated, social science research is comprised of not one but several paradigmatic approaches. The most important thing is not necessarily to judge which paradigm is the 'best' in the entire field of social science, but rather what paradigmatic logic 'best' works with the research purpose. All the paradigmatic approaches have their limitations and often 'new' paradigms emerge out of a critique of existing ones. Therefore, it is important that researchers locate themselves in the paradigm that best fits their purpose as they carefully, critically and reflexively choose between the different options. For each researcher to make an informed choice, we present the basic logics of each paradigm and also provide a brief account of how different paradigms have developed from each other. We want also to emphasise that we provide our reading of the nature of the social science paradigms. While this reading combines several attempts to trace the nature of paradigms, there are also other, often disciplinary-specific ways, to read the paradigmatic logics. In the table below (Table 2.1) we present one way of making sense of numerous ways of understanding the world of social science paradigms. We then detail the logic of each paradigm in more detail.

Table 2.1   Different paradigms

Paradigm				
logical empiricism	logical positivism	post positivism	humanism interpretive critical	poststructuralism/ postmodernism
Ontology				
one reality	one reality	one reality soft realism	one reality critical realism historical realism	multiple realities
one truth	one truth	one truth	one truth	multiple truths
Epistemology				
Objective	objective	objective/ subjective	subjective	subjective
Methodology				
quantitative	quantitative	quantitative qualitative	qualitative	qualitative

Logical empiricism and logical positivism:
The quantitative research logic

Logical empiricism refers to the logic of natural science research. This type of research focuses on examining through objective research conducted in laboratory settings how natural phenomena occur. Such natural science disciplines as biology, engineering, bio-medical research and physiology base their research on this logic. Consequently, exercise physiology and biomechanics follow a logical empiricist research paradigm. The social sciences, which focus on human behaviour rather than natural phenomena per se, also first followed the established logic of empiricism. However, human behaviour is not as easily dissected, experimented with or detected within laboratory settings similar to those used by the natural sciences and, thus, the social sciences adapted empirical logic to suit their own special needs. This meant that the ontology – the belief that the meaning of research was to understand and detect how things 'truly' happen – remained. As any subjective influence hampers the researcher's ability to find this reality, the research had to remain objective (epistemology). However, new methods, such as surveys, structured interviews or objective observations were added. All the methods were quantitative so that the researcher could objectively generalise the findings to represent 'the' reality. This quantitative social science research is referred to as **logical positivism** or **positivism**. This approach is based on acontextual, formal and standardised research that seeks analytically to separate distinct variables in an effort to prove causality – cause and effect. In other words, through formal measurement and conceptualising the social world as a system of variables, positivism traces facts or causes of certain phenomena, a truth that can be objectively obtained through the rigorous testing of hypotheses. As such, positivist researchers distance themselves from the particular phenomena under investigation, searching for a reality that is entirely independent of their opinions about certain phenomena: a measurable and objective reality that determines a universal truth.

In the research of physical culture, such varied approaches as large-scale surveys, analysis of media content or physical activity interventions come under the umbrella term of positivism. For example, a researcher can send out a questionnaire to a large randomly sampled population to test if increased promotion of physical activity has increased physical activity levels and reduced obesity levels. Or a researcher can analyse a large sample of media texts to test statistically the hypothesis that women athletes receive less media coverage than male athletes. Or a researcher can test the hypothesis that exercising with a peer mentor motivates the physically inactive to engage in continued exercise through an exercise intervention. This requires two groups: a group that engages in the exercise intervention with the peer mentor and a control group that has no peer mentor, but is provided with the same written exercise information as the intervention group. In addition, the researcher needs to measure the motivation levels before and after the intervention with the pre-validated questionnaire to provide an objective measurement of motivation. After a statistical analysis the researcher can then assert or negate that the presence of a peer mentor increased motivation (causality). See Chapter 3 for more examples of the deductive, quantitative logic of positivist research. To summarise, the positivist physical culture researcher investigates isolated variables to discover generalisable information that illustrates a universal truth. As such, a positivist epistemology is centred on controlled data collection, objective distance between the researcher and the subject, quantitative measurement, hypothesis testing and statistical analysis to prove direct causality.

Denzin and Lincoln (2005) refer to this moment in the development of social sciences as the *traditional* period, which is characterised by attempts to analyse human beings objectively. While positivism is the earliest clearly defined paradigmatic approach to the social sciences, it is by no means invisible. On the contrary, it still dominates many social science disciplines that favour quantitative research. It is important to note, however, that positivism is only one paradigm through which social scientists examine the world. Therefore, it is no more a 'true', 'authentic' or 'correct' way of conducting social science research than any other way. In addition it is important, if one adopts this paradigm, to follow its quantitative logic, which means that positivists, like other social science researchers, need to be aware of the philosophical underpinnings of their research. See Chapter 3 for more detailed discussion of the deductive logic of logical positivism. Nevertheless, as we are more interested in qualitative methods in this book, we now detail the paradigms that use qualitative research methods more carefully.

Post-positivism: Combining quantitative and qualitative research methods

Much of the history of research design, and indeed much of the current debate, centres around a quest by various groups of scholars to 'prove' that their way of conducting research is *the correct*, and thereby only, way to investigate the matter at hand. Therefore, there have also been critics of the foundational beliefs of positivism. Is it possible, for example, to totally detach oneself from the research? Or, is it possible to always find clear causes in human behaviour? For example, although previous research has demonstrated that most individuals know that physical activity is good for their health, the majority of the population remains inactive. How can this be explained? Surely everyone under- stands that it is good be healthy. Or why do the majority of exercisers quit their exercise programmes after 2 weeks even when they know that exercise is beneficial for them? Why does increased knowledge not lead to improved behaviour? Such questions lead to *post-positivist* work that often combines both quantitative and qualitative methods (Denzin & Lincoln, 1994; Guba & Lincoln, 1994). Denzin and Lincoln characterise this moment as the *modernist* phase, which is dominated by the collec- tion of qualitative data, which researchers attempt to fit to the canons of positivism (Denzin & Lincoln, 1994; 2005).

Post-positivists point out several shortcomings of quantitative research pertaining to research on human behaviour. Based on Guba and Lincoln's (1994) discussion we highlight some of these shortcomings to illustrate the paradigmatic logic that characterises post-positivism. First, quantitative research requires tight control of variables to obtain precise results. Therefore, research is often conducted in strictly control- led settings like laboratories or through strictly controlled methods like questionnaires. However, this research design can exclude variables that exist in the actual context and that might greatly alter one's results. For example, when some researchers have measured levels of physical activity, they have defined physical activity to include only moderate and high intensity exercise. Therefore, a person who walks two hours at low intensity every day will be reported as physically inactive despite engaging in a great deal of activity. It also means that the results can be properly applied only in other laboratory situations. For example, if an athlete's laboratory test results show higher VO2 max levels for him, they certainly indicate that his cardiovascular fitness has improved, but this does not mean that he can obtain his personal best in his next race because of multiple factors, such as mental pressures, the weather or other competitors' interference, present in the actual competition situ- ation. In addition, while generalisations based on quantitative research can be statistically meaningful, they do not have applicability in each individual case. For example, even if peer mentoring is statistically linked to increased exercise motivation, this does not apply to every individual case, as some exercisers might prefer to exercise alone and hate to be continually monitored by someone else. Consequently, post-positivists argue for qualitative data that is collected in more **natural settings**. Second, the post-positivist critics argue that quantitative methods tend to exclude the **meaning** and purposes attached by human actors to their activities (Guba & Lincoln, 1994). For example, while surveys on physical activity levels might indicate how often and at what intensity people exercise, they say little about what physical activity means in people's lives, what different ideas they attach to the ways they exercise, how they experience their physically active bodies and what exercise might mean for them in the first place. Third, post-positivists have identified a disjunction between the researcher's theoretical views and participants' everyday understandings. The theoretical approaches and hypotheses based on theory tend to have little meaning for the participants whose behaviour is investigated. For example, physically (in)active people might define physical activity very differently from the researchers who definitions invariably draw from the causal link between increased exercise and illness prevention. However, post-positivist critics point out, for theories to be valid they should be strongly **grounded** on the views of the people investigated, not only on the theoretical, scholarly literature. These critiques have led to the development of a grounded theory approach, spearheaded by the work of Glaser and Strauss (Glaser, 1992; Glaser & Strauss, 1967), to social enquiry. These researchers enter into natural settings, such as an exercise class, sport field or natural park, to obtain any data, using a variety of methods such as observation, informal interviews and/or textual analysis. Based on this data, they develop theories grounded on phenomena in their natural setting instead of theory-led research. We discuss the methodological implications of grounded theory in Chapter 3. In addition to grounded theory, qualitative data are often used to generate further research hypotheses for quantitative research. Such data sets are then used to develop questionnaires, concepts or ideas for further research. For example, a researcher interested in motivating currently inactive, obese children to exercise, might interview currently active children to obtain concepts and ideas that work with children as population and then develop a questionnaire.

In summary, post-positivist researchers promote qualitative research to accommodate the influence of natural exercise settings, to include participants' meanings and purposes, and to ground theories more firmly on participants' views. They assert that including qualitative methods in the study sufficiently addresses the shortcomings of quantitative research (Markula, Grant & Denison, 2001). Guba and Lincoln (1994) label their criticism an intra-paradigmatic critique, because although it points to problems inherent in quantitative research, it remains within the parameters of conventional positivist research: like quantitative researchers, post-positivists emphasise the importance of discovering a single theory with which to explain their results and stress external and internal validity when evaluating the research. Their main concern is to make a methodological adjustment, not to challenge the basic assumptions (ontology and epistemology) of positivist research.

Post-positivists, however, struggle with efforts to make round pegs fit into square holes: they use qualitative methods – such as observation – to test positivist theories. While post-positivists favour the use of some qualitative methods, like quantitative researchers, they still assume that knowledge that counts as legitimate research must be collected objectively. To remain objective, therefore, the researcher's influence on the results has to be minimised. Lather summarises that post-positivist research controls the values of the researcher and minimises the influence of the researcher in the research process in order to obtain precise, unbiased results. These limitations have led to further developments towards paradigmatic frameworks suitable specifically for qualitative work.

Anti-positivist paradigms: Humanism, postmodernism and poststructuralism

With the post-positivists' intraparadigmatic critique, it became obvious that the hallmarks of positivist social science are not well suited to capture the myriad perspectives or the contextual character of human interaction in the social world (Hammersley, 1989). The recognition of these limitations framed the emergence of the so-called interpretive turn that advocated human action and meaning in the construction of the social world as of primary importance to social science research (Hollands, 1985). The *interpretive* paradigm is founded upon the premise that the social world is complex, that people, including researchers and their research participants, define their own meanings. The aim of an interpretive project is to understand the individuals' behaviours, meanings and experiences within particular social settings. Qualitative methodologies centred on observation, participation, texts, conversation, interpretation, narrative and small scale and local interaction provide the approaches to gathering knowledge of multiple individual experiences.

Similarly to post-positivism, the interpretive turn provided the space for thinking about many of the inadequacies of positivism for understanding contextual human experience. However, many researchers wanted to move beyond intra-paradigmatic critique to define qualitative research in much broader terms. In addition to change in methodological practices, these researchers challenged the basic epistemological assumptions of positivist and post-positivist research. Denzin and Lincoln (2005) refer to this moment as the ***blurred or interpretive*** phase during which a range of theoretical narratives (e.g., symbolic interactionism, ethnomethodology, neo-Marxism, feminism, racial and ethnic theories) brought into question the 'golden age' of positivist social science.

Through their critique of objective knowledge production (the epistemology) extra-paradigmatic critics call for new understandings of social science research. They argue that objectivity is an impossible and unnecessary requirement because scientifically observed 'facts' are seriously influenced by the theory that defines the frame for the research and the statistical procedures through which the researchers 'work the data' (Markula, Grant & Denison, 2001). Because theory provides a focus for positivist research, scientific theories are constructions based on observation of only selected aspects of the 'reality', rather than objective observation itself. In addition, research on human subjects is interactive in nature: the researchers influence the results and the results influence the researchers. For example, when participants answer a physical activity survey, their answers are influenced by the researcher who has included only certain questions in the survey. Their answers, at the same time, influence the researcher's statistical and theoretical analysis. If a researcher is conducting an exercise intervention or has entered a sport field, school or leisure setting, this interaction is even more tangible. In these conditions knowledge, instead of being value-free, neutral and objective, is, in fact, created by the people involved in the research process. As Guba and Lincoln summarise: 'the notion that findings are created through the interaction of inquirer and phenomenon (which, in social sciences, is usually people), is often a more plausible description of the inquiry process than is the notion that findings are discovered through objective observation "as they really are, and as they really work"' (1994, p. 107).

Due to these criticisms, new forms of research knowledge, unlimited by objectivity, have emerged. Proponents of this type of research challenge the claims for objectivity and value-neutrality that are at the heart of the natural sciences and positivist and post-positivist enquiry. Some scholars label these approaches collectively as anti-positivist (Burrell & Morgan, 1979). Others, influenced by the interpretive turn we discussed earlier, call them 'interpretive' (Gratton & Jones, 2004) or yet some others, influenced by Denzin and Lincoln's (2005) moments of qualitative research, call them 'postmodern' as they all challenge that 'modernist' phase of post-positivism. We use the term anti-positivist as in this context we understand 'interpretive' as a part of the humanist paradigm rather than collective term for all qualitative social science research. While all these paradigms see social science as a subjective rather than an objective enterprise, they also contest each other's assumptions regarding research ontology, the role of the researcher in the research process, the nature of the interaction between the individual and society, and the nature of the human self in social science research. In this book, we have organised our discussion of anti-positivist paradigms into humanist (interpretive and critical) and postmodern or poststructuralist paradigms. To clarify their distinctions, we begin with the philosophical and theoretical premise of the interpretive paradigm.

Humanism: Interpretive paradigm

Interpretive researchers consider all knowledge fundamentally subjective and therefore, the research process is also subjective and interactive: humans create knowledge through a subjective meaning-making process. Some refer to this paradigm as the *constructivist* paradigm as it is based on individual and collective reconstructions of knowledge (e.g., Guba & Lincoln, 1989; Manning, 1997). Constructivist enquiry assumes a relativist ontology (individuals construct multiple meanings of reality), subjectivist epistemology (interactive researcher/participant knowledge-making process) and hermeneutic methodology (mutual construction of research products) (Manning, 1997). This means that constructivist researchers see the reality emerging from the research as co-constructed with the participants. The orientation is thus to the production of reconstructed understandings of the social world (Denzin & Lincoln, 2005). However, these researchers assert that certain interpretations of reality are more plausible than others when considering the specific context of the study (Kvale, 1992; Manning, 1997). For example, a constructivist enquiry of physical culture might focus on how individuals make multiple meanings out of their experiences of being injured in sport. These understandings of injury become more understandable against each participant's sporting background, the severity of the injury and their individual backgrounds. For example, it is likely that an elite sportsman who, after a spinal cord injury, becomes paralysed has different experiences and meanings than a recreational naturegoer who twists her ankle during a hike. Ethically, the interpretive paradigm often aims to reveal instances of various individual problems such as illness or abuse. In constructivist enquiry, the researcher and the people studied are engaged in an intersubjective and circumstantial dialogue in which it is acknowledged that the research participants affect the researcher and the researcher has an impact on the participants. Manning explains that the relationship between the participants and the researcher 'is interactive in the way the researcher's questions, observations, and comments shape the respondents' actions, whereas the respondents' answers and explorations influence the meaning ascribed and interpretation negotiated by the researcher' (1997, p. 96). For example, when a researcher is investigating sport injury experiences, her interview questions shape the participants' answers and the researcher's interpretation of the participants' meanings is then shaped by the answers to the interview questions. Because the main purpose of constructivist enquiry is to understand participants' meaning, these researchers use methods, such as interviews, analysis of symbols in observations or textual analysis (Manning, 1997) that allow an interactive process between the researcher and the participants and result in multi-voiced reflection of the meanings and experiences. Consequently, many interpretive researchers (e.g., Holstein & Gubrium, 2005) understand research as a narrative through which participants share their experiences with the researcher. For example, interviews that map participants' sport injury experiences can be understood as narratives through which these athletes share their life stories (see Chapter 6 for further discussion of narrative research). While interpretive researchers share some general principles, the interpretive paradigm, nevertheless, includes several theoretical approaches. On the nature of 'theory' in qualitative research, see Chapter 3.

The interpretive researcher's main aim is to understand the participants' subjective experiences and through these experiences, interpret the participants' meanings. One of the most diverse theoretical approaches to understanding individual meaning-making processes is phenomenology. The central aspect of phenomenology is the study of human experience and thus, it is commonly classified among the inquiries within the interpretive paradigm. Edmund Husserl's (1931; 1965) philosophical or transcendental phenomenology serves as a starting point for multiple strands of phenomenological enquiry. Like interpretive researchers today, Husserl argued that objective scientific practice has excluded the individuals' subjective experiences of the world: the 'lived experience'. To examine these experiences, Husserl developed a method for examining how the essence of phenomena are lived into existence by individuals and thus reveal essential, absolute 'true' knowledge of the world.

Following Husserl's (1965) systematic attempts to examine the realm of the subjective consciousness, the researcher is to reach into the 'real' subjective experience buried in one's 'pre-objective' consciousness. To tap into essential knowledge through the subjective, lived experience, researchers, by 'bracketing' out their own existing beliefs and presuppositions of the phenomenon, gradually reduce all of the superfluous knowledge and are then able to reach into the essence. Husserl later developed his work towards an understanding of every experience as intersubjectively constructed and his work has been later developed by Alfred Schutz (1970) into sociological phenomenology and Harold Garfinkel (1967) into ethnomethodology. Other phenomenologists, such as Husserl's student Martin Heidegger, argue that the researcher cannot be separated out of the knowledge production process or the world in general. Heidegger's (1962) hermeneutic phenomenology thus, emphasises meaning making as an interpretive process of 'being-in-the-world' (Dasein): the study of the modes of being in the world. Hermeneutics refers to the interpretive process of understanding one's self through reflection of other's understandings, which can lead to an understanding of the human condition in general. Heidegger termed this process the hermeneutical circle. The notion of the hermeneutical circle has been further developed by Hans-Georg Gadamer (1975), Paul Ricoeur (1991; for further discussion of Ricoeur see Chapter 9 on memory work) and Max van Manen (1990). The third strand of phenomenology draws from philosophical existentialism and the work of Jean-Paul Sartre and Simone de Beauvoir. Existentialism as a philosophical movement emphasises the 'authenticity' of individual experience as defining the nature of existence. In addition, while such experiences might be varied, freedom is considered universally important for individual existence. Freedom thus has value as 'self-making'. Maurice Merleau-Ponty (1962), a contemporary of Sartre, emphasises the centrality of perception in the construction of human existence. His strand of phenomenology aims to understand meaning making as a dialogue between the body, consciousness and the world. For Merleau-Ponty, the physical body is an important aspect of meaning making as the body perceives the world around it and, thus, individuals can experience the world on a deeply bodily, pre-conscious, pre-linguistic level. Therefore, 'embodiment' – living, sensing and understanding the world through the body – is a central aspect of Merleau-Ponty's work.

Many phenomenologists assert that phenomenology is a method of itself (e.g., van Manen) and there have been several attempts to trace the general principles of phenomenological process (e.g., Giorgi, 1985; van Manen, 1990). For example, for research in physical culture, Allen

Collinson, mixing different phenomenological traditions, identifies description (of the experience, of phenomenon), reduction (bracketing out the superfluous material, suspending taken-for-granted ideas), identifying essences and understanding the intentionality (of meaning making process) as fundamental steps for most phenomenological enquiry. Recently, there have been attempts, particularly within psychology, to develop phenomenologically informed methods for collecting empirical material. Interpretive phenomenological analysis (IPA) is such an attempt to use phenomenological grounding to make sense of participants' meanings. Many IPA researchers use semi-structured interviews to understand subjective experiences. However, some phenomenologists (e.g., Smith & Osborn, 2003) no longer see phenomenology as a theoretical approach grounding many of the IPA projects, which have come to resemble any interpretive, qualitative research projects that trace individuals' experiences (see Allen Collinson, 2009 for more exhaustive critique of IPA as phenomenological method).

In addition to phenomenology, the interpretive paradigm includes sociological approaches of Max Weber and Erwin Goffman and symbolic interactionism by Herbert Blumer. While different from phenomenology, they also focus on obtaining a holistic understanding of subjective experiences. Although aspects of Weber's work are used by different sociologists, interpretive researchers draw particularly from (1968) concept of 'Verstehen' (understanding) to focus on the individual's own meanings (e.g., Donnelly, 2000; Manning, 1997). Goffman's (1959; 1961; 1963; 1967; 1969) 'dramaturgical sociology' highlights the importance of everyday lives wherein individuals, through 'strategic interaction', construct meanings. Blumer's (1969) symbolic interactionism is also known more broadly as the Chicago School sociology. It emphasises the significance of language through which an individual makes sense of the world. An individual engages in the active interpretation of symbols and then acts accordingly. Social life then consists of these individuals aiming to fit together diverse forms of understanding, action and conduct (Blumer, 1969). As all these interpretive sociologies focus on individual meaning making in everyday situations, such methods as ethnography, participant-observation and semi-structured and informal interviews suit their research aims.

The interpretive approaches all assume a subjective ontology and thus they cannot be used together with positivist approaches that are based on objectivity. Therefore, in terms of the anti-positivist paradigms, the qualitative researcher has to be careful not to 'mix and match' theoretical perspectives. Drawing from different theoretical perspectives within the same paradigm is, of course, possible – as the positivists can use any theory within their own paradigm – but obviously borrowing from different paradigms leads to philosophical contradictions and, therefore, difficulties in the interpretations of the results. For example, a constructivist enquiry on overweight students' experiences in an outdoor education field trip can draw from Goffman's concept of 'stigma' and be framed within Chicago school's assumption of interaction as open-ended where such stigma can change when experiences change in an educational environment.

The subjective epistemology has led interpretive researchers to scrutinise their own roles in the research process more carefully. Earlier it was pointed out that researchers are understood as parts of the data collection process, but, in addition, they write the final research texts (i.e., journal article, book chapter, dissertation, thesis or book). Denzin and Lincoln (2005) observe that the constructivist sensibilities led to the moment of *the crisis of representation*, during which qualitative researchers began to question the taken-for-granted role of research writing. During this moment, qualitative researchers became increasingly aware of their privileged position as authors and, despite their criticisms of the dominance of positivism, reproduced its academic heritage through their writing practices. Against calls for multiple voices, interpretive researchers began to make writing more reflexive to rupture further the objectivism of such concepts as validity, reliability and objectivity. They also wanted to address questions of the race, gender and class of their participants, whose voices they were meant to represent in their research. The 'crisis' referred to the researchers' authority, ability to write the experiences of the 'other' and the recognition that this experience is created in the actual text 'written' by the researcher (Richardson, 2000a). Because society is constituted of multiple meanings, qualitative research allows multiple voices to emerge from the research text in a manner that was not possible through traditional representation of interview quotations. More vivid representations of everyday experience and more detailed attention to ways of writing research were needed. Forms of research writing that engaged the researcher's voice with her/his subjects' voices on a dialogue of physical activity and lived experiences became emphasised. We discuss the modes of qualitative research representation further in Chapter 8.

In summary, the interpretive paradigm is based on subjective epistemology and these researchers (e.g., Manning, 1997) assume what they call a relativist ontology. Individuals make multiple meanings of the social world based on their experiences: an understanding of reality is relative to an individual's context and experiences. This assumes local and specific co-constructed knowledges of a reality. This is often a contentious point: some strands of phenomenology assert that although knowledge making is a subjective process, the main research aim is still to map the reality to which the participants' multiple experiences point. In other words, while the participants make different meanings, they nevertheless, share the reality in which their lived experiences take place. By tapping into such 'real' authentic experiences, the researcher could reach the essence of phenomena in general. Consequently, credible research represents the 'real' experiences of the participants (e.g., Plummer, 2005). The relativist ontology also points to the most commonly presented critique of interpretive paradigm.

Interpretive researchers are interested in individuals' lived experiences to obtain knowledge in general. In spite of answering the call for more subjective perspectives on research, interpretive research has been criticised for focusing too narrowly on subjective experience. Interpretive researchers seem to assume that individuals' meanings are a result of the interaction between people who knowingly control their experiences: their meanings and consequently, their knowledges are unaffected by other factors in life. This assumption refers to the 'humanist self': the individual who can, without consideration of external factors, lead the life of her/his own choosing. This notion also tends to imply that as long as one so decides and tries hard enough one will succeed, as there are no other barriers than self-determination for the chosen direction of life. Interpretive, constructivist enquiry is claimed to assume a universal 'human being': 'a common humanity that blinds us to wider differences and positions in the world' (Plummer, 2005, p. 364). This individual, the 'humanist self', is at the centre of action and attention as a powerful 'agent' of her own destiny. Critics of the interpretive paradigm argue that such project results in overt individualism in favour of social constraints that also structure experiences, meanings and actions. They further argue that few people in the world are free to create their own meanings, because the construction of individual meanings is influenced by the historical, political, cultural and economic context of one's experiences and, therefore, individuals' thoughts, meanings and knowledge are constructed within societal power relations (Markula, Grant & Denison, 2001). With this critique, issues of power have become a central part of some anti-positivist paradigms.

Humanism: Critical paradigm

While constructivist researchers understand the behaviours and experiences of human beings as socially constructed in interaction with others, they do not commonly discuss issues of power. Researchers in the critical paradigm locate individual actions within relations of dominance and subordination that, according to them, characterise the world we live in. Such approaches as ***critical theory***, some strands of ***social constructivism*** and the ***participatory/cooperative*** paradigm as described by Guba and Lincoln (2005) (see Chapter 7 for participatory action research as a method) follow this paradigmatic focus. Vivian Burr (1995) observes that the term social constructionism is almost exclusively used by psychologists who are 'only just discovering' the ideas of power. She further notes that there is no single definition for social constructionist psychology but rather that it is an umbrella term of such perspectives as critical psychology (e.g., Fox & Prilleltensky, 1997), critical social psychology (e.g., Gough & McFadden, 2001) and discursive psychology (e.g., Edley & Wetherell, 1995; Edwards & Potter, 1992; Harre & Stearns, 1995). (For further discussion of critical psychology and social constructionist psychology of the body see Riley et al., 2008). Each of these have common assumptions, and indeed the boundaries between them are often fluid and can be crossed, yet they share certain guiding principles.

The *critical paradigm* encompasses many different fields and theoretical formations that generally draw from the ideas of Karl Marx (1967), who critiqued capitalism for enabling and maintaining unequal class relations. In this system, the masters of production (the owners) and direct producers (the workers) compete for power (Marx, 1967). In this competition, the owners exploit the labour of the workers by suppressing them economically and politically (denying an access to capital and decision making). This leads to the continual alienation and impoverishment of the workers. Such economic activities constitute the base structure of society and also influence the structure of political and cultural activities, which Marx termed the superstructure (e.g., Rigauer, 2000). At Marx's time, most aspects of what we now understand as physical culture (dance, sport, leisure pursuits, education) would have come under the superstructure and would then be dictated by the ruling, 'owners' group. Since then the cultural condition has changed and currently sport, for example, could also be understood in terms of class conflict between the owners of the professional teams and their workers, the players. In addition, more people now have access to the superstructure of cultural, political and leisure activities. Due to the complexity of current society, pure Marxist analyses of physical culture are now quite rare, but critical perspectives deriving from Marx's original ideas abound. Marxism has since developed into political practice (through Marxist-Leninism and the development of communist parties and the communist regimes) and Marxist theory for philosophy, political economy and social sciences (Rigauer, 2000). We focus on the derivatives of Marxist theory in this chapter.

Neo-Marxism opposes the 'economic determinism' of Marxism. This means that neo-Marxists assume an interactive, dynamic dialogue between the base structure and superstructure rather than the dominance of the base structure that characterised Marx's theory. Neo-Marxists are sometime referred as the 'Frankfurt school' as they were all members of the Institute of Social Research founded in Frankfurt am Main in Germany (Rigauer, 2000). Such scholars as Max Horkheimer, Theodor Adorno, Herbert Marcuse, Walter Benjamin and later Jürgen Habermas are credited with developing so-called critical theory and focus particularly on the analysis of the superstructure. As noted earlier, the majority of what we define as physical culture would be part of the superstructure, yet neo-Marxist research on physical culture is quite rare. However, Habermas's (1972) critique of science remains pertinent for all qualitative researchers of physical culture.

With some variety, all theoretical perspectives within the critical paradigm assume that unequal power relations are based on the ideological control of the individual in society: all humans are subject to belief systems or ideologies that make certain ways of life, values and knowledges seem natural and just. However, ideologies benefit those powerful groups who control and dominate the rest of society through a conception that ideological beliefs will work for the benefit of all (Markula, Grant & Denison, 2001). Because dominance is still based on access to capital, the base structure controls the ideological construction of the superstructure. Universities and thus also research culture, are part of the superstructure and also permeated by ideological control. Habermas (1972) demonstrates that the requirement of objectivism has resulted in 'scientism', a belief that the only valuable knowledge is produced by objective, value-free research practices. Thus, in order to control research it is necessary to challenge the neutral objectivity of science and counteract the ideological construction. Habermas argues that scientism excludes other ways of knowing and creates arrogant scientists, who take objectivity for granted ignoring the subjective aspects of their actual research practices. Critical researchers, Habermas advocates, need to be 'awakened' to understand the ideological construction of academic power structures to uncover the ideological power of 'scientism' and to become aware of themselves as observing, knowing, thinking and interpreting human beings (for a more detailed discussion of this as it relates to research in physical culture, see Silk, Bush & Andrews, 2010).

The French critical scholar Louis Althusser is often discussed in connection with critical theory, although some writers trace his theoretical inclination from structuralism identifying him as a structural Marxist (Rigauer, 2000). Althusser (1971) argues for a very strict ideological control of ideas in a capitalist society. He believes that capitalism, through institutional or structural control, dictates social relations always in the favour of the ruling class. This is possible through the ideological state apparatus (e.g., the legal system, education, the political system, the media, the family) that organises the production of ideas so tightly that there is no room for critique. Individuals are 'interpellated' or indoctrinated into the ideological belief system so entirely that they hardly realise the extent to which they are controlled. With his ideas, Althusser represents the ultimate 'determinism': in a capitalist society individuals are so controlled or 'duped' by the ideological system that they do not consider resisting or asking for change. From an Althusserian point of view, sport, leisure activities or art would be ideologically controlled by the state apparatus to reproduce the ideals of the dominant group. Althusser's structural Marxism has been criticised for not crediting individuals with any voice in society and not theorising how change in ideological control might take place.

One critical theorist who challenges Althusser's determinism is Antonio Gramsci. If the other critical theorists are relatively seldom used to analyse physical culture, Gramsci's theory of hegemony is widely embraced. Gramsci (1971) believes that neither the superstructure nor the base structure can entirely determine people's actions or the construction of dominant ideologies. While the upper or middle classes might have advantage in terms of the access to both structures, the lower classes have established their own organisations (such as labour unions) through which they can influence the workings of the society. This creates an interchange between the different groups in society that then mediates between the two structures. The relations of dominance and the ideologies that support them are historically determined and context specific. Gramsci further emphasises the importance of the 'popular': how popular, everyday actions are important to supporting or resisting ideological control. Gramsci's hegemony theory thus credits individuals with 'agency', an ability to resist the dominant ideologies. We will discuss hegemony theory in more detail in Chapter 5 where we detail how this theory informs critical textual analysis.

Research in physical culture, particularly in sport sociology, has been strongly influenced by hegemony theory and such perspectives as critical feminism (e.g., Birrell & Theberge, 1994; Davis, 1997; Hall, 1996;

Lenskyj, 2000), cultural studies (Andrews, 2002; Andrews & Loy, 1993; Birrell & McDonald, 2000; Hargreaves, 1987; Hargreaves & MacDonald, 2000; King, 2005; Rowe, 2004) and critical race theory have been influenced by Gramscian ideas of the interplay of ideological dominance and an individual's agency. In addition, critical pedagogy (e.g., Kirk, 2006; Tinning, 2002; 2004), inspired by hegemony theory, has come to inform research in physical education. While these contextual approaches differ from each other, they are all committed to critical enquiry and social criticism of the unequal, ideologically produced power relations. For example, critical researchers of physical culture might look at an event (such as the Beijing Olympic Opening ceremony), a sport or leisure organisation, school physical education, fitness centre or sport club to read how ideologies construct them in a specific historically situated context. In addition, these researchers might focus on individuals' experiences within a specific activity (e.g., a sport, fitness class, outdoor education camp, school sport club, computer games, hip hop dancing) to examine how the participants might be influenced by and/or resist the ideologies shaping the activity. Critical researchers of physical culture can employ methods such a document analysis, participatory action research, participant-observation, ethnography or interviewers to interrogate the ideological structures and individuals' reactions to them.

Because of their critical stance, researchers within the critical paradigm presume a subjective epistemology: all knowledge is the result of a subjective research process. As the critical paradigm is inherently political in its critique of existing power structures, the researcher also has a strong political inclination towards critique of the current social world. Researchers within the critical paradigm aim to expose the workings of ideology to reveal how powerful groups, who benefit at the expense of the majority, maintain ideological constructions. Their work is, consequently, inherently 'liberatory': to 'generate knowledge in ways that turn critical thought into emancipatory action' (Lather, 1992, p. 94). With the ultimate goal of emancipatory action, the researcher assumes the position of a political advocate who takes up an openly ideological stance to fight imbalances between powerful and marginal groups. Marginalisation is often defined as ideological exclusion based on identity factors such as gender, class, race/ethnicity, sexuality, disability or age. It is also acknowledged that exclusion might happen within the intersections of several marginalised identities (Collins, 1990; 2004). For example, poor black women tend to face more ideologically constructed exclusion than white women. Intersectional analysis of gender, race, sexuality and nationalism has inspired particularly feminist readings of sport media representation (e.g., Birrell & MacDonald, 2000; Borcila, 2000; Douglas, 2005; Elling & Luijt, 2009; Hills & Kennedy, 2009; McDonald, 2008; Spencer, 2004; Stevenson, 2002). In such an analysis, a researcher aims to read how differential media presentations of gender, sexuality, race and nationalism further marginalise women athletes by sexualising and trivialising them.

So-called cultural studies work could also be defined as a part of the critical paradigm as it advocates an understanding of the physically active body as ideologically, socially and culturally situated (see King, 2005). Like critical theorists, (physical) cultural studies researchers operate under an assumption that societies are fundamentally divided along hierarchically ordered lines of differentiation (i.e., norms of class, ethnic, gender, ability, generation, nation, race and or sexuality). Physical cultural studies (see Andrews, 2008) involves identifying an 'event', almost in an abstract sense, that is implicated in hierarchical, iniquitous, unjust power relations and effects for a potentially important focus of critical enquiry. While a diverse field, (physical) cultural studies can be characterised by several unifying themes. First, those working in physical cultural studies are committed to 'working the hyphen' (Fine, 1994) between private concerns (e.g., the exercising body) and public interests (power relations). This involves starting with the particular (an instance of physical culture, an experience, a text such as a sport film), the 'scrap of ordinary or banal existence', and then working outwards, upwards, internally, sideways and across to unpack the density of relations and intersecting social domains that inform it (Frow & Morris, 2000, p. 327). This allows for connections and attachments to be made from the lives of private individuals, texts and institutions to structures (racial, gendered, economic, national, global) to expose the often hidden ideological structures of physical culture. Therefore, there is a specific recognition that physical cultural forms (practices, products, institutions or experiences) can only be understood through the way in which they are *articulated* (Grossberg, 1992) within a particular set of complex social, economic, political and technological relationships that comprise the social context. Given the focus on the operations of power within the social formation, there is an unequivocal 'commitment to progressive *social change*' (Miller, 2001, p. 1). Physical cultural studies researchers therefore attempt to produce knowledge that would *make a difference*. Although cultural studies commonly accepts a plurality of theoretical approaches, we have included cultural studies in the critical paradigm because of its defining feature of a perpetual unity in difference (Hall, 1992). Researchers in cultural studies may be influenced by various forms of neo-Marxism and various poststructuralist approaches, but unite in a common commitment to change in ideologically constructed power relations.

In summary, if the interpretive paradigm emphasises the participants' subjective meaning making, the critical paradigm strongly acknowledges the researcher as a politically oriented, subjective producer of knowledge. While the researcher's critical politics is openly celebrated, this does not necessitate including the researcher's voice openly in research writing. Nevertheless, specific qualitative research methods (e.g., critical discourse analysis, see Chapter 5) have been developed to reveal how ideological power naturalises certain phenomena. However, the critical paradigm has been critiqued for imposing certain theoretical notions of what emancipation means without enough understanding of the diversity of subjective experiences in society. As an answer to this criticism, such methods as participatory action research – that is judged on the ability of the work to produce praxis or emancipatory action – has emerged. This method is based on a participative, co-created, subjective-objective reality (ontology); an experiential, propositional, practical epistemology producing co-created findings; and a practical methodology centred on political participation in collaborative action enquiry and a language that is grounded within a shared experiential context (Lincoln & Guba, 2000). To emphasise research as coproduced between the researchers and the participants, the ways research is written and used are also problematised. We will discuss participatory action research in more detail in Chapter 7. However, local and small scale approaches, such as participatory action research, have produced critical social science research that has become a site for critical conversations about democracy, race, gender, class, nation-states, globalisation, freedom and community (Denzin & Lincoln, 2000) while retaining reflexivity (see Chapter 8 for further discussion of research representation).

While critical theorists assume political advocacy with clear subjective, yet theoretical, visions of justice for a certain underprivileged group in society, they often come from a more privileged position in society. Consequently, discrepancies between visions can arise. As Lather cautions: 'there is a growing concern with the dangers of researchers with liberatory intentions imposing meanings on situations, rather than constructing meaning through negotiation with research participants' (1992, p. 95). There is a danger that the researcher assumes a group with rather uniform life situations, aspirations and goals: an essential, universal prototype for an underprivileged person that then comes to represent all the members of that group. This notion of the 'self' embraced by the critical paradigm is closely connected to its ontology.

Ontologically, the critical paradigm embraces what can be termed a historical realism – an understanding that ideological constructions stemming from certain social, political, cultural and economic reality shape identities. In this sense, it opposes the interpretive paradigm that advocates a view of individuals – the humanist self – who consciously, free of social constraints, make meanings based on their experiences. Nevertheless the critical paradigm, with its emancipatory ethos, advocates that humans can find their 'true' selves and make more conscious meanings once the ideological clouding has been revealed to them. For example, the critical researcher, after exploring the ideological construction of 'scientism', is free to engage in research that more truthfully reflects 'the' reality. Consequently, once free from ideological constraints, each individual sees the reality and can then make more informed choices about her/his life. For example, critical research of physical culture aims to demonstrate how women's advances in sport are constrained by masculine ideology that trivialises, sexualises and marginalises women athletes. Through this critique, the ideological barriers should be removed and the female athletes freed to embark on successful careers. This position is akin to the humanist self of the interpretive paradigm and, consequently, the critical paradigm can be classified as a form of humanism. The difference between interpretive and critical humanism is that interpretive researchers embark on analysing the experiences of an individual directly, but critical researchers need first to reveal the oppressive ideological structures that limit the individual's free and conscious actions. Similar to the interpretive paradigm, however, after the external constraints are critiqued or removed, the individual can lead the life of her/his own choosing. For example, an individual woman is then capable of choosing to participate in any sport without ideological oppression. Consequently, the individual continues be a powerful 'agent' of her/his own destiny.

Because of the limitations arising from humanist assumptions of realist ontology and the humanist self, some anti-positivists have turned to alternative modes of theorising. Instead of focusing on certain groups as either dominant or subordinate, researchers have looked at how all individuals, including the researcher advocating liberation, are participants in power relations. The most vocal challenges of the humanist paradigms come from poststructuralism and postmodernism.

Poststructuralism/postmodernism

Similar to the other paradigms, postmodernism and poststructuralism consist of multiple different theoretical strands. It is often claimed that postmodernism, particularly, cannot be captured in one clear definition. What complicates any efforts to define is that postmodernism, similar to Marxism, can refer to a social and cultural movement as well as a theoretical research perspective. The beginning of postmodernism as a cultural movement is often credited to those arts, particularly architecture, that as a reaction to modernism had already in the 1960s begun to challenge the very nature, form and meaning of art (e.g., Rail, 1998). For example, in dance the postmodern movement was strong from the 1960s to the late 1970s (e.g., Banes, 1994). Consequently, some define postmodernism as a time period probably from the 1960s onward in the western world. As a scholarly perspective, it is difficult to define postmodernism, but, for example, Kvale understands it not as a systematic theory or a comprehensive philosophy, 'but rather diverse diagnoses and interpretations of the current culture, a depiction of a multitude of interrelated phenomena' (1992, p. 32). Poststructuralism is occasionally used interchangeably with postmodernism, particularly in North American scholarship (e.g., Andrews, 2000; Rail, 1998) and therefore the distinction between these two theoretical perspectives tends to be blurred. However, poststructuralism was born as a reaction to a theoretical perspective called structuralism and it is, thus, clearly located within academic debates rather than a cultural condition. Because we focus on research paradigms, our discussion draws from postmodern/poststructuralist critiques of humanist qualitative research: critique of universal metanarratives, critique of dualistic understanding of power relations and critique of the humanist self.

Critique of universal metanarratives: Multiple, fractured realities

Francois Lyotard was one of the first scholars to introduce postmodernism as scholarly thought. Against modernist narratives of rationality and progression, he calls for an 'incredulity towards metanarratives' (1989, p. xxiv). This means that he is critical of previous attempts to legitimise science through the appeal to grand narratives such as emancipation or progress. Instead of a world unified through universally generalisable theories that represent the true 'reality', postmodernism and poststructuralism favour cultural pluralism. These scholars understand the world as fragmented into multiple worlds that resembles more of a pastiche (Jameson, 1983) or a collage (Kvale, 1992). Such a world is further characterised by constant cultural change that is an ongoing, active, yet unpredictable and often irrational process. Rapid changes do not turn into coherent narratives or often do not have any meaningful relation to each other, but are organised in a series of fragmented presents (Jameson, 1983). Jean Baudrillard (1983) adds that current reality is transformed into images and this 'unreal' image world becomes more real than the original world: simulacra. This creates confusion between the real and the models of the real (Giulianotti, 2004). For Baudrillard, the media is central in the creation of hyperreality, and the digital age makes this further possible. For example, watching a football match at home in a high definition, digital large screen television with multiple slow motion replays, the possibility to zoom in, expert commentators, hi-fi sound and instant player statistics can become a more *real* spectator experience than actually attending a cold, crowded, dirty stadium where one can barely see the players, cannot hear anything but the noise of the other fans and is offered no other visuals besides the actual game. The images in the era of hyperreality are meant to be consumed and enjoyed on this surface level as intense moments of different sensations (Featherstone, 1991), which has lead to an increased fragmentation of how an individual experiences the world. In terms of qualitative research, postmodernism points to the signs of constant change in social theory, society or our everyday experiences within an image-based culture. These examinations might use any qualitative method to collect empirical material. For example, qualitative researchers in physical culture could focus on how media texts represent a fragmented, hyperreal narrative of sport performance, health or identity. Or through interviews, they could analyse how individual users of the 'new' (or old) media consume the rapidly changing mediascape to understand, for example, how and why they follow their sport idols through Twitter or communicate with their 'virtual' friends through Facebook.

Similar to interpretive research, postmodernism/poststructuralism observe multiple meanings. Unlike interpretive research, however, the multiple interpretations of reality become valuable only when reflected against the social and historical context of the knowledge making (Markula, Grant & Denison, 2001).

Critique of dualist understanding of power

Similar to the humanist paradigms, poststructuralism and postmodernism assume subjective epistemology: individuals make multiple meanings and the researchers' meanings are an integral part of the research process. Similar to critical humanism, poststructuralism and postmodernism acknowledge that the researchers have a political agenda in terms of social critique. In addition to critique, however, poststructuralists and postmodernists aspire to create change in the world. This is possible as they understand power as relational. This is different from the critical humanist dualist understanding of power as dominance and subordinance. Poststructuralists have particularly theorised the practice of power in postmodern society.

Poststructuralism has its roots in contemporary French philosophy. Often philosophers such as Jacques Lacan, Jacques Derrida, Michel Foucault and Gilles Deleuze are considered to be at the heart of poststructuralist theorising. While Lacan's psychoanalysis, Derrida's deconstruction, Foucault's theory of discursive power relations and Deleuze's rhizomatics differ from each other, one way or another they each draw from critiques of structuralism. Structuralism as a theoretical approach was developed at the turn of the twentieth century by Ferdinand de Saussure and was adopted, particularly in anthropology, by Claude Levi-Strauss, to provide a universal theory of how meanings are created through language structures (in the case of Levi-Strauss, how cultures are created). Once established, Saussure argues, meanings become fixed forever and thus the point is to theorise the exact process in order to predict and explain the nature of language. Against this background, it is important to note that the 'structuralism' in poststructuralism does not refer to structures of power, even less to the idea that poststructuralism assumes 'no structure', but rather an opposition to Saussure's universalist theory of how meanings are made through structures of language. Derrida (1978; 2004) was one of the first to clearly theorise that meanings, instead of being fixed, are constantly changing through the process of continual difference (from other meanings) and deferral (delayed meaning-making process). This change is deeply embedded in the structures of power that allow certain meanings to emerge and become dominant. As language is the prime means of communication for humans, privileged terms in language also tend to structure behaviour. For example, if terms associated with masculinity (such as determination, assertiveness ruthlessness, aggression, desire to win, strength) are continually considered desirable, masculinity will also become a positive characteristic over other (feminine) characteristics. How the 'good' meanings become attached to masculinity, for example, is then a question of who can define masculinity and is thus a question of power relations. Foucault has theorised further how power operates within society.

Foucault (1978; 1980a/b; 1983) argues that power is not the possession of certain dominant groups who then actively oppress and marginalise other groups. Rather power is relational: by engaging in relationships with others, individuals are always necessarily part of power relations.

As most individuals have to interact with others, everyone is a part of some power relations. This does not mean equality: instead of possessing power, dominant individuals or groups have arrived at their positions through the strategic use of discourses. Discourses, simply defined, are ways of knowing. All the knowledge, then, rather than neutral or objective, is deeply embedded in power relations. Power relations, for Foucault, are supported by knowledge. Discourses (ways of knowing) are not credited to a single person or a group of people who actively use them to oppress others but, rather, their exact origin is unclear and they operate through everyday practices. In addition, discourses change over time and they are not necessarily oppressive, but rather their effects depend on how they are used. A Foucauldian researcher would consider, for instance, the discursive construction of health within the current society and how the current understanding of 'health' has come to dominate. At the moment, health research is dominated by biomedical science that views 'health' primarily as the absence of illness. Consequently, much health research funding, health research education and health research publications actually concern illness (e.g., how physical activity can prevent diabetes). In addition, significant amounts of governmental health policy are devoted to decreasing the cost of illnesses. As a result, researchers of 'health', instead of outsider critics or neutral producers of scientific knowledge, are part of the power relations that significantly shape the meaning of this word and the related practices. A Foucauldian researcher would further connect this discourse of health with power relations to look at the social consequence of this particular understanding of health, and, finally, analyse what type of social change is needed for creating a broader meaning for health where resources, in addition to illness prevention, might for example be directed to general well-being that benefits a wider part of society.

Consequently, poststructuralism is a deeply political project in which society is considered a site of constant political struggle with continual competition for dominance depending on who dominates the meaning field at the time (Markula, Grant & Denison, 2001). We discuss the differences between a critical humanist view of power and Foucault's conceptualisation of power relations in more detail in Chapter 5. Poststructuralists nevertheless assert that language powerfully structures social meanings, power relations and individual consciousness. The focus on language has led many poststructuralists to analyse meanings embedded in cultural texts. In addition, several of the poststructuralist philosophers have developed their own methods for this purpose. For example, Derrida (1978) titles his method **différance**.

Foucault (1970, 1972, 1977; 1978; 1980a/b) developed **archaeology** and **genealogy** for his analysis power/discourse nexus. Deleuze (Deleuze & Guattari, 1988) created **rhizomatic** analysis in order to find ways to create social change. As qualitative sport researchers, it is important to respect the original method developed with the theoretical stance the researcher takes. For example, to attempt a Foucauldian analysis of the meaning of health related fitness, the researcher should consider, in the first place, using genealogy, as this was developed by Foucault in connection with his theoretical approach (see Chapter 5 for further discussion of Foucauldian discourse analysis).

The role of the individual: Critique of the 'humanist self'

Because poststructuralist analysis originates from a critique of structuralism, a theory of how meanings are structured through language, poststructuralism is sometimes considered only suitable for the analysis of texts. Consequently, poststructuralism has been critiqued for its overt emphasis on language at the expense of the body, embodiment or lived experiences that also define the core for analyses of physical culture. While poststructuralist theory might originally stem from an interest in language, it has since been applied widely to the examination of power relations, everyday practices and the body. For example, Foucault (1991) finds the body an important site for power relations, but also considers everyday body practices as ways of coping with and transforming the discursive construction of power relations. Similarly, Deleuze (Deleuze & Guattari, 1988) assigns the physical body a crucial role in transforming the current structures of dominance. In this sense, then, poststructuralist theories can be fruitfully used by those researching physical culture to examine the meanings of sport and physical activity, but also how these meanings can be recreated or transformed through such practices as policy making, sport competitions, physical activity participation, coaching, teaching, fitness instruction or managing sport organisations. Therefore, many poststructuralists employ such methods as interviewing, narrative writing, participant observation or ethnography to examine how individuals practice and understand physical culture in a particular discursive context. Nevertheless, poststructuralism differs from critical humanism in terms of the role of the individual within the negotiation of the power relations. This stems from the different understandings of power within these two paradigmatic positions.

While language creates a strong social context for understandings of reality, individuals actively produce multiple meanings which are, through language, products of society and culture (Weedon, 1987). At this point, poststructuralism differs from the interpretive paradigm and its understanding of subjectivity possessed by the free and self-determining individual to argue for social construction of meaning making (an understanding of 'a self' as socially produced in language). Furthermore, each individual is a part of power relations and, thus, part of the negotiation, circulation and alteration of discourses. It is not possible, therefore, to be outside power or discourse as these are continually formed through human interaction. The individual, or the self, is also continually being formed and shaped within this power/discourse nexus. The individual comes to understand her/himself in relations to this nexus and creates a corresponding identity. In a poststructuralist sense, there is no core, or unchanging 'true self' to be found, but an individual becomes a subject within power relations and continually creates an understanding of a self or assumes an identity suitable to a specific social context. For example, while an athlete might be born with certain biological and physiological characteristics suitable for a certain sport, he will actively have to construct an identity (the looks, behaviours, attitudes, cultural understandings) required of him within his particular sport. It is obvious that different sporting contexts tend to produce different athletic identities. For example, snowboarders embody a different identity from distance runners or football players. In addition, other pre-formed social constructions (such as gender, race/ethnicity, age, ability) shape the identity construction. For example, often women and men in the same sport assume quite distinct identities from each other. Or athletes with different ethnic and/or national backgrounds create distinct identities. This identity will be reconstructed with the changes of context, for example in retirement. In this sense, poststructuralism differs from the critical paradigm that tends to presume that the true essential, universal self (e.g., an athlete's self, a male self, a gay self, a disabled self) can be discovered once the ideological structures have been removed. Foucault (1988), for example, argues that a subject (or individual or the self) is a form (rather than a fixed substance waiting to be discovered under oppressive ideologies) that can be modified under different cultural conditions. The notion of the subject as a form also allows poststructuralists to think of social change: if a certain understanding of an individual or identity is currently limiting, it can be changed. In the humanist paradigm, only the ideologies can be changed or removed. For example, a critical humanist researcher would demonstrate that the ideology of masculinity currently oppresses women athletes by marginalising, trivialising and sexualising them. Therefore, the ideology of masculinity needs to be removed. However, what emerges after that is unclear – what is the universal, true athletic self that then operates in the sport world without ideology of masculinity? The aggressive, competitive, violent, tough (male) self? Is this the true self for women athletes? It this a positive self? From the poststructuralist view, both male and female athletic selves are socially constructed through certain ways of knowing about sport. They are not essential, universal or even necessary. Thus, both the current masculine and feminine athletic selves can be problematic, but can also be continually reconstructed through discourse (not found only in their absence). Poststructuralists thus understand the 'self' as constructed (even the idea that there is a 'true' self is a construction, not a truth) within the intersections of individual, power relations and knowledge. They do not negate identity construction, but rather see individuals continually creating or problematising identities against certain cultural conditions.

In sport studies generally, as with the social sciences and humanities, poststructuralism and postmodernism have often been seen as contradictory, mysterious, incomprehensible and even apolitical research paradigms. They have been accused, in turn, of relativism (individuals are seen to make multiple meanings without social constraints – a paradigmatic position of the interpretive paradigm) or determinism (individuals are so constrained by power relations that they have no ability to make any of their own meanings – a common critique of such Marxist theorists as Althusser). When debated in these modernist terms, poststructuralism and postmodernism appear to escape clear definitions, sparking fury among already confused researchers. Nevertheless, both of these research approaches share common paradigmatic assumptions to posit that there are multiple realities that individuals actively construct within the context of certain power relations. All individuals are part of power relations, yet some have achieved more dominant positions through the strategic employment of discourses (or ways of knowing). Therefore, language and meaning making (knowing) are central aspects of analysis. Poststructuralists are particularly interested in the formation of current power relations and often critique how discourses are used for dominance. By understanding this process, suggestions for change become possible. The individual's self is understood as a 'form' continually constructed through discourses. While the construction of the self can be dominated by discourses, the individuals, as part of power relations, can also actively construct selves that while still informed by the discourses, are less dependent on them.

Summary

After formulating the purpose (e.g., mapping a field, social critique, social change), a qualitative researcher proceeds to think about the paradigm in which the research is located. A paradigm refers to the researcher's assumptions of reality (ontology), knowledge (epistemology) and ways of gathering knowledge of reality (methodology). Therefore, we emphasise that methodological practices derive from paradigmatic concerns.

In this chapter, we discussed three paradigms for qualitative research: post-positivism, humanism and postmodernism/poststructuralism. Post-positivism provides an intra-paradigmatic critique of quantitative, positivist paradigm to call for research in participants meanings in natural setting. Theory, it argues, should be grounded in data collected from these natural settings. Consequently, post-positivists call for the use of some qualitative methods. They nevertheless share an epistemological (objective knowledge production) and ontological (the search of true reality) basis with positivism. These factors will influence how post-positivist researchers analyse their data (see Chapters 4–7) and judge the quality of their research (see Chapter 9). Unlike the post-positivists, humanist researchers assert that knowledge production is subjective process, but like post-positivist researchers, they tend to search for the universal, one reality (ontology). We divided humanism into interpretive and critical paradigms. Interpretive researchers are interested in how multiple individual experiences can collectively reveal the reality. Critical researchers focus on oppressive ideological constructions of these experiences. They assume that such constructions work universally to benefit certain groups and marginalise others. Like humanists, postmodern/poststructuralist researchers find knowledge production a subjective process (epistemology) but, unlike humanists, assert that there are multiple realities (ontology). These paradigmatic assumptions further determine the methods, analysis of collected empirical material and quality judgements of qualitative research within each paradigm (see Chapters 4–7 and Chapter 9).

Because these paradigmatic approaches are all social constructions, they are subject to changes in emphasis, substance and influence. How each researcher chooses to locate her/himself within these paradigmatic structures is a choice based on their research problem. A researcher's location within these paradigmatic debates will depend on the purpose of the research and what they want to achieve. Some paradigmatic approaches are clearly better suited to understanding physical bodies within a particular context than others. Some are clearly better suited to genetic investigations on cancer cells. Some may be drawn by some of the sensibilities of the participatory action research and thus draw from the hallmarks of critical theory. However, it is impossible to draw on sensibilities from, for example, positivism and the poststructuralist/ postmodern paradigm when the underpinning philosophies are too distant from each other. Because of the important differences between paradigms (Denzin & Lincoln, 2005; Fine et al., 2000; Lincoln & Guba, 2005), the qualitative researcher cannot afford to be naïve to the onto-logical, epistemological and methodological assumptions of each. As research becomes increasingly interdisciplinary, qualitative research is also a 'messier' enterprise: while having plenty of choices, the researcher also has to actively negotiate between the multiple paradigms, mul-tiple theories and multiple methods to create research that matters. Consequently, the qualitative research process is, in many ways, more complex to master than following the clear rules of positivist, quan-titative social science research. However, qualitative research, in its multiplicity, also offers flexibility, variety, excitement and chances for experimentation for those interested in understanding multiple voices in multiple social contexts with the possibility of creating social change. In the next chapter, we examine the **process** that might be used by qualitative researchers of physical culture.

Further reading

Phenomenology of Physical Culture:

Allen Collinson, J. (2009). 'Sporting embodiment: Sport studies and the (con-tinuing) promise of phenomenology'. *Qualitative Research in Sport and Exercise*, 1, 279–96.

Kerry, D. S. & Armour, K. M. (2000). 'Sports sciences and the promise of phenom-enology: Philosophy, method, and insight'. *Quest*, 52, 1–17.

Nicholls, A., Holt, N. L. & Polman, R. C. J. (2005). 'A phenomenological analysis of coping effectiveness in golf'. *The Sport Psychologist*, 19, 111–30.

Ryba, T. V. (2008). 'Researching children in sport: Methodological reflections'. *Journal of Applied Sport Psychology*, 20, 334–48.

Warriner, K. & Lavallee, D. (2008). 'The retirement experiences of elite female gymnasts: Self identity and the physical self'. *Journal of Applied Sport Psychology*, 20, 301–17.

Young, I. M. (1980). 'Throwing like a girl: A phenomenology of feminine body comportment motility and spatiality'. *Human Studies*, 3, 137–56.

Interpretive sociology of physical culture:

Donnelly, P. (2000). 'Interpretive approaches to the sociology of sport'. In J. Coakley & E. Dunning (Eds), *Handbook of sport studies* (pp. 77–91). London: Sage.

Birrell, S. & Donnelly, P. (2004). 'Reclaiming Goffman: Erwin Goffman's influence on the sociology of sport'. In R. Giulianotti (Ed.), *Sport and modern social theorists* (pp. 49–64). Basingstoke: Palgrave Macmillan.

Marxism and physical culture:

Gruneau, R. (1983). *Class, sports, and social development*. Amherst, MA: University of Massachusetts.
Ingham, A. G. (2004). 'The sportification process: A biographical analysis framed by the work of Marx, Weber, Durkheim and Freud'. In R. Giulianotti (Ed.), *Sport and modern social theorists* (p. 11–32). Basingstoke: Palgrave Macmillan.
Rigauer, B. (2000). 'Marxist theories;. In J. Coakley & E. Dunning (Eds), *Handbook of sport studies* (pp. 28–47). London: Sage.

Neo-Marxism and physical culture:

Carrington, B. & McDonald, I. (2009). *Marxism, cultural studies and sport*. London: Routledge.
Inglis, D. (2004). 'Theodor Adorno on sport: The jeu d'espirit of despair'. In R. Giulianotti (Ed.), *Sport and modern social theorists* (pp. 81–96). Basingstoke: Palgrave Macmillan.
Morgan, W. (2004). 'Habermas on sports: Social theory from a moral perspective'. In R. Giulianotti (Ed.), *Sport and modern social theorists* (pp. 173–86). Basingstoke: Palgrave Macmillan.

Structural Marxism on physical culture:

Brohm, J.-M. (1978). *Sport: A prison of measured time*. London: Ink Links.

Gramsci's hegemony theory in physical culture:

Rowe, D. (2004). 'Antonio Gramsci: Sport, hegemony and the national-popular'. In R. Giulianotti (Ed.), *Sport and modern social theorists* (pp. 173–86). Basingstoke: Palgrave Macmillan.
Hargreaves, J. A. & MacDonald, I. (2000). 'Cultural studies and the sociology of sport'. In J. Coakley & E. Dunning (Eds), *Handbook of sport studies* (pp. 48–60). London: Sage.

Physical cultural studies:

Adams, M. L. (2005). 'Death to the Prancing Prince': Effeminacy, sport discourses and the salvation of men's dancing. *Body & Society*, 11(4), 63–86.
Andrews, D. L. (2002). 'Coming to terms with cultural studies'. *Journal of Sport and Social Issues*, 26, 110–17.
Atkinson, M. (2007). 'Playing with fire: Masculinity, health, and sports supplements'. *Sociology of Sport Journal*, 24, 165–86.
Dickson, G. & Schofield, G. (2005). 'Globalization and globesity: The impact of the 2008 Beijing Olympics in China'. *International Journal of Sport Management and Marketing*, 1, 1/2, 169–79.
Fusco, C. (2006). 'Inscribing healthification: Governance, risk, surveillance and the subjects and spaces of fitness and health'. *Health & Place*, 12(1), 65–78.
King, S. (2006). *Pink Ribbons, Inc.: Breast Cancer and the Politics of Philanthropy*. University of Minnesota Press.

Spielvogel, L. (2003). *Working out in Japan: Shaping the female body in Tokyo fitness clubs*. Durham: Duke University Press.
Wheatley, L. (2005). 'Disciplining bodies at risk: Cardiac rehabilitation and the medicalization of fitness'. *Journal of Sport & Social Issues*, 29, 198–221.
Woodward, (2004). 'Rumbles in the jungle: Boxing, racialization and the performance of masculinity'. *Journal of Leisure Studies*, 23, 5–17.

Postmodernism and physical culture:

Giulianotti, R. (2004). 'The fate of hyperreality: Jean Baudrillard and the sociology of sport'. In R. Giulianotti (Ed.), *Sport and modern social theorists* (pp. 225–40). Basingstoke: Palgrave Macmillan.
Rail, G. (1998). *Sport and postmodern times*. Albany, NY: SUNY Press.
Rojek, C. (1995). *Decentring leisure: Rethinking leisure theory*. London: Sage.

Poststructuralism and physical culture:

Andrews, D. L. (2000). 'Posting up: French post-structuralism and the critical analysis of contemporary sporting culture'. In J. Coakley & E. Dunning (Eds), *Handbook of sport studies* (pp. 48–60). London: Sage.
Markula, P. (2009). '"Acceptable bodies": Deconstructing the Finnish media coverage of the 2004 Olympic Games'. In P. Markula (Ed.), *Olympic women and the media: International perspectives* (pp. 87–111). Basingstoke: Palgrave Macmillan.
Markula, P. & Pringle, R. (2006). *Foucault, sport and exercise: Power, knowledge and transforming the self*. London: Routledge.
Rail, G. (1998). *Sport and postmodern times*. Albany, NY: SUNY Press.

3
The Process of Qualitative Research in Physical Culture

In this chapter, we will

- Compare the quantitative and qualitative research designs;
- Discuss the different parts of a qualitative research project;
- Discuss the researcher's role in a qualitative research process.

Within this chapter we begin to delineate our third P, the actual *process* of conducting a piece of physical cultural research. As has already become obvious, different researchers can approach the same physical site, event or concern from a different angle because of their paradigmatic positions that will inform their methodological practices. It is nevertheless possible to consider what these different qualitative projects have in common and in this chapter we consider what a qualitative research process might look like. We suggest a qualitative research structure that can inform writing theses and dissertations as well as journal articles. We offer this as a helpful starting point that, in our experience, has also proven an effective and clear way of constructing publishable work. In addition, we provide a more detailed account of what should be included in a section dedicated to qualitative methodological practices. We begin by contrasting qualitative, logic with quantitative, deductive logic to highlight the differences between these two forms of research. The point here is not so much to argue for the superiority of either one, but rather to provide insights into thinking qualitatively versus quantitatively.

Qualitative research process

While different paradigmatic assumptions shape different qualitative research projects, it can be argued that all qualitative research follows a similar, logic as its basic design. While qualitative logic can be characterised in several ways, one way of demonstrating its defining qualities is to compare it to the deductive logic that underpins quantitative research.

Deductive, quantitative research design

It is important to remember that quantitative social science research is characteristically located within the logical positivist paradigm that, as explained in Chapter 2, assumes that the reality can be 'truly' captured by objectively collected, numerical data. Because these researchers have not yet mapped all facets of 'the reality', they keep testing the truthfulness of previous theories based on their empirical data. In this sense, logical positivism aims continually to envelop the 'true' picture of the reality. A research design based on these assumptions is called deductive design. This design is characteristically a 'top-down' process (see Figure 3.1):

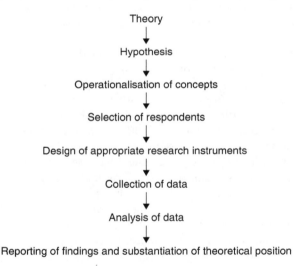

Theory
↓
Hypothesis
↓
Operationalisation of concepts
↓
Selection of respondents
↓
Design of appropriate research instruments
↓
Collection of data
↓
Analysis of data
↓
Reporting of findings and substantiation of theoretical position

Figure 3.1   Deductive design

To obtain objective data to test effectively the previous theoretical assumptions it is necessary to follow the above order. Therefore, it is important to note that quantitative research should always provide a test for previous theorising – merely collecting numerical data and conducting statistical analysis does not qualify as research. Below are some examples of hypothetical deductive designs for physical culture (see Figures 3.2, 3.3).

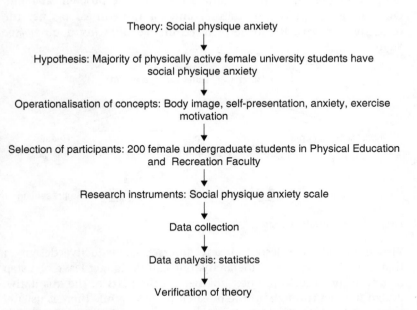

Theory: Multidimentional self-esteem model (Shavelson, Hubner, & Stanton, 1976)

↓

Hypothesis: An injury results in low self-esteem in majority of ice-hockey players

↓

Operationalisation of concepts such as self-esteem and injury

↓

Selection of participants: Requires a large sample for example, 5 professional teams, 5 university first teams, 5 lower level teams

↓

Research instruments: Injury questionnaire, self-esteem measurement instrument

↓

Data collection

↓

Data analysis: statistics

↓

Verification of theory

Figure 3.2 Example 1: Self-esteem in injured male ice-hockey players

Theory: Social physique anxiety

↓

Hypothesis: Majority of physically active female university students have social physique anxiety

↓

Operationalisation of concepts: Body image, self-presentation, anxiety, exercise motivation

↓

Selection of participants: 200 female undergraduate students in Physical Education and Recreation Faculty

↓

Research instruments: Social physique anxiety scale

↓

Data collection

↓

Data analysis: statistics

↓

Verification of theory

Figure 3.3 Example 2: Social physique anxiety in physically active female university students

Qualitative research design

Rather than taking steps to test a theory, qualitative research design assumes a more flexible form. As qualitative research is always subjective and self-reflexive, it is not necessary to follow a rigid, pre-set order of tasks. In addition, qualitative researchers do not develop hypotheses that focus research on a narrow, predetermined aspect of 'reality'. A hypothesis is always an assumption based on previous theory rather than a problem that evolves from the researcher's previous experience, reading or interaction. Because qualitative researchers are interested in mapping people's lived 'realities', critiquing existing conditions or creating social change, they do not base their projects on assumptions derived from previous theories, but rather want to be open to what is taking place in world. This does not mean, however, that qualitative research is atheoretical. Rather, theory is used to frame and analyse the topic of interest and often used to connect the topic with larger social and cultural issues. To account for multiple stories and realities that might evolve through the research project, qualitative researchers develop research questions that guide the research design, yet leave it open enough to capture multiple facets of the problem at hand. Qualitative design is thus messier and far from linear (as per the deductive sidebar). It can be pictured in the following manner (see Figure 3.4):

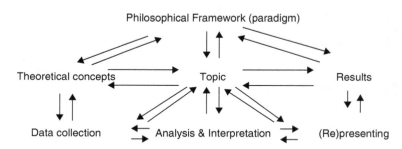

Figure 3.4   Qualitative design

Visually, qualitative design already differs from deductive design in that there is no ladder of hierarchy: one can no longer leave one step behind to proceed to the next. Rather, all the parts of the qualitative design interact throughout the research project. While there is usually an order, it is possible that these moments can take place simultaneously. For example, a researcher may be conducting ethnographic observations based on previous literature about hyper-masculine behaviours in a male sports team. While 'in the field' the researcher will constantly be making decisions about which players to watch, which events to attend, what to write down, who to talk to and how to act. While recording observations, the researcher is also interpreting them by choosing which field notes to make and how to write such notes. At the end, the researcher may read through the notes, write some up formally and refer back to a previous article on masculinity and sport which forms part of the basis for the next set of observations. As such, in a qualitative design, the boundaries between steps or moments are rather fluid and messy. A qualitative design is a flexible design in which all the parts will continually be shaped during the research project. It is advisable, however, that a researcher begins a qualitative project from a clear research question, concern or topic that will aid in the selection of paradigmatic approach, theoretical concepts and appropriate methodological practice(s) in the most efficient manner. Therefore, this approach will also provide 'deep' empirical material with the greatest potential for meaningful results. We further discuss the structure of qualitative research project later in this chapter. Below are two examples (see Figures 3.5 and 3.6) for qualitative research projects that stem from similar topics to the earlier examples of quantitative, deductive design.

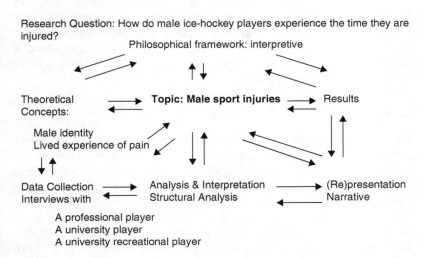

Figure 3.5 Example 1: Research question: How do male ice-hockey players experience the time they are injured?

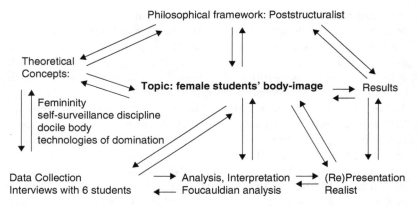

Figure 3.6 Example 2: Research question: What do physically active female university students think of their bodies?

Structure of a qualitative research project

Most qualitative research projects (at least within formal university structures) contain the following components: introduction, literature review and theoretical grounding, methodological practices section, analysis/discussion of empirical material, conclusion, notes, references and appendices. The order might vary. For example, sometimes there is a separate section for analysis and discussion; some research does not contain notes or appendices. However, given that such a structure is likely to frame the majority of projects, we detail below what is commonly included in each section.

Introduction

It is clear that an introduction should guide the reader to the project ahead. In this sense, it should also entice readers to engage with the research. This is often more difficult to achieve than one might first think and it is common for the qualitative researcher to write this section last to provide a better structure for it. Regardless, it is important to provide an interesting and well written introduction as this is the reader's first meeting with the project. If this section is dull and disjointed, it is unlikely that anyone will continue to read. In qualitative research, the introduction is usually relatively brief (about 500 words). It does not contain a review of previous literature (as is often the case in quantitative research), but rather builds to state the overall purpose of the study.

While one can state the purpose in the first sentence of the introduction, it is more inspiring to build up the purpose by beginning with a general statement that connects the study to what is previously known about the topic, or to current cultural, societal, or political events. Through this discussion the researcher should point to a problem to which her/his research asserts to attend. For example, in a research project of women athletes' media representation during the Olympic Games, the researchers might begin the introduction by first stating the importance of the Olympic Games as a cultural event, also as an important event to the women athletes. The researchers can then move into the importance of the media in producing meanings of the Olympic Games and then narrow the discussion down to the particular medium they plan to focus on in their study (e.g., television, newspapers or magazines).

The main purpose of the introduction is to introduce the project, but one can also consider recounting a recent incident or event that might have inspired the research as an introduction. For example, if one's research project concerns drug use in sport, one can begin with a story of a recent case of an athlete who has allegedly used drugs and thus illustrate the importance and meaning for a scholarly study of drug use. In some cases, it is very appropriate to begin with a personal experience that has inspired the researcher to undertake the particular topic. Whichever way one decides to entice the readers to engage with the project, it is important to finish the introduction by detailing what one is planning to do in the paper, dissertation, thesis or book chapter (e.g., in this paper, I will first … I will then … Finally, I will conclude by …).

Literature review

The literature review is the key part of a qualitative study: it sets up the entire study as it makes the case for the research and locates the work in the existing academic literature. The case is usually made by critically analysing previous research on the topic and then identifying a gap, problem or deficiency that provides a reason to conduct the intended research. While the purpose of the literature review appears obvious, many qualitative researchers, and not only students, have difficulty in structuring a comprehensive literature review. Because literature reviews have proven one of the most difficult aspects of writing qualitative research – even many experienced researchers struggle to provide a literature review that is in-depth but at the same time provides a tight, concise focus for the research at hand – we offer below a substantial discussion of the various components and indeed pitfalls associated with them.

The aim of a literature review is to show the reader (a tutor, a second marker, an external examiner, a journal editor, a fellow academic) that the researchers have read, and have a good grasp of, the main published work concerning a particular topic or question in the field. The review will be guided by the research topic, by the various contexts (social forces) within which the work is located, the paradigmatic and theoretical location, and by the central argument. It is crucial to incorporate an array of contextual and specific works that provide the analytical, interpretive and theoretical tools to use for analysis and discussion. This will allow the researchers to connect particular issues with the wider context and thus avoid mere description. It is very important to note that the literature review should not simply be a description of what others have published, but should be a critical discussion that shows insight and an awareness of differing arguments, theories, approaches and contexts. As a synthesis and analysis of the relevant published work, it should be linked at all times to the research purpose and rationale. In a literature review, the researchers may compare and contrast different views on the same topic, critique various methodological approaches (e.g., 'As stated, all previous work has been conducted using surveys, yet no research to date has asked how participants experience the issue. This research utilises a design that will allow for the voices of participants ...'). They might locate their work in relation to previous studies or in relation to prominent theoretical positions (e.g., Foucault's position on disciplined bodies). The purpose is, nevertheless, to explicate why some previous works are exemplary and why others need to be expanded, and most importantly to reveal gaps in research with which to build a research question. The literature review should demonstrate where the study fits within the previous literature of the topic and the broader social context to argue why a further examination of the topic is important. This means that the reader will be given a clear indication of the research problem and why it is unique through a critical discussion of the reviewed work. A good literature review therefore provides an analysis of what has been written previously in the research topic, identifies areas of controversy, raises questions, contextualises the proposed research and identifies areas that need further research.

Given that the literature review creates the space for the formulation and communication of the research problem or issue, it is critical that it is written before embarking on the actual collection of empirical material. While the research problem or issue may change, or indeed may arise from everyday practice (for example, problems in how coaches treat the athletes, dancers getting commonly injured, certain people are excluded from certain sports), a research project should always link these problems to the previous research literature. Otherwise the problem is not a research problem, but rather a practical issue that needs to be set right through practical means.

Because all qualitative research is embedded in a certain paradigm, implicitly or explicitly, it is important, particularly in PhD work, to address the paradigmatic locations of the previous research and the researcher's intended paradigmatic stance. Further, qualitative research should be embedded in theory and it is therefore important to address the theoretical perspectives of the previous research as well as the researcher's intended theoretical stance. Because 'theory' in qualitative research is located within a range of paradigmatic options, the researcher needs to know which paradigm to locate each theory (see Chapter 2 for further clarification). As each paradigm has its own ontological and epistemological assumptions that each theoretical stance will also follow, it is important not to 'pick and choose' randomly between concepts from different theories. Because different paradigmatic stances are also critical of each others' assumptions, careless borrowing of concepts across theories that are located in different paradigms creates contradictions that demonstrate the researchers' inexperience in providing a sound theoretical grounding for her/his work. It is important to observe that one social research paradigm can contain several 'theories' and it is possible in one's research project to draw from several theorists located within the same paradigm. For example, Foucault, Derrida and Deleuze, while having developed their own distinct theoretical vocabularies, are generally considered poststructuralists and therefore share ontological and epistemological assumptions. Likewise, those working in the critical paradigm will likely draw from a range of (neo-) Marxian thinkers. Similarly, quantitative social science research is invariably located within the logical positivist paradigm and theorists located within this paradigmatic approach share the same philosophical assumptions. Consequently, it is possible to mix and match different concepts from different quantitative researchers without creating contradictory assumptions. The key point is to be able to assess critically the paradigmatic underpinnings of each theoretical tradition and then locate a space for one's own research paradigm and theory(ies) through a critical examination of the previous research on one's topic.

Structure of the literature review

The overall structure of the literature review will depend largely on the thesis topic or research area. It is clear, however, that the literature review should contain research related to the researchers' topic. For example, a team of researchers might be interested in homophobia in women's sport. However, after looking for literature on this topic, they realise that existing research has approached this topic from several theoretical perspectives, through several methods, looked at several sports and dealt with different types of participants (e.g., coaches, officials, athletes, administrators, journalists, athletes). In addition, there is an existing literature on sexuality in sport. It is clear that the researchers, while including this type of literature, also need to decide upon a more specific focus for their project. In addition, the researchers need to think about how to organise the existing literature to build towards their specific focus. It is likely that one's specific research issue will be linked to other related issues and social forces. For example, homophobia is related to issues around sexuality in society. Therefore, it is important to acknowledge such connections, but to retain the focus on one's topic. It is important not to begin from an issue too distant from the actual topic. For example, if a qualitative researchers intend to examine who attends 'after school' physical activity programs, they do not need provide a lengthy review of literature regarding the connections between physical activity and obesity although this issue has been used to justify the importance of after school physical activity programmes.

To help their reader follow their thought process, the researchers should address the logic of their literature review in a brief **introduction**. It is often helpful to begin introducing the literature review with a generic sentence that acknowledges the link to larger social issues (e.g., 'In recent years, there has been increasing interest in issues of sexuality in sport') and provide references to major research in the topic. Similarly to the introduction to the actual study, the researchers should explain what exactly they discuss in the literature review. Articulating the structure will help not only the readers but also the researchers to think what it makes sense to include in the literature review.

Because a good literature review is not only a descriptive list of studies, the researchers also have to decide on an analytical order in which to present the literature. In this sense, a literature review forms a type of coherent narrative that builds into a conclusion: the research questions. One way is to organise the literature review **chronologically**, beginning from the earliest research on one's topic. This is probably the least analytical way to construct a literature review. To provide a deeper reading into the literature, the researchers would need to think what are the similarities and differences between the different studies. These can be based on different **theoretical** approaches. For example, a researcher can identify positivist studies of the prevalence of homophobia, post-positivist studies that examine attitudes of homophobia, interpretive research that maps individuals' experiences of homophobia, critical studies of the ideological construction of homophobia, or poststructur-alist studies of homophobic practices in identity construction. In case all the existing literature draws from similar theoretical perspectives, the researchers need to focus on other differences and similarities. There can be differences in the choice of **methods** and participants. These can also be linked to theoretical differences. For example, interpretive stud-ies may use interviews to examine the experiences of different people involved in sport whereas positivist studies have used questionnaires. There might also be similarities and differences between **findings**, and a good literature review aims not only to state these differences, but to analyse from where these differences stem (e.g., theoretical and methodological issues). Therefore, the idea is to analyse the previous literature – including various approaches, perspectives and findings – in a critical and coherent manner, not to ignore positions different from one's own. It is important to incorporate various perspectives and then explain the main disagreements (e.g., unsuitable or insufficiently justi-fied choice of method, weak theoretical analysis).

It often seems difficult to contain the literature within the parameters of one's study (literature should comprise no more than 1/3 of one's study). For example, a typical research journal article is about 8000–9000 words (about 25 double spaced pages). If one's literature review by itself is 4000 words (or 15 pages) there would not be enough space for one's actual findings. How much detail, then, is required from each reviewed study? How many articles should one include in a literature review? This is difficult to ascertain decisively. One can, for example, include several studies in one sentence that provides a generic background for one's research and then focus in more detail on studies that are closest to one's focus in terms of their theoretical or methodological approach or their findings. For example, if the researchers aim to look at homophobia in women's sport through a lens of critical paradigm, they can address previous studies of sexuality in women's sport in one sentence. They can then discuss other studies that draw from critical theory to link sexual-ity and homophobia in women's sport. They can then further narrow down their discussion by focusing on the studies that discuss specifically lesbian athletes' experiences of homophobia and compare and contrast different theoretical perspectives and findings to argue for a case for their specific focus. These studies can then be discussed in further detail. The researchers might conclude that there is more need to look at the experiences of homophobia in certain sports; or there might be a need for a critical approach to such experiences; or they might conclude that the previous research has ignored whether male to female transgender athletes experience homophobia. Therefore, the researcher should make choices as to what studies and what detail to include, but it is important, nevertheless, to demonstrate that one has read broadly around the chosen topic and not ignored major research in the area. In summary, it is important **not** just to describe what one writer says, and then go on to give a general overview of another writer (book or article). The structure of the review should be determined by topic area, theoretical arguments and the critical analysis of varying approaches and findings.

The literature review should conclude with the gap in previous literature (e.g., in topic, theory, methodology or sample) that justifies conducting the research project. In qualitative research, it is necessary to formulate **a research question** or questions based on the gap(s) identified in the literature review. The research question(s) captures the research purpose or the research problem in a question form. Each research project should have at least one main research question that can then be divided into smaller research questions. However, a research question clarifies what the researcher is intending to examine through his/her research project. Therefore, it is necessary to state one's research question explicitly. Typical qualitative research questions begin with 'how' or 'what'. For example, an interpretive researcher might ask: How do lesbian women coaches experience homophobia? Or a critical theory researcher might ask: What are the ideological constructions that support homophobia in men's football?

Further general advice

Good literature reviews have a clear line of argument. The researchers should make it easy for the reader, who may never have thought about the topic before, to understand the pathway they are taking through the literature. Further, it is important to make sure that there is always a link between the main purpose and the literatures included in the review. All researchers should use quotations from the literature to support their discussion. However, because researchers structure the literature review to build their own research question, not to describe previous findings, they should avoid long direct quotations. These can really only be used to showcase an important point or issue. In most cases, it is more useful to paraphrase (or rewrite in one's own words) other authors' work. This convinces the reader that the researchers actually understand what they are talking about. Literature reviews do tend to be written in a formal, academic style. Therefore, it is important to keep the writing clear and concise and avoid colloquialisms and sloppy (slang) language.

We are often asked how to go about finding literature on a topic. It is important to conduct a wide literature search to become familiar with as much literature on one's area as possible. To check this, one can ask the following questions:

- Have I gone back historically?
- Have I read the key journals in the field and looked through their back issues to ascertain what has been written on the topic?
- Have I looked outside of those books and journals associated with physical culture?
- What has been written, for example, in the cognate disciplines on my topic?

With technological development, internet search engines such as Google scholar can be extremely helpful in finding relevant literatures, as can library based databases that often provide access to a wide-variety of full-text journal articles. However, it is important to distinguish between peer-reviewed scholarship (the types of articles in scholarly journals and books) and those found on a web source such as Wikipedia. Beginning researchers often rely on such 'non-scholarly' or popular sources to obtain previous information. It is, of course, absolutely fine to cite a journal article accessed electronically. But it is very different to consistently cite from a non-peer reviewed source, such as a blog or a dictionary entry. This should be avoided in qualitative research literature review. All sources should be carefully referenced in line with the accepted referencing style (of the journal, the department or the discipline of the work) within the literature review to ensure correct acknowledgement of the works of others and to avoid plagiarism. Further, we often are faced with statements from students who have identified an important topic, but have not been able to find 'any' literature on the topic. While there are, indeed, previously non-researched issues, it might also be that one's research for literature has been superficial or limited to computerised search engines that are often based on finding the most appropriate key word(s) for one's search. Qualitative researchers often prefer 'catchy' titles that do not necessarily have the key words of the research in the title (e.g., 'See Spot Run'; 'Mow My Lawn') and thus key research articles are often missed in purely computerised searches. It is therefore useful to identify key journals and texts in one's area of research in addition to computerised searches and actually look through these sources for appropriate research and that way identify further sources. If there is absolutely no research in one's chosen topic, then one can refer to the literature that uses a similar theoretical perspective, uses a parallel topic (if you are looking at women's field hockey, research on other women's team sports such as soccer might be helpful) or shares concepts with one's research (e.g., masculinity or race) (see the earlier discussion on qualitative research design).

In summary, a good literature review

- Contains an assessment of related previous literature (no other reflections or opinions);
- Provides a logical and clear discussion of the main issues, concepts and approaches to one's research topic;
- Is written in clear, 'tight', analytical and critical manner;
- Opens a gap in the literature that leads into a research question(s).

Methodological practices section

The methodological practices section is the major focus for the next section of the book: 'Doing' qualitative research and forms the basis of the 4th and 5th P's, Practices and the Politics of Interpretation. While we provide the generic description of this section here, we will present more details on how to structure this section in connection to different qualitative method(s) in the subsequent section. In addition to the parameters or boundaries of action which are set by the paradigmatic stance, this section should be clearly structured around information that the readers require in order to understand how the empirical material for research has been obtained. While the information needed might differ slightly depending on the methodological practices chosen, the following is generally essential for qualitative research methods section:

Epistemological and ontological basis of project

- Clear and logical understanding of the philosophical basis for the project;
- Appropriate to the purpose and meaning of the study.

Explanation of the research setting

- Critical discussion of the research setting and the practices;
- Sampling: Selection of participants / texts / site (e.g., number of participants, number of texts chosen, justification for using a certain population);
- Ethical concerns.

Methodological practices chosen

- Clear explanation for the chosen methods and their link to the ontological or epistemological base of the research;
- Justification for the practices chosen.

Interpretation, representation or validation

- Clear explanation of the analysis process;
- Consideration of the ways in which the work will be written/presented, commensurate with the boundaries of action defined by the paradigmatic stance;
- Criteria for qualitative research validation.

We present a more detailed description of each of these topics in the subsequent chapters.

Interpretation, analysis and discussion

This section is perhaps the most crucial place in which to add new knowledge to a topic matter. Its length will vary dependent on the output. In a published paper or in a Masters thesis, the analysis is usually contained within one section. A PhD dissertation, however, typically contains more than one chapter that discusses the results. Further, this section does far more than just present the results from the research. Unlike quantitative research, qualitative researchers often discuss the analysed empirical material together with references to previous research. It is often impossible to provide qualitative empirical material on its own (e.g., excerpts from texts or interview transcripts do not make sense on their own) and therefore this section provides space for the researcher's analysis of the empirical material and discussion of it in the light of previous research that was presented in the literature review. This section thus provides a crucial connection between the literature review and the results of the research. The researcher's task is, therefore, to make sense of the empirical material in the light of their analysis and comparisons to the previous research findings. This section then demonstrates the researchers' skill at synthesising their empirical material with previous literatures, theoretical positions and wider social issues.

In the analysis process, the researcher has to be able to work through volumes of empirical material, mostly in the form of words, and work with this material to select coherently certain segments for inclusion within the discussion section. For example, empirical material that contains volumes of interview transcripts based on female body image, cannot all, within the confines of a journal article or even a PhD thesis, be incorporated. Rather, the researchers need to go through a careful process of selecting certain portions of these transcripts in order to produce an account that critically discusses the collected empirical material in relation to previous literatures and theoretical perspectives. Obviously, based on the empirical material the researchers make decisions on common themes, the voices to include and their interpretation through theory and previous literature. In essence, in this section, the researchers decide what story to tell about their research and indeed how they want to tell it. Further, the researchers return to the purpose of the study. For example, in the hypothetical study on female body image, it would be remiss to leave the study as a description of 6 students' thoughts and reflections on their own bodies, but it is important to connect these findings to what is previously know about body image and physical activity and provide a theoretically sound analysis of what these new results mean. It must be noted that qualitative research results are not aimed at generalisability, but map lived experiences, critique social constructions of body image or aim at changing the forces that create negative body image. The discussion section creates a connection, then, between the empirical material, literature and theory through which the researchers produce a meaningful account from the empirical material.

Conclusion section

This section should detail the major contributions of the research project. This is often the last part of a research project and it is common to feel out of ideas of what to include in this section. However, as this section focuses on what is most important in the study, it is of great importance to the readers. While there is no definite way of structuring this section, we suggest the following aspects that can help conclude one's research in a meaningful manner.

One can begin this section by summarising the major results. It is important, however, not to repeat the analysis/discussion provided in the previous section, but rather to provide a concise summary to remind the reader about the major findings. This summary can lead to implications that the current research has for the field, for the development of theory, for practice or for society in general. Here the researchers should ponder the meaning of the research in the larger context of one's scholarly field, examinations of one's topic, social policy or for practitioners of the sport, physical activity or body practice.

In this section, the researcher should also reflect on the limitations of the project. For example, did the collection of the empirical material go as planned? Should this process be improved? Should there have been more or different participants? Based on these limitations, the researcher can also suggest future research that stems from the current project. This can include projects that expand from the current project or projects that draw from different theoretical perspective(s), use different methods or focus more narrowly on a certain aspect identified in the current research project.

The subjective qualitative researcher: Self-reflexivity

As we indicated in the introduction, the researcher is an integral aspect of the qualitative research process. Throughout the research process, and indeed, throughout this text, there are a number of considerations or pathways that the qualitative researcher will be negotiating. Such negotiations will, however, differ depending on the paradigmatic approach that provides the boundaries for research.

Researchers in the positivist paradigm assume an objective epistemology and thus carefully aim to exclude their researching selves from the research process. The search for 'truth' takes place without influence from the individual researcher ensured through the deployment of specific methodologies, protocols and experimental conditions. Postpositivists, despite entering into 'natural' settings, would also champion the discovery of one reality and thus attempt to remain as objective and detached as possible. Those in the anti-positivist paradigms, however, recognise that knowledge is shaped by a variety of factors including the researcher. They believe that there are no 'objective observations, only observations social situated in the worlds of – and between – the observer and the observed' (Denzin & Lincoln, 2005, p. 21).

Anti-positivist researchers are thus involved in a continual process of negotiating the I–thou (me, other) dialogue 'between the researching self and sources of different kinds' (Johnson et al., 2004, p. 77). This dialogue is also internal as it happens 'within the researcher' as she/he revises, critiques and reformulates the understandings (Johnson et al., 2004, p. 77), makes decisions about people, about who to talk to, what to ask, which pieces of evidence to use or discard. In this regard, qualitative researchers hover between self and other, between the different empirical materials and self, and between interpretation and self, maintaining an 'in-betweeness' (Johnson et al., 2004) throughout the research process.

There are important paradigmatic differences within the anti-positivist paradigms and these also impede on the role of the researcher's self in the research process. Some interpretive researchers acknowledge their impact on the research process, yet deploy a set of practices that will attempt to soften their impact. For example, the researcher may employ methodological triangulation – the deployment of different methods (such as interviews, observations, documents) – or analytical triangulation (such as member checking or peer debriefing) in an attempt to reveal how, through different practices, the researcher is capturing the same phenomena. These are both efforts to diminish the researcher's influence despite acknowledgement of the impact of the researcher's self on the project (for a further discussion of this type of validation see Chapter 9). Richardson (2000a) suggests replacing types of understanding of the researcher's self with a more interpretive stance. She visions self-reflexivity more like a crystal. When looking through a crystal, from whatever angle, the researcher will see something different. Whoever else looks, even from the same angle, will also see something different. As Richardson describes: 'what we see depends on our angle of repose' (2000a, p. 934). The researchers acknowledge that they are only able to gain a partial understanding of the topic under interrogation. Instead of 'capturing' lived experience, it is always 'created' in the research process and social text produced by the researcher (Denzin & Lincoln, 2005).

In the critical paradigm, the poststructuralist and postmodern paradigms of the self frame all aspects of the research as the researcher's own views may shape the entire process. In the critical paradigm, a researcher takes sides with a marginalised population to uncover an instance of exploitation and work with participants to overcome their exploitation. However, it is important to reflect upon the impact of different backgrounds (i.e., many critical researchers are often from privileged backgrounds) between the researcher and the participants. One of us (see Silk, 2005; 2008) for example, has reflected on the difficulties in negotiating his own situated (middle-class, white, male) researcher identity in his ethnographic practice in Malaysia. In his critique, Silk (2005) suggested that his position of relative privilege meant that those with whom he took sides – marginalised groups in Malaysia – were totally absent from his written accounts. However, self-reflexivity should be a visible part of the critical researcher's project. A researcher's self-reflexivity, as it engages with the role of the researcher, can break down the hierarchical borders between the researcher and the researched. Giroux, for example, advocates 'border crossing' that allows for recognition of the borders between the critical 'scholar', the 'participant' and the activist, artist or social worker as partial, fluid and open to forms of community or social engagement (2001, p. 6). Giroux's position aims to keep justice and ethical considerations alive through producing progressive research that can have an impact on the development of knowledge in physical culture that has a use for both academics and indeed for those outside the academy.

From a poststructuralist point of view, the entirety of knowledge production – qualitative research – is embedded within power relations. Poststructuralist researchers, as knowledge producers, have to locate themselves as integral aspects of these relations as they create, structure, conduct and write up each qualitative research work within the constraints of a particular social/academic context. However, in their view it is difficult to take clear sides (as the critical researchers would do) because everyone is, to a certain extent, a user of power, including the researcher who actually has considerable impact on how a research project takes shape, how the participants are represented and how the research results are distributed. Poststructuralist researchers thus aim to think how to use their power ethically, with a minimum of domination, but with a maximum of ethical impact. This means that a poststructuralist researcher of fitness, for example, would need to consider her research topic (what is meaningful research in terms of the field of fitness: mapping, critiquing or creating social change?), her research practice (what are the research methods that provide the most ethical research results and how can the researcher ensure this), her research writing (how will the results be presented to affect the scholarly, theoretical understanding as well as 'popular' understanding of fitness) and, finally, what type of change might the researcher be able to create through the research project (what is the meaning of this research to the fitness field?). Some poststructuralist researchers, in addition to obtaining 'views from the field' (like the critical researchers), are participants of the field and, thus, producers of multiple understandings of the events in it. However, poststructuralist researchers also actively problematise the discursive construction of field, its practices and its identities. For example, as a fitness instructor and a poststructuralist researcher, one of us (Markula, 2004; 2009) has continually had to problematise her role as a practitioner/researcher when creating more ethical fitness practices within the constraints of the fitness industry.

Qualitative researchers of physical culture must, then, one way or another deal with being self-reflexive. The visibility and extent of self-reflexivity depends on the researcher's paradigmatic approach. An internal dialogue regarding self-reflexivity characterises qualitative research: How much of the self to let in and leave out? Schwandt (2000, p. 204) proposes that qualitative researchers should focus on the choices about how they want to live the life of social inquirers in terms of practical and moral knowledge and question: 'How should I be towards these people I am studying?'.

Summary

In this chapter we have illustrated how the qualitative research process works. In addition, we have provided a generic structure (introduction, literature review, method/practices, analysis/discussion, conclusion) for a qualitative study. Finally, we have considered the role of the self-reflexive researcher in the research process and the potential practical application of qualitative research in physical culture. As a summary we suggest, adapting Johnson et al. (2004), the following approach for the process of qualitative research:

1) **Starting point**: At the beginning of the qualitative project, the researcher should consider an issue to be mapped, critiqued or needing change. Answering the following will further help locate the project into a paradigmatic and theoretical framework: What makes a topic important for the researcher? What is the **purpose** of the research project? Which paradigmatic approach and theoretical grounding provides the basis for the research? Where do I fit? How should I be throughout the process? What is the practical impact? Who will care about this research?

2) **Previous literature**: A thorough review of previous literature on the issue under investigation will help locate the qualitative research project within the broader research context. Answering the following

questions will help to identify the types of literature relevant to the project: What is previously known about the topic? What is the starting point for literature search? What are the historical / political dimensions surrounding the topic? Where does researcher exist in relation to previous arguments of the issue under investigation? Against the previous knowledge, what are **the research questions** for the current project?

3) **Practices:** A qualitative researcher needs carefully to design the research project to answer the research questions. This means that the actual methods or practices of collecting empirical material need to draw from the researcher's paradigmatic and theoretical stance and the previous literature. Answering the following questions will help to decide upon the actual methods for a qualitative research project: What empirical material will be collected for the study? How will the researcher decide on appropriate sampling? How will the ethical procedures for qualitative research be met? What methodological practices, or indeed a combination of practices, are appropriate to addressing the topic?

4) **Analyses/discussion:** This section brings together the results, the previous literature and the researcher's theoretical stance. Answering the following questions will help to formulate this section: What are main themes that emerged from the empirical material? What stands out immediately? Is there an argument emerging? Which passages might the researcher use to elaborate the key arguments? What seems to be missing? What are the silences? Did the research questions change? How do the findings synthesise with the literatures read? With the emergent argument, is it necessary to extend, elaborate upon and rewrite the results? For what purpose? Is the researcher taking sides? How can the researcher show the reader that the particular reading is interesting, comprehensive, in-depth, thorough?

Part II
Doing

In this section, we address the fourth and fifth Ps of Research: *Practices* and *The Politics of Interpretation*. We consider the term *practising* to be a more accurate description of the actual process of doing qualitative research, but use also the term 'method' to describe a way of collecting empirical material. While qualitative researchers often use multiple methods, we have divided our discussion into four chapters that introduce different methodological practices: interviewing, textual analysis, narrative analysis and field methods. We provide actual 'steps' for using each method, but we also discuss how these relate to the wider theoretical and philosophical debates that surround the 'choice' of each method. This will help qualitative researchers with their paradigmatic and theoretical assumptions of physical culture research as well as to align their research practice with their research purpose.

We also address the sixth P, the **Politics of Interpretation** within these chapters. We combine Practices and the Politics of Interpretation deliberately for two reasons. First, as discussed in Chapter 3, these are not always distinct phases in research, but can take place throughout the research process. Second, empirical material collected through different practices can be interpreted in different ways and it is thus logical to discuss the process of analysis in connection with each 'method'. The following four chapters provide an introduction to the most common practices and analytical approaches of qualitative research in physical culture.

4
Practice and the Politics of Interpretation: Interviewing

In this chapter, we will

- Detail the types of qualitative interviews;
- Discuss developing an interview guide;
- Discuss the selection of the interview participants (sample);
- Detail how to analyse qualitative interviews.

In the current society, we often encounter interview situations. According to Atkinson and Silverman (1997), interviews have become even more pervasive due to the contemporary mass media that effectively transmits such conversations around the world. Consider all the television shows where invited guests are interviewed, documentaries based on face-to-face interviews, radio chat shows and interviews published in magazines or in various Internet spaces. Fontana and Frey note also that everyday interactions contain plenty of interview situations: 'interviews are everywhere, in the forms of political polls, questionnaires about doctor's visits, housing applications, forms regarding social service eligibility, college applications' (2000, p. 646), not even considering job interviews that most people confront at least once in their lives. Finally, a significant proportion of the qualitative research articles draw from interview data. Consequently, Atkinson and Silverman label the current society as the 'interview society', in which it is assumed that the only way to know anything interesting, 'truthful' or 'accurate' is to interview people. In this way, interviewing has become 'a means of contemporary storytelling' (Fontana & Frey, 2000, p. 647). Most interviews focus on the individual and thus 'seek various forms of biographical description' (Fontana & Frey, 2000, p. 467). Qualitative researchers also commonly seek to solicit individual's feelings, experiences or knowledge(s) through interviewing. Interviewing is, indeed, so common that most qualitative research guides devote major space to this particular method. While we are about to do the same, we also want to caution anyone planning to embark on interviewing to consider carefully whether this choice is made based on the research problem and research question rather than a common sense notion that qualitative research must include interviewing. A qualitative researcher must be particularly careful not to 'idealise' interviewing as the way into the 'lived experiences' or the 'true', absolutely reliable understanding of the interviewee. In addition, it is important to link interviewing to one's paradigmatic stance to deliberate whether this is, indeed, the method that provides the best empirical material for answering the research question. With these precautions in mind, we discuss interviewing as a qualitative method. In addition to the general considerations for a method section we alluded to in Chapter 3, a method section for an interview study should include at least the following sections:

Box 4.1 Content of a method section for qualitative interviewing

- Qualitative framework;
- Type of interview (format);
- Interview guide (frame);
- Sampling of participants and the interview situation;
- Ethical concerns (see Chapter 1);
- Pilot interview;
- Analysis of empirical material;
- Issues of representation (see Chapter 8);
- Validation (see Chapter 9).

In this chapter, we will now address each of these sections in more detail.

Qualitative interviewing

If interviewing is not the best choice for all qualitative inquiries, when should the researcher opt for this method? Kvale (1996) reminds that an interview is a conversation with a purpose. Therefore, qualitative researchers must define their research purpose clearly and then develop a research question(s) that can be answered through talking to other people. One way of doing this is to fill in the qualitative research model we discussed in Chapter 3 and return back to the research question determined in the literature review section of one's research.

Before embarking into an interview study, it is important to consider whether the research question can be answered based on information available through previous research, other methods (such as participant observation) or through the media. For example, it is not necessary to interview people to know what happens in football practice – one can obtain that knowledge by observing such practices. Neither is there a need to interview the players to know about their player statistics if these are available from the club's website. However, if the researcher is interested in the players', coaches' or managers' experiences or meanings of playing football in the club, interviews might be the appropriate method for the investigation. After determining that interviewing is, indeed, the best means to obtain the information to answer the research question, the researcher then needs to consider:

- The appropriate interview format: How do you talk to your participants?
- Interview questions: What do you talk about?
- The appropriate interview setting: To understand participants' meanings and experiences, do you need to speak to them personally in a 'formal' environment?

We now discuss how to choose the format, appropriate questions and the setting for the interviews.

Interview format and questions

Because there is a rather substantial literature regarding qualitative interviews, there are also a myriad of terms that researchers use to characterise their particular interview techniques. Terms such as semi-structured, open-ended, in-depth, standardised, informal, unstructured, postmodern, feminist, conversational and face-to-face are often used to describe the type of interview used in a particular study. Sometimes these terms are also used interchangeably although they are, by no means, synonymous with each other and refer to different aspects of the interview process. To provide some clarity on how to use these different terms, we have organised them under four headings characterising the interview process (see Table 4.1): type, setting, interaction and participants.

Table 4.1   Types of interviews

Type	Setting	Interaction	Participants
Structured	Formal	Face-to-face Telephone Electronic	Individual Focus group
Semi-structured	Formal	Face-to-face Telephone Electronic (e.g., Skype)	Individual Group
Unstructured	Informal	Face-to-face	Individual Group

Organised this way, it is clear that there are actually only three types of interviews and all the other terms detail how these types of interviews are conducted. We have included structured interviews in our classification although they follow the quantitative deductive logic and are designed to maximise the objectivity of the information gathered. Structured interviews always take place in a formal environment entirely reserved for the purpose of the interview. The interviewee(s) come to this situation solely to be interviewed. These interviews can be conducted individually or in groups. The term 'focus group' usually refers to structured group interviews. Structured interviews can be conducted 'face-to-face', when the interviewer and interviewees are both present in the same location, or over distance through telephone or electronic means.

Semi-structured interviews are arguably the most common type of qualitative interview technique. Like structured interviews, they can be conducted formally face-to-face or over distance, individually or in groups. Unstructured interviews differ from semi-structured interviews in terms of their setting. These interviews are used in everyday settings and take place in the middle of other action or practices. Therefore, informal interviews do not require the interviewer to reserve time or location specific to the interview. The differences between the types of interviews become more obvious when we consider the role of the interviewer and types of questions in each interview type (see Table 4.2).

During quantitative, structured interviews, the interviewer has to remain objective to ensure that she/he does not influence the information given by the participant. Therefore, she/he has entirely control the situation entirely to prevent any unexpected 'disturbances' that might influence the objectivity of the situation. The questions asked

Table 4.2 The role of interviewer and types of interview questions

	Interviewer	Types of questions	Type of information
Structured	Objective	Closed	To identify adequate indicators for chosen variables
	Controlling leader		
Semi-structured	Subjective leader (participant)	Open ended	In-depth
Unstructured	Subjective Participant	Open ended conversational	In-depth

in these interviews are closed. These questions require yes/no answers or the interviewee is provided with numerical scales (e.g., Likert scale from 1–5) to choose as an answer. These questions ensure that the interviewee give answers to the intended questions without straying to give opinions or long explanations that are un-codable for statistical analysis. Consequently, it is ensured that the interview provides information regarding the predetermined variables and eventually either confirms or negates the research hypotheses.

As qualitative research is not limited by claims of objectivity, semi-structured and unstructured interviews allow the researcher to be an active participant in the interview situation and 'probe' further information or discuss issues that arise during the interview situation. The interviewer can also share her/his own experiences. However, as the main interest is in interviewee's meanings, one should be careful to give voice to the interviewee without dominating the conversation. While both types of interviews use open-ended questions – the answers are expected to be several sentences, rather than short yes/no – the interview situation (formal versus informal) creates a difference in terms of the purpose of the interview. Semi-structured interviews in their formal setting are more interviewer led. Therefore, there is more time to prepare the open-ended questions carefully (this is the interview guide that we discuss later in this chapter) to meet the purpose of the research. Usually the length of these interviews range from one to three hours in order to gather in-depth knowledge of people's experiences. Unstructured interviews take place spontaneously and are most commonly used as a part of ethnographic field work where the researcher engages in brief everyday conversations with people in the field (see Chapter 7). Unstructured interviews aim to gather deep knowledge, but because they are brief there usually needs to be other means of collecting empirical material (e.g., participant observation in the field) for these interviews to obtain their aim. Note, however, that strictly speaking there are no open-ended interviews, but rather semi-structured and unstructured interviews that use open-ended questions. Similarly, there are no in-depth interviews, but rather semi-structured interviews that aim to gather in-depth knowledge. Therefore, to avoid any confusion, one should state, for example, that 'I use semi-structured interviews with open-ended questions to acquire in-depth knowledge on footballers' experiences of playing in a second division football club'.

While interviews can be used by all qualitative researchers, we want provide the following summary of how one's paradigmatic position might influence the type if interview suitable for the project:

Box 4.2 Type of interview & researcher's paradigm

Structured	Positivist, post-positivist
Semi-structured	Post-positivist, humanist, poststructuralist/postmodernist
Unstructured	Post-positivist, humanist, poststructuralist/postmodernist

The interview guide

The interview guide includes the questions that the researcher plans to ask during the interview. In a structured interview the guide is set and the interviewer is not to deviate from it to ensure that all the interviewees are asked exactly the same questions in exactly the same order. Semi-structured interviews are based on a pre-prepared guide that is, nevertheless, designed to be flexible to adjust to each interview situation and each interviewee's experiences. Unstructured interviews do not use interview guides as the need for these spontaneous interviews arises from the specific situation. Consequently, we focus here on how questions for a semi-structured interview are prepared to ensure that the purpose of the interview is achieved.

While most texts refer to interview guides, such terms as an interview schedule are also used. For example, Patton (2002) refers to an interview schedule that contains a detailed set of questions and probes, whereas an interview guide is usually organised around a series of topics or themes with a set of appropriate questions underneath each theme. While there are several ways to develop an interview guide, the questions should always help to answer the research question(s). Based on the literature review the researcher should be able to identify themes that either help obtain more in-depth knowledge than the previous research or that are new and previously unexplored issues. The following diagram (Figure 4.1) helps to conceptualise the interview guide approach further:

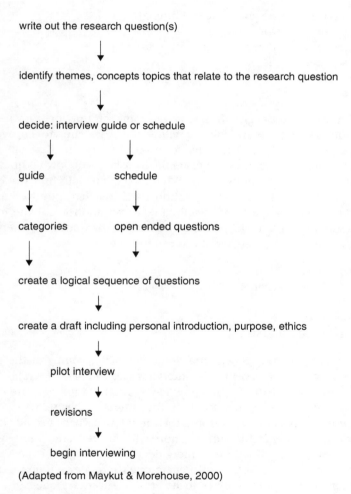

write out the research question(s)

↓

identify themes, concepts topics that relate to the research question

↓

decide: interview guide or schedule

↓   ↓

guide   schedule

↓   ↓

categories   open ended questions

↓   ↓

create a logical sequence of questions

↓

create a draft including personal introduction, purpose, ethics

↓

pilot interview

↓

revisions

↓

begin interviewing

(Adapted from Maykut & Morehouse, 2000)

Figure 4.1   The interview guide approach

As we pointed out earlier, qualitative interviews – semi-structured and unstructured interviews – are based on open-ended questions that allow the interviewee to elaborate at some length on the issues at hand. To maximise this opportunity, one should avoid closed questions that evoke a discrete response of yes or no. Such questions typically begin with: 'Are you ...? Have you ...? or Do you ...? For example, consider the following interview where the researcher is interested in player's experiences of pain and injury:

Interviewer: Are you currently injured?
Response: No.
Interviewer: Have you ever been injured?
Response: Yes.
Interviewer: Do you consider playing injured acceptable?
Response: No.

While these responses give the researchers some information, they hardly warrant 'in-depth' knowledge or allow the researcher to engage in a meaningful analysis. The interviewer could have had a chance to elaborate on the responses, for example, by asking a follow-up question about the player's previous injury (What type of previous injury did you have?). However, the original question itself solicited only 'yes' as an answer. To facilitate a more meaningful conversation about the topic, the researcher should ask open-ended questions that move the interview dynamically along. These questions can begin with

- What do you think ... ?
- How do you feel about ... ?
- In what way ... ?
- How might ... ?
- Why do you find it ... ?

Some qualitative researchers offer more detailed accounts of the tasks that each question serves in the interview (see sidebars of Kvale, 1996 and Patton, 2002). To ease the interviewee into the interview situation, it is sometimes recommended that the interview begins with 'easy' questions, such as those regarding the interviewee's background. These questions require factual information without reflection and, thus, might serve as introductions to more detailed accounts of experiences. In any case, it is important to prepare one's interview guide carefully based on the research themes to determine the exact questions and their logical relationship to each other.

Box 4.3 Types of interview questions

Kvale (1996):

- Introducing: Can you tell me about ... ? Do you remember an occasion when you performed really well?
- Follow-up: You stated that drug use is common in sport – how often have you seen someone administering drugs?
- Probing: Could you say something more about this? Can you give a more detailed description of what happened when your coach talked about using drugs?
- Specifying: Questions that obtain more specifying descriptions: How did you actually feel when ..? How did you react then?
- Direct: Have you ever taken drugs to improve your performance? Have you ever cheated?
- Indirect: How do think other athletes or coaches perceive drug use in sport?
- Structuring: Breaking up long answers that are not relevant for the structure of interview to introduce another topic: I would now like to introduce a new topic ...
- Silence: Allowing pauses during the interview for the interviewee to reflect and then break the silence him/herself.
- Interpreting: What do you mean when you say that everyone is taking drugs? Is it correct that you believe the medical team has given permission for the coaches to administer drugs?

Patton (2002):

- Behaviour/experience: Questions about the interviewee's previous experiences (e.g., what type of involvement has the interviewee had with drugs in sport?)
- Opinion/value: Questions that map the interviewee's opinions on, for example, drug use in sport (e.g., Is it justified or right in general?)
- Feeling: Questions about how the interviewee feels about, for example, drug use in sport (e.g., What are the interviewee's personal feelings about drug use in sport?)
- Knowledge: Questions to find out factual information, for example, a medical doctor will be able to provide facts about the types of drugs used in sport.

- Sensory: Questions about what is seen, heard, touched, tasted or smelt.
- Background/demographic: Questions about identifying characteristics of the interviewee such as age, education, occupation, ethnic background.

The interview situation

As stated earlier, semi-structured interviews usually require a formal setting designed to allow the participant to focus on the discussion at hand. Here the term 'formal' refers to a place dedicated to the interview, but otherwise, it can take place in the setting chosen by the interviewee (e.g., at the clubhouse after the practice, in an empty dance studio or class room, a café) that is quiet enough for an uninterrupted, purposeful conversation. Interviews usually take place in a 'public' setting (see Chapter 1 for ethics of conducting interviews in private settings such as participant's home).

While a qualitative, semi-structured interview is a conversation between two or more people, it is, nevertheless, designed for a specific research purpose determined by the researcher. At the same time, although the topic is chosen by the researcher, the intention is to gain the participants' viewpoints. The participants have volunteered their time to provide information for the researcher and, therefore, it is important that the researcher is fully appreciative of their efforts to help the researcher. While the researcher should guide the direction of the interviews, it is crucial that the participants should do most of the talking as their feelings, views and experiences are of the most interest. To encourage this, the researcher should use everyday language or the types of terms that participants would use in their lives. It is important to act professionally and avoid academic or theoretical terms even though the interview themes might be derived from academic, theoretical literature. This is particularly important if the participants come from a different cultural background from the researcher. Keep in mind that the idea is to understand the participants' viewpoint, not necessarily cast judgment on whether they are right or wrong. Consider the following interview situation:

Interviewer: In my research I am interested in how dominant masculinity is constructed through pain and injury in sport.
Participant: OK.

Interviewer: So, what do you think of that?

Participant: Think of what?

Interviewer: Dominant masculinity?

Participant: In my sport it is necessary to gain dominant position in the game – that is the only way to score …

Interviewer: and that leads to injuries?

Participant: No, not necessarily, only if you are unfit or you get tackled in a bad way and after all, this is a contact sport and …

Interviewer: So violence is a common cause of injuries in your sport.

Participant: I wouldn't call it violence. For example, tackling and some fighting are necessary parts of our sport.

Interviewer: But it is wrong to fight! That is not justifiable, you have rules and referees to prevent that!

Participant: Anyone who can't take the physical aspect, should not play – without it this is not a real sport. If you get injured, you are just weak, or you just have to suck it up!

Interviewer: But that is a terrible attitude – no wonder you players are injured all the time …

In this interview, it is obvious that the participant is not familiar with the term 'dominant masculinity' and begins to discuss his own understanding of 'dominance', which the interviewer interrupts to return to the research topic with a rather (mis)leading question. This leads to an exchange where the interviewer (mis)interprets the answers based on his research background and ends up judging the participant's ideas without an attempt to understand or listen to the participant's experiences, which while strong and perhaps misinformed from the researcher's perspective, are nevertheless indicative of his lived experiences – which should be the researcher's main interest! No doubt, this interview will be quite short and not result in in-depth knowledge of how masculinity is constructed in a particular sport. To obtain 'better' empirical material the interviewer should first have thought how he can ask questions about 'dominant masculinity' with words to which the participant might relate and then listen the participant's explanations with appropriate follow-up questions. For example,

Interviewer: I am interested in what type injuries you have had during your sport career. What was the last time you got injured?

Participant: I was driving forward – hard – I got tackled and my knee got dislocated.

Interviewer: That sounds like a serious injury. How long did you have to stay out?

Participant: I had to have an operation and then I went to rehab, so it was about 6 months without training and then I got back to training, but didn't play in a match until about 9 months.

Interviewer: How did you feel about having to take this much time off?

Participant: I have always been considered a tough guy, one that can be put into the frontline and who can take it and then having to not just do anything, having to just lay on the bed and sit and such ... I was beginning to think that I might no longer have it, I mean, not being able to play anymore after all that time. The pain is still there, but rehab is the worst, so much pain before you are even fit to train.

Interviewer: How does being injured influence your attitude to playing the game now?

Player: Yeah, I do have to think about it – like, not getting injured again, but you know, you can't show that, you can't let them know that you are avoiding something, or that you are not driving so hard anymore – you can't win with that attitude. Being able to take pain and not to avoid the tackles and even to fight sometimes is a necessary part of this game.

Interviewer: In what way are they necessary?

In this interview, the researcher carefully uses open-ended questions that encourage the participant to talk about his life. However, all the language used is familiar to the player and the interviewer is able to obtain relatively long answers from him. The researcher does not judge the participant's responses but is, instead, interested to know why the participant might think certain way about his sport. It is also obvious that the researcher has made the participant talk about 'dominant masculinity' (being tough, not showing pain or fear, having to 'fight') without using the theoretical term itself.

It is common that the interviewees consider the researcher as the expert in the topic of the interview and occasionally ask advice from the researcher. How do we act in such a situation considering that we are interested in the interviewee's experiences, not imposing our expertise on anyone? This is a difficult situation, because a qualitative interview is not a discussion between an expert and a client, unlike an interview in a doctor's office where the physician is interested in the patient's life only to provide health advice. In a qualitative interview the participant is actually the 'expert' whose knowledge is important per se. However, if someone acquires your research expertise, for example on injury treatment or training practices, this request should not be denied but the researcher might offer to discuss it in more detail after the interview is over.

A pilot interview

A pilot interview refers to 'a practice interview' that the researchers can conduct to 'test' their skills as interviewers and their interview guide as a research tool. It is common to conduct at least one pilot interview that can be done with an acquaintance to seek feedback of the interview protocol. Based on this feedback, the researcher might want to make some alterations to the interview guide or improve her/his interview skills to ensure the best possible material from research interviews.

Selection of participants

The number of participants in a qualitative interview study can range from 1 to 100 and it is therefore difficult to determine conclusively the number and the type of participants in a qualitative study. However, there are qualitative sampling techniques that help the researcher to determine who or what, and how many, one should include in the projects.

The target group of participants should be determined based on the research topic and research question. For example, if the research question is – How do serious female contemporary dancers understand injury? – it is clear that the actual sample has to come from women who are defined as serious contemporary dancers and who might have had an injury to reflect upon. How many of these dancers are chosen to participate in the study constitutes the sample. In qualitative research, samples are selected, not randomly to ensure objectivity as in quantitative research, but purposefully to seek answers to a specific research question. As Patton states: 'The logic and power of purposeful sampling lie in selecting *information-rich cases* for study in depth. Information-rich cases are those from which one can learn a great deal about issues of central importance to the purpose of the inquiry, thus the term of *purposeful* sampling' (2003, p. 230, italics in the original). Consequently, many qualitative researchers simply call their sampling technique 'purposeful sampling'. Patton, however, presents several 'sub-categories' for purposeful sampling. The following list is adapted from Patton (2003):

- Extreme or deviant case sampling: selected participants are information rich because they are unusual or special in some way. For example, one could try to interview winners of the Paralympic Games.

- Intensity sampling: information rich participants that manifest the phenomenon of interest intensely (but not extremely). For example, one could interview participants in the Paralympic Games.
- Maximum variation sampling: capturing and describing central themes that cut across a great deal of variation. One could select inactive and elite sport people with diverse types of mental and physical disabilities.
- Homogenous samples: selecting a small, homogenous group to describe some subgroup in depth. For example, one could interview male Paralympic wheelchair racers.
- Typical case sampling: selecting typical participants for study. For example, one could interview people with disability who typically take part in physical activity.
- Critical case sampling: selecting participants that exemplify the researcher's point dramatically. For example, one could interview people with disabilities whose quality of life has improved significantly due to participation in physical activity.
- Snowball or chain sampling: starting with a person well-situated to be interviewed about a special topic and then asking this person for more participants: 'Whom else do you know that I should talk to about this issue?' This way the sample gets bigger and bigger like a snowball as the researcher accumulates more information rich participants. For example, one could begin by interviewing one spinal cord injured athlete and then ask who else this participant would know with a similar injury.
- Criterion sampling: to review and study all participants that meet some predetermined criterion of importance. For example, all participants must be women over 18 years old who have gone through knee surgery, rehabilitation and returned to their sport.
- Theory-based sampling: 'The researcher samples incidents, slices of life, time periods, or people on the basis of their potential manifestation or representation of important theoretical constructs' (Patton, 2003, p. 238). For example, one chooses to interview sport people who illustrate an involvement in 'technologies of the self' (a theoretical concept by Foucault).
- Theoretical sampling: used by grounded theorists and defined as 'method of data collection based on concepts/themes derived from data' (Corbin & Strauss, 2008, p. 143). The purpose of this type of sampling is to maximise opportunities to develop concepts.
- Convenience sampling: selecting participants based on convenience such as time-efficiency, cost or location. For example, one can interview injured athletes in the sports teams of one's own university.

While all qualitative research uses purposive sampling, it is important to consider carefully which type of purposive sampling best serves one's research aim – it is unusual to adopt more than one sampling technique unless the research project contains several phases that require several, different samples.

How many participants to select is a less clearly defined issue. There is no clear rule in qualitative research regarding the sample size. The exact size depends mostly on the research purpose: how many people, cases or settings are needed in order to answer the research question(s)? What are the researcher's resources and time? For example, most likely it is not feasible to conduct 50 two-hour semi-structured interviews for a masters thesis where the student is to conduct all the interviews and also transcribe them. For such purpose, a sample of 10 or fewer participants might be more appropriate. It is equally unfeasible to think that a sample of three one-hour semi-structured interviews provide enough evidence for a qualitative PhD thesis. Therefore, for student work, it is best to negotiate the sample size carefully with one's supervisor. In other words, qualitative work in physical culture needs to present a rationale for the sample size in addition to the sampling technique and thus justify that the sample size is, indeed, purposeful for the particular research.

Transcribing an interview

Most qualitative researchers audio-tape their interviews into digital files and then transcribe them into a 'text-document' that can be printed and analysed. Transcribing can be done 'in verbatim' where all the 'utterances' and words during the interview are faithfully transcribed. Consider the following 'verbatim' interview transcript:

Interviewer: I would like to ask you some background information so that is not directly regarding the injuries and things, but kind of contextualises them
Participant: OK.
Interviewer: what we talk about later. So how long have you been dancing?
Participant: Um, well I started dancing when I was a little girl; I was probably like seven years old but intensely probably when I was in grade 11
Interviewer: OK so that makes you
Participant: grade. I moved to V to go
Interviewer: AHHH

Participant: yeah, I left, I'm from F
Interviewer: Aha
Participant: and I left in grade 11 to go to high school in V to go to preprofessional ah, ballet school
Interviewer: Aha
Participant: Called Arts and Ballet
Interviewer: mmmhmm
Participants: so almost like
Interviewer: so maybe ...
Participant: 20 years
Interviewer: Yeah, yeah
Participant: Yeah
Interviewer: 'cause of your dancing career
Participant: yeah, yeah
Interviewer: yeah, yeah and I know that you teach ballet but
Participant: yeah
Interviewer: what other types of dance do you teach?
Participant: ah, it's funny, um, ah, I've regularly was teaching jazz
Interviewer: mmmhmm
Participant: ah, ballet
Interviewer: mmmhmm

Transcribing absolutely everything obviously records the discussion faithfully. However, it can also unnecessarily lengthen the transcript. The discussion above only established that the participant has been dancing 20 years and is at the moment teaching ballet. In the actual interview situation this could have taken probably only a couple of seconds and adding all the 'utterances' does not seem to add anything conceptually interesting into the analysis (however, see discourse analysis discussed later in this chapter to explore how these types of 'utterances' can be used in an analysis). In addition, writing down spoken language sometimes makes the speakers appear incoherent and non-fluent although in the actual interview situation the conversation flows naturally. Therefore, the researcher might consider a 'cleaned' version of the interview situation, particularly if one is transcribing the interview oneself. The same conversation could be 'cleaned up' in the following manner without changing to the participant's meaning:

Interviewer: I would like to ask you some background information that is not directly regarding the injuries, but kind of contextualises what we talk about later. So, how long have you been dancing?

Participant: I started dancing when I was a little girl; I was probably like seven years old but intensely probably when I was in grade 11. I moved to V to go … I'm from F and I left in grade 11 to go to high school in V to go to pre-professional ballet school called Arts and Ballet. So, almost 20 years.

Interviewer: I know that you teach ballet but what other types of dance do you teach?

Participant: It's funny, I've regularly been teaching jazz; ballet …

When planning a qualitative interview design, the researcher should keep in mind that transcribing is time-consuming: if you transcribe yourself, calculate that one hour of audio-taped interview requires a minimum of three hours to transcribe if you are an experienced typist, have good equipment and the interview sound quality is good.

Interview analysis

Although a qualitative researcher is continually interpreting the collected material during the process of each interview by, for example, asking follow-up questions, the systematic analysis process begins after the interviews are transcribed. The analysis, while a crucial aspect of qualitative research, is an invisible process in the final research article or thesis. However, this is an important aspect of the qualitative research process as it determines the quality of the results of the study. In general terms, data analysis refers to working with the collected empirical material. In quantitative research, data analysis consists of statistical analysis that provides objective, numerical data to support or negate the research hypothesis. As qualitative interviews are subjective and draw from several paradigmatic orientations, there are also multiple analysis techniques. However, Corbin and Strauss (1990) present a useful division between pure data, data description and data interpretation. For example, the interview transcript is considered pure data that has not been analysed in any way. Therefore, it is not sufficient to present the transcripts as the research results. The material in them needs to be interpreted in some way to answer the research questions. Description could refer to listing what each interviewee answered for each question. While the data is organised differently from the transcripts, it is only described, not interpreted and, thus, description does not provide sufficient research knowledge. Therefore, empirical material for qualitative research needs to be interpreted which requires a further analysis process from the researcher. Kvale and Brinkmann (2007) understand analysis as a process in which the researcher focuses on the meaning of the interviews. This process, similar to other aspects of qualitative research, depends on the researcher's paradigmatic orientation. As qualitative research moves further away from the positivist paradigm there are fewer detailed data analysis techniques. For example, post-positivists have developed elaborate and lengthy processes for analysing their data whereas poststructuralist/postmodern researchers tend to rely more on their theoretical approach to analyse their empirical material. We thus present interview analysis techniques specific to each paradigm.

Post-positivist analysis of interviews: Coding

While post-positivism consists of multiple research traditions, they all, while using some form of qualitative research, assume an objective reality that the researcher aims to map together piece by piece. To ensure the objectivity of their results, several strands of post-positivist research have developed detailed data analysis techniques. For interview analysis, we detail here grounded theory, discourse analysis and conversation analysis.

Grounded theory data analysis

Grounded theory has been an integral aspect of the post-positivist movement and an elaborate system of analysing has evolved within this tradition. Corbin and Strauss (2008) have played a major role in developing a system of coding for the data analysis for grounded theory. Because the purpose of grounded theory is not to test hypotheses deductively, but rather to develop theory inductively (yet objectively), theory is grounded in the collected data and, therefore, working with the interview data by coding it in increasing detail is an integral part of a grounded theory approach. In a grounded theory approach the analysis moves from developing categories to finally theory through different levels of coding. The constant comparative method by Maykut and Morehouse (2000) illustrates the basic process (see Figure 4.2 below):

Strauss and Corbin's analysis is based on a continual and simultaneous process of categorisation of concepts through open and axial coding. Open coding refers to 'breaking data apart and delineating concepts to stand of blocks of raw data' (2008, p. 195). While open coding usually begins the data analysis as it identifies the basic concepts from the data, axial coding, which refers to 'crosscutting or relating concepts to each other' (p. 195), takes place once any concepts emerge from the raw data. Concepts obtained through these analyses are then refined into

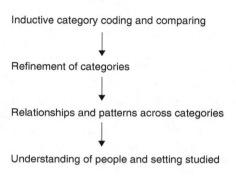

Inductive category coding and comparing

Refinement of categories

Relationships and patterns across categories

Understanding of people and setting studied

Figure 4.2   Constant comparative method

categories. These categories are fully developed when there is sufficient data saturation to create clear properties and dimensions, yet account for the variation. Based on the categories, the researcher can then trace the theory evolving from the data. An important aspect of this analysis process is 'memoing', where the researcher carefully records the names of the different codes, how they were drawn from the data and how they evolve into different categories. Based on the memos, the researcher can develop diagrams, 'visual devices that depict relationships between analytic concepts' (Strauss & Corbin, 2008, p. 117). For a more detailed account of the complex process of constant comparison through coding, see Strauss and Corbin (2008) and for a more contemporary reading of the grounded theory approach, see Charmaz (2005).

The new computer-assisted analyses of interviews are also based on coding (Kvale & Brinkmann, 2007). Some researchers use software packages designed specifically to aid qualitative analysis (Richards & Richards, 1998). There are a small number of software packages available, such as AnSWR, ATLAS.ti, HyperRESEARCH, Ethnograph, QCA, QSR NUD*IST and TextSmart that can aid in the management of qualitative data, the coding and retrieval of pieces of data, the indexing and exploration of data and the formation of theory (Richards & Richards, 1998). While perhaps intuitively appealing to the researcher, using these packages is the most suitable for post-positivist researchers who need to distance themselves from the data to increase the reliability of the interview process. Some have accused such packages of killing off the intuitive art of qualitative analysis (Richards & Richards, 1998; Stroh, 2000). Patton reminds us that 'Computers and software are tools that *assist* analysis. Software does not really analyze qualitative data. Qualitative software programs facilitate data storage, coding, retrieval, comparing, and linking – but human beings do the analysis' (2002, p. 442, italics in original).

Discourse analysis

Discourse analysis focuses on how language is used in context by looking at discursive strategies of particular people in particular socio-cultural situations. Discourse here refers to people's everyday conversation. This analysis technique characterises particularly discursive psychology (e.g., Edwards & Potter, 1992). Discursive psychologists are interested in talk as an interactional site 'in which speakers enact social roles and negotiate identities' (Brooks, 2009, p. 363) and they analyse how individuals build, manage and make their interests known within interactions. They are interested in how talk is used to construct certain accounts as valid. For example, they might analyse how interview participants use psychological and medical language to talk about their anxieties with food. Or they might analyse how interview participants 'psychologise' the meaning of exercise by emphasising 'blame' and guilt in their discussion.

While discourse analysis is mostly recommended for naturally occurring data such as informal interviews, it can also be used for the detailed analysis of semi-structured interview data. Discourse analysis, however, is not suitable for textual analysis (see Chapter 5 for further discussion of textual analysis). The emphasis is on how texts are made meaningful in the process of speaking and, therefore, the functional value of words (what the interviewee is doing with words) rather than the meaning of the words is under analysis. The idea of discourse analysis is to make explicit the implicit forms of language use. Therefore, the focus of the analysis is strictly on the language used and not on how the meanings are produced within the larger societal context. Therefore, discourse analysis differs from critical discourse analysis (CDA) or Foucauldian discourse analysis, which both examine how language reflects the power relations in society (see Chapter 5 for further discussion of these textual analysis techniques). To trace the function of a particular utterance in a particular social situation (e.g., in an interview) at a particular place, the researcher detects transactions – exchanges, moves and acts – in a conversation. Consider the following exchange in an elementary school class recorded by Mills (2004, p. 121):

Teacher: Can you tell me why do you eat all that food? Yes.
Pupil: To keep you strong.

Teacher: To keep you strong. Yes. To keep you strong. Why do you want to be strong?

In this short conversation, a discourse analyst first detects the type of exchange it represents. In this case, it is a conversation where the teacher elicits information from the students. The analyst then examines how this conversation was moved along through different transactions by the participants. For example, in line 1, the teacher uses an initiating move to begin the conversation; the student provides a responding move in line 2 by answering the question; the teacher again provides a feedback move as the first part of her answer and an initiating move again with a further question. Finally, the discourse analyst considers the function of different speech acts. For example, the teacher's first 'Yes' constitutes a nominating act as it chooses a pupil to answer the question whereas the second 'Yes' is a confirming act as it reaffirms the student's answers. This way it is possible to analyse how words can have different functions in the interaction. However, discourse analysis requires detailed attention to the ways talk is used: here only three lines of conversation provided a relative lengthy analysis.

Conversation analysis

Conversation analysis, in many ways, resembles discourse analysis. It is also an analysis of talk-in-action. However, the purpose of this analysis is to move from understanding an interview as expressing the speakers' internal thoughts to understanding talk as a social activity. However, 'social' here, similarly to its use in discourse analysis, refers to an interview situation as a social act between people (not to larger social structures that might produce the meanings of the talk) and, similarly to discourse analysis, the focus is on the interaction rather than the meanings produced in the talk. According to Kvale and Brinkmann, conversation analysis focuses on 'the sequencing of talk, in particular upon turn-taking sequences and report of turn-taking errors' (2007, p. 221). It provides minute details of 'talk-in-interaction' and thus focuses on 'what a specific speech segment accomplishes' (Kvale & Brinkmann, 2007, p. 221). It follows closely the verbal interaction between the speakers rather than interprets the meanings of their speech. While conversation analysis is intended for situations independent of a researcher's intervention/objective such as unstructured, informal interviews, it is also often used to analyse formal, recorded interviews. In conversation analysis, the talk is understood as a jointly constructed interaction between the interviewer and interviewee: how speakers constitute their reality in face-to-face situation. Therefore, the central goal of conversation analysis is:

> The description and explanation of competences that ordinary speakers use and rely on in participating in intelligible socially organised interactions ... the analyst is not required to speculate upon what the interactants hypothetically or imaginably understood ... instead analysis can emerge from the observation of the participants.
> (Atkinson & Heritage, 1984, p. 1)

A special feature of conversation analysis is orthographic transcription where all words and all expressive features such as pauses, partial words, elongation and volume of speech are recorded. This type of transcription requires special skills, but all these features of talk are considered an integral part of how the talk-in-action becomes an intelligibly organised social interaction. For example, Finley and Faulkner (2003) examined how athletes managed attributions – how they 'explained' the cause for the outcome of their sport action (particularly losing) – through their interview conversations. The interview transcripts demonstrated the athletes' struggle and reluctance to discuss losing: they 'bought time' through hesitation and 'put off' answering such questions in the interview. A detailed analysis of the orthographic transcription clearly illustrated these features in the interactions where the athletes employed numerous pauses and took their time to struggle through the interview.

Conversation analysis and discourse analysis share many similar features and they are sometimes used interchangeably to describe a detailed analysis of the function of talk. They both subscribe to the paradigmatic assumptions of the post-positivist paradigm in that they aim objectively, in detail, to trace how talk functions in everyday interactions. This type of analysis is devoid of any interpretation of meaning as that cannot be objectively supported by visible transcribed data, the actual talk. In addition, talk interactions are assumed to represent stable and generalisable patterns of talk, which the participants demonstrate in their particular conversations (Smith & Sparkes, 2005). Therefore, emphasis is on empirical evidence, the conduct, in favour of the motives of the speaker that cannot be detected clearly from the transcript. Both discourse analysis and conversation analysis consequently focus on how things are said in a conversation leaving the 'whats' (i.e., what the conversation means) outside the analysis (Smith & Sparkes,

2005). In short, these techniques focus on description of practices and patterns of interaction in immediate conversation context instead of theory driven analysis of how meanings are made within a larger social context. In addition, discourse analysis, particularly, aims to eliminate the researcher's impact on the situation and favours naturally occurring conversations in which the researcher does not participate. However, many researchers also clearly distinguish between these two interview analysis techniques (e.g., Smith & Sparkes, 2005). Faulkner and Finley (2002), for example, understand conversation analysis as a microanalytic variety of discourse analysis that, rather than mere focus on function of the words, also traces the cognitive content (beliefs and sources of the beliefs) in talk interaction. In addition, conversation analysis is more cognisant of the interviewer's impact on the conversation. In any case, these analysis techniques are unsuitable for critical and poststructuralist analysis of interviews that require a more theoretical approach for the analysis of how meanings are constructed within a larger social context. It also is important not to confuse post-positivist discourse analysis with Whetherell and Potter or Fairclough's critical discourse analysis (see Chapter 5), which are both inspired by critical theory, or Foucauldian discourse analysis (see Chapter 6).

Interpretive interview analysis: Focus on meaning units

The interpretive paradigm focuses on an individual's experiences and meanings; therefore, interviews are often used to collect data within this paradigm. The interpretive paradigm assumes that there is one reality, but there are multiple openings to that reality, and thus the focus is on individual meaning making. As noted in Chapter 2, phenomenology is often located within the interpretive paradigm. Many phenomenologists claim, nevertheless, that phenomenology is a philosophical approach as well as a method. This understanding defines the entire research process and is not limited to a specific data analysis phase. Therefore, while empirical material can be collected by interviewing people, it is important, the phenomenologists claim, to assemble 'descriptions' of lived experiences unlimited by, for example, semi-structured interviews that are influenced by the researcher's theoretical viewpoint. Giorgi (1985), inspired by Husserl, suggests the following process that can be use to analyse phenomenologically informed interviews:

- The collection of concrete, naïve description of the phenomenon (through interviewing);

- The adoption of the phenomenological attitude;
- An impressionistic reading for each description;
- The in-depth reading to identify 'meaning units' to capture specific aspects of the whole;
- The identification of explicit psychological significance of each meaning unit;
- The production a general description of the structures of the experience.

(Adapted from Giorgi, 1985).

For other phenomenological analysis process see, for example, van Manen (1990). Other qualitative researchers have modified the phenomenological process for a more general use. Kvale and Brinkmann, for example, offer an interview analysis technique based on phenomenology and hermeneutics. They characterise the phenomenological analysis as meaning condensation: through analysis '[l]ong statements are compressed into briefer statements in which the main sense of what is said is rephrased in a few words' (2007, p. 205). The process consists of five steps (see Figure 4.3) (see also Groenewald, 2004):

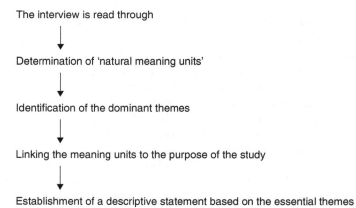

The interview is read through

Determination of 'natural meaning units'

Identification of the dominant themes

Linking the meaning units to the purpose of the study

Establishment of a descriptive statement based on the essential themes

Figure 4.3   Five steps of meaning condensation

Holstein and Gubrium's (2005) analytic bracketing draws from the interpretive premise of individual meaning making. Unlike the post-positivist discourse and conversation analyses, which focus solely on how language is used, analytic bracketing aims to analyse both discursive practice (how language is used) and discourse-in-practice (what is said). For a more detailed description of this analytical technique see narrative research (Chapter 6).

Similar to Groenewald (2004), Ritchie and Spencer (1994) developed an interpretive approach titled 'Framework' as an analytical process by which to analyse unstructured interview material. Framework involves a number of distinct yet highly interconnected stages. This approach relies on the creative and conceptual ability of the analyst to determine meaning, salience and connections (Ritchie & Spencer, 1994). Somewhat adapting Ritchie and Spencer (1994), the five stages of the approach are:

1. Familiarisation (the researcher reads transcripts, re-reads, uses memory, thoughts or feelings).
2. Identifying a thematic framework (the process of identifying emergent themes).
3. Indexing (literally going through the empirical material and coding it for the various themes, either physically using numbers, highlighter pens or other systems that work well, or copying and pasting on a computer).
4. Charting (linking the relationships between the various themes).
5. Mapping and interpretation (picking various instances within themes and relating to various literatures and wider social forces).

The framework approach was used by Lee, Avis and Arthur (2007) in their work with older people. In particular, Lee et al. were interested in understanding the role of self-efficacy on the amount of exercise conducted by this population. The design of the study initially centred on a large walking intervention trial. Following this intervention, a subset of older people from the trial were interviewed to understand more about their experiences and views of walking as an exercise. Interviews were analysed using the framework technique described above. Lee et al. (2007) report that the technique allowed for the structured and systematic generation of themes from the interview data, but also the opportunity to return to earlier stages of the process to rework ideas and thematic development.

Interview analysis for the critical paradigm

Johnson et al. (2004) suggest an analysis process more aligned to the critical paradigm. This approach recognises both the self-reflexive role of the researcher and the complex political and ideological agendas that are often hidden in one's work. Their concept of dialogic interpretation asserts that each stage, aspect or moment of interpretation involves a dialogue between the researcher (self) and other (others' words). Their approach is useful because it allows the researcher to 'connect' the empirical material with wider social structures and contexts. In this sense, this approach enables the researcher to socially situate the research and the researcher, and thus 'work the hyphen' between the private world of that researched and the public worlds of the wider social context. Johnson et al. (1994) suggest four dialogic moments of interpretation, which we have somewhat adapted below:

> <u>Dialogue 1</u>: *Recalling*: The researcher thinks about the impressions accumulated (this should happen at the start of data collection), confirms or internally debates hunches, rethinks hunches or assumption, thinks about the insights gained into the particular instance of physical culture. The process may be mundane or it may be more visceral. It may be create excitement about the collected empirical material, a chunk of material may literally cause the researcher to worry, to become anxious, or, conversely, it may be a cause for joy or happiness. It is important not to focus purely on such 'nuggets', remembering that the banal data may well be as important. These types of interpretation can take place during and after the collection of empirical material and involve using memory to recall events.
>
> <u>Dialogue 2</u>: *Listening Around*: This is the second dialogue that takes place between the researcher and the actual materials collected (e.g., transcriptions). This process, similar to Ritchie and Spencer's Framework (1994), involves becoming familiar with the empirical material (the researcher reads transcripts, re-reads, uses memory, thoughts or feelings). Further, it involves a process of transcription, coding and indexing to highlight the emergent themes. Here the researchers ask whether the material is adequate to answer the research question/address the issue and whether more material is needed. This dialogue is also designed to help locate the empirical material within existing literatures to investigate whether the researcher's hunches, ideas or assumptions need revision.
>
> <u>Dialogue 3</u>: *Close reading*: At this point the researcher should have a good knowledge of the material and have a sense of possible arguments to ask the question: what now? Key themes will be recognised in the empirical material. The researcher will start to think about how to construct a story, for what purpose, for which audience?

The 'so what' question also needs to be addressed at this point: What difference will this research make, will there be a practical impact? How am I going to turn these data into a piece of work that connects them to social forces? How am I going to 'work the hyphen': to reveal how the words reflect the ideological construction of the social world. How am I going to present it in a socially meaningful story? Which key instances from the themes developed shall I use to develop understandings and explanations of power? What are the typical cases for arguments? What are the apparent exceptions and differences? Does it matter if I reveal differences of opinion and produce a messier text that is less logical and coherent (but reflects that which I interpreted) in terms of my argument for the ideological production of reality? Or will I produce work that agrees with the previous literature and my political position as a researcher? In essence, at this point, the researchers focus on how meanings and identities (including the researcher's identity) are produced in current ideological contexts of research, recognise who they do not address and identify how various absences or silences illustrate the ideological workings of power.

Dialogue 4: *Representing Self & Others*: This is the 'writing-up' stage of the research. This is not a simplistic process. There are many political, structural and aesthetic issues that must be taken into account, including how research writing fits with the purpose, political motivation or praxis orientation of a critical researcher. We discuss the issues around research writing further in Chapter 8.

(Adapted from Johnson et al., 2004))

Interestingly, within published work, the analysis phase is often invisible. This is due to space limitations (e.g., in a journal article) or a lack of consideration for the actual process of analysis. Indeed, this phase is often overlooked in the design of a study, yet it is crucial given that critical interpretation and reflection may well mean the researcher goes back into the field, or perhaps changes the focus of the questioning or, indeed, how they act towards certain people within the research setting. Newman (2007; 2010); Newman & Beissel (2009) who conducted intensive ethnographic work on the pervasive racial politics surrounding the symbolism of the Colonel Rebel mascot at Ole Miss University (see Newman, 2007) offers a rare example of the critical analytic process. Newman initially conducted a series of interviews with University administrators and ancillary groups (e.g., booster clubs, alumni groups) and then cross-referenced these interview findings with a series of historical documents. Throughout his work, and particularly as he reflected on his findings, he began to feel discomfort with what he was finding, and indeed on his own positionality within the research setting. Newman returned to the field, interviewing as many participants as possible during game day festivities, until he felt he had reached saturation point. The next stage of analysis meant that he linked the everyday festivities at Ole Miss to wider social forces. Through working the hyphen, he does not present his observations in an ahistorical or acontextual fashion, but rather points to the inextricable links between the academic institution and its sporting icon, and idiomatic and systematic formations of longtitudinal racial oppression. Further, he also critically reflected on the notion that his ability to contact these informants and collect these data, and thus tell a story of continued racial oppression, is in part due to the access afforded him given his own gendered, regionalised and racialised identity politics – that of being Southern (identifiable in regional diction and drawl), white and male.

Poststructuralist and postmodern interviews: Theory-based analysis

Researchers from a poststructuralist or postmodern paradigm are often vague about how they work with their empirical material. This is partly due to their subjective epistemology, which does not necessitate detailed verification of the research process to ensure objectivity. There is a much stronger emphasis on understanding individual meaning making within a social, political, historical and economic context. This does not mean that these researchers do not need to go through an analysis process in order to interpret their interview material. On the contrary, a well conducted analysis process strengthens the interpretation and provides a convincing final analysis. Poststructuralist/postmodern researchers require a clearly articulated theoretical frame for interpreting the meanings in interviews (Kvale & Brinkmann, 2007). Therefore, researchers from these paradigmatic orientations should clearly stipulate how they analyse their empirical material through their theoretical lenses. In addition, they should be cognisant of analysis techniques for their theoretical orientation. For example, poststructuralists such as Foucault (genealogy), Derrida (deconstruction), Deleuze (rhizomatics) and many psychoanalysts have developed very specific theory-based analysis techniques that researchers claiming to use their theoretical perspective should respect. While there are theoretical specifications, the following general patterns for interview analysis can be helpful for poststructuralist and postmodern researchers:

- Identification of themes:
  - The themed interview guide will aid in this step;
- Analysis of the themes:
  - Intersections with themes;
  - Discrepancies with themes;
  - 'New themes';
- Connection with power relations, theory and previous literature.

In his work on rugby, Pringle (Markula & Pringle, 2006; Pringle & Markula, 2005) framed his interview study within Foucault's theory of discourse. The guide for the semi-structured interviews was constructed to highlight the discursive construction of men's lived experiences of rugby and consequently consisted of three interrelated themes: personal sporting histories; rugby experiences of fear, pain and pleasure; and understandings of masculinities, gender relations and rugby. The last two themes reflected previously known dominant discourses (or ways of knowing) of rugby (rugby as a high contact sport with physical pain and fear of contact, but also a pleasure of playing the game; and rugby as a 'masculine' sport). The first theme was designed to locate the discourses within the participants' sporting backgrounds. The interview analysis was then guided by Foucault's 'cautionary prescriptions' (Markula & Pringle, 2006, p. 106) about discourses: it is not a simple task to identify discourses or divide them into either dominant or marginalised ones, but the researchers should look for 'numerous and even contradictory discourses' that 'govern the interviewees' perceptions' (p. 106). Furthermore, the analysis followed specific techniques of analysis provided by Foucault (1978):

- To identify enunciations that are required, but also those that are concealed;
- To identify their effects;
- To identify who is speaking and the speaker's position of power;
- To identify the institutional context.

Finally, the interview analysis aimed to reveal the 'tactical productivity' of discourses evident in the men's interviews: how 'discourses were drawn upon to (re)produce sporting identities and shape gender relations' and how 'the interviewees *strategically* used these discourses to position themselves and others' (Markula & Pringle, 2006, p. 107, italics in original).

Validation for interview research will be discussed in Chapter 9.

Summary

While interviews are among the most often used sources for empirical material in qualitative research, they are not suitable or necessary for every qualitative project. Therefore, the researcher should carefully consider what types of interview can provide the best answers to the research question at hand. In addition, the researchers should carefully consider, based on their paradigmatic approaches, how to interpret their empirical material from the collected interviews. A successful interview study has the following characteristics:

- The type of interviewing (semi-structured, unstructured) is selected based on a clearly defined purpose;
- The interviews have clearly defined, paradigmatic and theoretical logic;
- The themes and questions in the interview guide are based on a well developed review of previous literature on the topic;
- The sampling of participants is conducted purposefully;
- The interview is conducted by a well prepared, skilled and professional interviewer;
- The transcript is mostly filled with the participants' words and provides in-depth knowledge for a qualitative analysis;
- The results are derived through a clearly articulated and appropriate analysis technique.

Further reading on qualitative interview analysis

Grounded theory:

Cote, J., Salmela, J. H. & Russell, S. (1995). 'The knowledge of high-performance gymnastics coaches: Methodological framework'. *The Sport Psychologists*, 9, 65–75.

Kihl, L. A., Richardson, T. & Campisi, C. (2008). 'Toward a grounded theory of student-athlete suffering and dealing with academic corruption'. *Journal of Sport Management*, 22, 273–302.

Kihl, L. A. & Richardson, T. (2009). '"Fixing the mess": A grounded theory of a men's basketball coaching staff's suffering as a result of academic corruption'. *Journal of Sport Management*, 23, 278–304.

Discourse analysis:

Brooks, S. (2009). 'Radio food disorder: The conversational constitution of eating disorders in radio phone-ins'. *Journal of Community and Applied Social Psychology*, 19, 360–73.

Wiggins, S. (2009). 'Managing blame in NHS weight management treatment: Psychologizing weight and "obesity"'. *Journal of Community and Applied Social Psychology*, 19, 374–87.

Conversation analysis:

Faulkner, G. & Finley, S. (2002). '"It's not what you say, its the way you say it!" Conversation analysis: A discursive methodology for sport, exercise, and physical education'. *Quest*, 54(1), 49–66.
Finley, S.-J. & Faulkner, G. (2003). '"Actually I was the star": Managing attributions in conversation'. *Forum: Qualitative Social Research*, 4(1), no page nos.
Potter, J. & Hepburn, A. (2005). 'Qualitative interviews in psychology: Problems and possibilities'. *Qualitative Research in Psychology*, 2, 281–307.

Interpretive analysis:

An, J. & Goodwin, D. L. (2007). 'Physical education for students with Spina Bifida: Mothers' perspectives'. *Adaptive Physical Activity Quarterly*, 24, 38–58.
Lee, L., Avis, M. & Arthur, A. (2007). 'The role of self-efficacy in older people's decisions to initiate and maintain regular walking as exercise: Results from a qualitative study'. *Preventative Medicine*, 45(1), 62–5.

Critical analysis:

Newman, J. (2007). 'Army of whiteness: Colonel Reb and the sporting south's cultural and corporate symbolic'. *Journal of Sport & Social Issues*, 31(4), 315–39.
Newman, J. I. (in press). [Un]Comfortable in my own skin: On articulation, reflexivity, and the duality of the self. *International Review for Qualitative Research*.

Postmodern/poststructuralist analysis:

Markula, P. (2004). '"Tuning into one's self": Foucault's technologies of the self and mindful fitness'. *Sociology of Sport Journal*, 21, 302–21.
Pringle, R. & Markula, P. (2005). 'No pain is sane after all: A Foucauldian analysis of masculinities and men's experiences in rugby'. *Sociology of Sport Journal*, 22, 472–97.

5
Practice and the Politics of Interpretation: Textual Analysis

In this chapter, we will

- Discuss how to select written texts for qualitative analysis;
- Detail three different textual analyses: critical discourse analysis, Johnson's cultural studies approach to textual analysis and Foucauldian discourse analysis.

This chapter focuses on the analysis of texts as a way of practising research in physical culture. As written communication has become the dominant form of communication in today's society, social analyses of different types of 'texts' have also become increasingly common. Physical culture is also often examined through how it is written about in various sources, ranging from popular texts to scholarly analyses. Consequently, several methods, exclusive to text analysis, have evolved. Textual analyses differ from the other ways of practising research because the researchers do not actually assemble empirical text material themselves. In an interview study, for example, the researcher needs first to collect the interview 'texts', which are then analysed and interpreted (see Chapter 4). Or during participant-observation, the researcher writes field notes that are then analysed and interpreted (see Chapter 7). A textual analysis focuses interpreting the content and meaning of already existing texts, most commonly written by someone else. In this sense, textual analysis is, strictly speaking, a form of data analysis technique. We treat it, however, as a way of practising research because it can provide the main methodological framework for a research project on physical culture.

In addition to the generic features we laid out in Chapter 3, a method section for a study using textual analysis should include at least the following sections:

Box 5.1 Content of a method section for qualitative textual analysis

---

- Qualitative, inductive framework;
- Sampling;
- Type of textual analysis;
- Validation.

We will now detail sampling for textual analysis and three different types of textual analyses. We discuss the 'validation' of a textual analysis in Chapter 9.

Selection of texts

As we are surrounded by different forms of written communications, there is no difficulty in finding sources for textual analysis. While the most common 'texts' in terms of research are probably literature, popular media and policy texts, any written (e.g., newspapers, magazines, drama, text messages, internet websites, blogs, emails), visual (e.g., film, photographs, television broadcasts, visual art), audible (e.g., lyrics, conversations) or combination of these texts can be chosen as sources of analysis. How to choose exactly what texts for analysis?

To select a sample for their textual analysis, the researcher needs to consider:

- The type of medium (e.g., newspapers, magazines, books, films, television, radio);
- The type of text (e.g., written articles, photographs, spoken text, moving images or a combination);
- The time frame (e.g., one week, one month, a length of event coverage such as Olympics, one year);
- The number of text sources (e.g., how many newspapers, magazines, television channels, books, films);
- The number of texts (e.g., how many newspaper articles or photographs from the selected newspapers or magazines, what television programs/episodes).

Therefore, as the sample size for a textual analysis depends on all these factors, it is difficult to determine conclusively a suitable number and the type of texts for a qualitative study. As in other types of qualitative studies, the number and type of sample depends on the research topic and research question. For example, a researcher can ask: how were British women athletes represented in British newspapers during the Vancouver 2010 Winter Olympics? It is then clear that the time frame for this study should include the two weeks in which the Olympics take place. However, the researcher still needs to decide exactly what newspapers should be included in the study. Should both tabloid and broadsheets be included? How many of each? Should all the issues be analysed? Should the entire newspaper coverage be analysed or just the sport pages? Should both pictures and textual material be analysed? Should all women athletes in the British team be included or should the researcher focus only on some who receive substantial coverage?

It is obvious that samples for textual analyses, as in all qualitative research, are selected, not randomly to ensure objectivity like in quantitative research, but purposefully to seek answers to a specific research question. As Patton states: 'The logic and power of purposeful sampling lie in selecting *information-rich cases* for study in depth. Information-rich cases are those from which one can learn a great deal about issues of central importance to the purpose of the enquiry, thus the term of *purposeful* sampling' (2002, p. 230, italics in original). It is important, therefore, that the researchers carefully think of the purpose of their textual analysis in order then to select the texts that provide the best information to answer the research question. It is also important to detail how one selected one's sample in the method section for a textual analysis. Patton's 'subcategories' for purposeful sampling can also be used to determine the exact sample for textual analysis. The following typology of sampling is adapted from Patton (2002):

- Extreme or deviant text sampling: selected texts are information rich because they are unusual or special in some way. For example, selecting articles that with an unusual topic or special focus during Olympic newspaper coverage.
- Intensity sampling: information rich texts that manifest the phenomenon of interest intensely (but not extremely). For example, selecting articles that focus on women athletes of colour during the Olympic Games newspaper coverage.
- Maximum variation sampling: capturing and describing central themes that cut across a great deal of variation during a certain

timeframe or in a certain medium. For example, selecting articles of the most successful and most unsuccessful male and female athletes during the Olympic Games newspaper coverage.

- Homogenous samples: selecting a small, homogenous group of texts to describe a specific phenomenon in detail. For example, selecting all articles on women gold medal winners during Olympic news-paper coverage in the sports pages of one tabloid newspaper.
- Typical case sampling: selecting typical text for study. For example, including all newspaper articles that focus on previewing matches of a major sport (such as football).
- Critical case sampling: selecting texts that exemplify the researcher's point dramatically. For example, selecting articles that dwell on women athletes' failure to demonstrate the construction of empha-sised femininity.
- Criterion sampling: to review and study all texts that meet some pre-determined criterion of importance. For example, selecting newspaper articles that portray only gold medal winners in the Olympic Games.
- Theory-based sampling: texts are selected for their potential to repre-sent important theoretical constructs. For example, selecting newspaper articles that illustrate how nationalism as an ideological construction works through sports reporting.
- Convenience sampling: selecting texts based on convenience such as time-efficiency, cost or location. For example, selecting a newspaper generally available in the researcher's hometown.

While all qualitative research uses purposive sampling, it is important to consider carefully which type of purposive sampling best serves one's research aim – it is unusual to adopt more than one sampling technique unless the research project contains several phases that require several different samples.

How many texts to select is a less clearly defined issue. There is no clear rule in qualitative research regarding the sample size. The exact size depends mostly on the research purpose: how many texts are needed to answer the research question(s)? What are the researcher's resources and time? For example, most likely it is not feasible to analyse all the content in a sports magazine during 12 months, or all the television coverage dur-ing the Olympic Games for a masters thesis. For such purpose, a homo-geneous sample of 10 articles or critical case sample of certain segments of the television coverage are more appropriate. It is equally unfeasible to think that a sample of three 2-page magazine articles provides enough information rich texts for a qualitative PhD thesis. Is one sport film a big enough sample for textual analysis? The researcher would need to think carefully about the context of the text, and whether this text is appropriate to the research problem or concern. For example, reading a text such as the Lingerie Bowl (the annual pay-per-view broadcast timed to coincide with the Super Bowl), might be important as an extreme case of gender politics. It is therefore important to be clear about the research assumptions and research question and then find an appropriate sample size. For student work, it is best to negotiate the sample size carefully with one's supervisor. In other words, qualitative work in physical culture needs to present a rationale for the sample size in addition to the sampling technique and thus justify that the sample size is indeed purposeful for the particular textual analysis. In addition to selecting a sample, a researcher needs to consider the type of textual analysis to employ. There are several textual analysis methods and the selection of the specific methods depends on the researcher's paradigmatic and theoretical framework.

Types of textual analysis

Similar to interviewing, textual analysis can be conducted quantitatively or qualitatively. Quantitative textual analysis is commonly referred to as content analysis (e.g., Deacon et al., 1999; Riffe, Lacy & Fico, 1998; Wimmer & Dominick, 2003). It aims to represent a body of messages accurately 'to understand what the media produces by systematically quantifying media content, using pre-determined categories, and analysing the results statistically' (Bruce, Hovden & Markula, 2010, p. 31). This type of textual analysis follows a deductive logic, through which hypotheses derived from the current theory are proven correct or incorrect. It provides numerical measurements of textual content. For example, content analysis is often used to analyse the amount of media coverage on a specific issue. It is possible to analyse the amount of sport coverage devoted to women's sport versus that of men's sport in newspapers or televised sport broadcasts (e.g., Bruce, Hovden & Markula, 2010). As content analysis focuses on the amount of coverage, it will not provide a great deal of detail about the type of content. In other words, it explores what is in the text, but not how it is presented. Contrary to content analysis, qualitative textual analyses focus on the meaning(s) of the text.

Qualitative textual analysis is a methodology that draws from several distinct theoretical traditions. Researchers interested in phenomenologically derived analysis of lived experiences presented through texts should consult Chapter 4 where phenomenological analysis is discussed in the context of interview texts. Researchers interested in other forms of interpretive analysis of texts should consult Chapter 6, where narrative analysis is discussed. In this chapter we focus on textual analysis from critical and poststructuralist perspectives. This type of textual analysis is based on the idea that text has several meanings, some of which are more obvious than the others. All of these meanings, however, will influence how the text is interpreted. Therefore, the researcher aims to reveal several meaning layers in the text, but also to examine how these meanings are constructed in their particular context. According to Stuart Hall's (1980) seminal theory media texts have:

- Denotative meaning: obvious, intended meaning; and
- Connotative meaning: hidden meaning.

Therefore, multiple readings are possible, but texts are not open to any reading. Their meanings are:

- Encoded by the text producers:
  - preferred reading;
- Decoded by the audience who can read:
  - preferred reading;
  - negotiated reading;
  - oppositional reading.

Analysis of text is often referred to as 'discourse analysis'. In its most common meaning discourse refers to 'language' and, as we discussed in Chapter 4, spoken language can also be considered as 'discourse'. In the table below we have identified several analysis methods that use the term 'discourse', but differ in terms of how they contextualise the meaning of discourse. In this chapter we focus on analysis of written texts and detail Fairclough's critical discourse analysis (CDA), Johnson et al.'s textual reading as practice and Foucauldian discourse analysis as ways of interpreting text content (see Table 5.1).

Critical discourse analysis

While interviewing can be used across several paradigms and theoretical orientations, textual analysts have developed methods based on a very specific theoretical grounding and thus they provide the best results when used with their 'proper' theoretical approach. We will first detail critical discourse analysis (CDA), which draws from critical theory to analyse texts in their social context.

Table 5.1   Types of discourse analysis

	Theoretical approach	Theorist	Power	Definition of discourse
Discourse analysis See Chapter 4	Post-positivist	Edwards and Potter	No connection to power	Spoken language
Critical discourse analysis (CDA)	Ideological hegemony	Fairclough	Hegemonic power	Written, spoken, visual, texts
Social-constructionist discourse analysis	Ideological hegemony/ Foucault	Wetherell and Potter	Hegemonic power	Written and spoken language, visual texts
Foucauldian discourse analysis	Foucault	Foucault	Power as relational	Written and spoken language, visual texts

While CDA is a general term that encompasses a variety of methods for social critique (Blommaert, 2005), Norman Fairclough has systematically developed 'a set of philosophical premises, theoretical methods, methodological guidelines and specific techniques' to analyse texts (Phillips & Jørgensen, 2002, p. 60). The central focus of CDA is to critically investigate and address social problems through examining *ideological workings* of the text. In this sense, CDA draws from critical social theory such as the Frankfurt School and neo-Marxism (Blommaert & Bulcaen, 1997). To further understand the theoretical premise for CDA, we present a simplified version of how critical theorists conceptualise ideology and how it is linked to language use and text. This version draws mainly on Gramsci's theory of hegemony (see Figure 5.1) (see also Chapter 2):

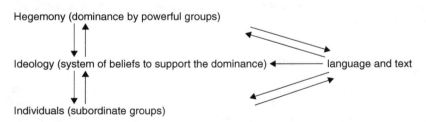

Hegemony (dominance by powerful groups)

Ideology (system of beliefs to support the dominance) ← language and text

Individuals (subordinate groups)

Figure 5.1   CDA

In this context, dominant groups hold the power in society and work to maintain their position of power through distributing belief systems that, while they support the dominance, appear natural, justified and beneficial for all groups. Image/text/language serves to transmit the ideologies from the dominant group to the individuals. Analysis of language can be used to examine how the subordinate groups influence the dominant groups and thus, serve to change the ideologies. The dominant group is assumed to have access to more media sources than the subordinate groups. Therefore, CDA is designed to disclose the ideologies and, thus, make explicit how dominance works through texts and language (Liao & Markula, 2009). Fairclough uses the term 'discourse' as a 'particular way of conceptualizing ... language' (2006, p. 9) that includes written texts, spoken words, visual images, body language and various semiotic forms. Each text is read as a 'communication event' (Blommaert, 2005; Phillips & Jørgensen, 2002) that contextualises the language use within a specific field. In other words, a CDA researcher is interested in what way speaking gives meaning to experiences from a particular perspective in a particular event and social field.

It is obvious that CDA scholars approach the analysis of texts from a political perspective. The purpose is to understand the intersection of language use and social and political structure, particularly how language use, or discourse, functions ideologically to contribute to the creation and reproduction of unequal power relations. This analysis is possible through textual analysis because language is considered to contribute to the constructions of social identities (both dominant and subordinate identities), social relations between individuals and groups and finally, the systems of knowledge and meaning used to maintain the power differences. CDA thus, is designed to examine the relationship between language use (discursive practices), events and texts and the relationship between texts and broader social and cultural structures, relations and processes. Therefore, Fairclough (1995, 2002) is concerned about how ideology constrains language use and how language used in communication events transforms meanings. The analysis thus has to take place at three levels that comprise the communicative event:

Communicative event:

- Text:
  - speech, writing, visual image, or combination;
- Discursive practice:
  - production and consumption of text;
- Social practice.

(Adapted from Fairclough, 1992)

Fairclough defines the three analytical steps as description of the content of the communications event (text), intertextual analysis (discursive practice) and connection to ideological dominance (social practice). We have modified Fairclough's conceptual model to provide a 'user-friendly' way to conduct CDA to examine the ideological construction physical culture through text.

Box 5.2 Conducting critical discourse analysis

- Step 1: Analysis of text and picture images.
- Step 2: Analysis of connections to existing narratives.
- Step 3: Connection to ideology.
- Step 4: Connection to power.

Step 1 of our modified CDA model consists of a detailed description of the text at hand. In this step the researcher should really focus on 'what is' in the text without attempting to analyse its content further. For example, an analysis of written texts at this stage should include description of

- Vocabulary, wording:
  - key words and terms;
  - what words are used to describe people;
  - types of adjectives used;
- Grammar;
- Syntax;
- Sentence coherence;
- Metaphors.

An analysis of a visual text that depicts people should include

- Clothing;
- Groupings;
- Positioning;
- Gestures;
- Facial gestures;
- Appearance;
- Context of picture.

In addition, one should focus on visual analysis of camera techniques:

- Camera angle;
- Close up;
- Full figure;
- Colour.

Box 5.3 Meanings of camera angles

- A full body shot signifies a social relationship;
- A close up signifies intimacy;
- A camera panning down signifies power and authority;
- A camera panning up signifies smallness and weakness;
- A camera zooming in signifies observation and focus on the object.

(Adapted from Berger, 1982)

Step 2 focuses on what Fairclough (1992) labels discursive practice: How people use language to produce and consume texts and how authors draw from existing discourses and genres. While it is important to understand how people use and consume texts, CDA has been criticised for neglecting this aspect of analysis. To determine how readers actually use texts would require an interview study. Consequently, we focus on the second aspect: how authors draw from existing discourses or narratives to construct their text. It is possible to detect this in the texts by now thinking what the text is about. At this stage the analysis should include

- Context of the picture or text (where is it situated in magazine, newspaper or TV programming);
- Contrast or contradiction of text and pictorial content;
- What themes or narratives emerge? What is the text about?

At **step 3** the researcher aims to connect the narratives to the ideological effects within which the text operates. This means connecting each narrative to a particular ideology (e.g., nationalism, masculinity, heterosexism, racism, ablebodiedness, competition, commercialism, healthism). Through this step, the researcher aims to reveal how texts are used for ideological purposes.

Table 5.2 Critical discourse of a *Health* magazine cover

Text		Narrative connection	Ideological effect	Hegemony	Notes
Key words	Flat belly Burn fat Stop cravings Live less Cancer Headache Health	Losing weight, Illness prevention/cure	Healthism (individual to take responsibility of illness prevention) Emphasised femininity (thin body is attractive) Consumerism (selling of health related products)	Powerful dominant groups push the responsibility of health to the individual rather than the state. The publishing industry	The picture connects with thinness, but not with illness. Thinness and attractiveness seem to be connected to 'health'
Clothing	Green spaghetti string top that reveals cleavage, black bottom, necklace	Reveals an attractive, thin body	Emphasised femininity Consumerism	Male dominance through narrow definition of femininity The publishing industry	Physical activity does not seem to be part of 'health'
Grouping	n/a				
Positioning	Centre, model sitting leaning on her chin, upper body shot	Sedentary, but attractive	Emphasised femininity (passive body)	Male dominance (patriarchy)	

Gestures	Model leaning her chin on her hand, arms folded		Emphasised femininity	Male dominance (patriarchy)
Facial gestures	Smiling, looking straight to camera	attractive	Emphasised femininity	Male dominance (patriarchy)
Appearance	Mid-length, brown hair, white teeth, thin, not muscular	Attractive, ideal looking thin body, not physically active	Emphasised femininity Consumerism	Male dominance (patriarchy)
Context of the picture	Studio?			
Camera angle	Straight, but the model is looking slightly up with a slightly tilted head	Attractive looking	Emphasised femininity	Male dominance (patriarchy)
Type of picture	Half-body shot			
Colour	colour	Costuming supports the colour of the title	Emphasised femininity Consumerism	Male dominance (patriarchy) The publishing Industry

Step 4 connects the ideological structure to power relations: What are the dominant groups that create a particular ideological structure through the text and to what effect?

As an example of CDA, we offer a reading of a women's health magazine cover (*Health*, May 2009). On this cover, a smiling woman is pictured sitting down and leaning her chin on her hand (see more details below). This cover contains both image(s) and text and it is important to analyse both the visual content and the language used in this cover. We have created a table (see Table 5.2) in which we illustrate how both the picture and the accompanying text are connected to narrative structures to create a certain ideological effect and finally, how these create links with power.

This analysis of the image and text points to intertwined narratives of health and beauty in women's lives. The way health is talked about on the cover also assigns individual women the responsibility for avoiding illness. The belief that individuals are solely responsible for their health denotes an ideology of healthism. In addition, the texts strongly connect health to the looks of the woman on the cover. The cover model exemplifies the 'traditional' attributes of feminine beauty: youthfulness and thinness combined with attractive smile, tight, cleavage revealing clothing and a feminine pose. Curiously, in this magazine cover, healthy femininity is not connected to a physically active body. All these representations exemplify the ideological construction of 'emphasised' femininity that continues to connect desirable femininity to women's looks, thin body size and inactivity. Who are the powerful groups that benefit from such a representation? The state health system will benefit from increased individual responsibility for health because investments into social issues (such as poverty) that cause diseases are not needed. The visible emphasis on femininity would point to continued patriarchy in the society. The magazine publishers appear to benefit in the maintenance of intertwined emphasised femininity and healthism because they can provide advice on individual health and beauty concerns and thus increase their sales in a consumerist society.

Johnson's cultural studies approach

While Fairclough's CDA is specifically developed to detect ideological construction of a given text, this approach gives very little attention to the researcher's role in the process of textual analysis. However, as discussed in Chapter 2, many critical, cultural studies researchers find a self-reflexive approach to critical analysis essential. Therefore, while the ideological underpinnings of a text can be analysed through CDA, we have modified

Johnson and his colleagues' (2004) cultural studies approach, which emphasises the researcher's role for the use of textual analysis. The aim of this approach is to aid the researcher think through why any given text (e.g., a sport film) is important with regard to understanding power relations in any given social formation. By asking 'why this text now', researchers are able to identify dominant meanings (power) within the text and connect these to external social forces. Johnson et al.'s (2004) approach provides a systematic and coherent guide for the researcher in the practices of textual reading. These stages do not necessarily take place in the presented order as it is likely the researcher would track back and forth between stages with each stage informing analysis of other stages.

Box 5.4 Johnson's cultural studies approach

- Step 1: Close reading of the text: researchers' dialogue between the text and themselves.
- Step 2: Narrative: the bones of the text, the underlying deep structure.
- Step 3: Organisation of meaning: a contextual understanding of how the plot and story of a text are imbued with ideological dimension and indeed with how characters, situations and locations are often ordered through binary opposites, such as good and bad.
- Step 4: Relationship to other media texts.
- Step 5: Tracing the relationships between textual and cultural formations.
- Step 6: Asking the question: Why this text now?

Their approach is based on 'pulling out' the underlying meanings embedded within certain texts. Because the self-reflexive researchers are involved in a continuous dialogue between themselves and the text, there are likely to be multiple, polysemic and perhaps contradictory readings about certain texts. In this regard, the readings of texts are termed 'close' readings as opposed to 'closed' readings (Johnson et al., 2004) to acknowledge their self-reflexive positionality and partiality. As with any methodological practice, important questions over process dominate this approach. Somewhat adapting the work of Johnson et al. (2004), the researcher will invariably grapple with, and likely have to justify, questions over the number of texts to 'read for dominance'.

The researcher would then have to think about the dialogic reading of the text(s) itself, thinking about the actual structural practices and conventions alluded to above (e.g., rhythm, flow, narrative, form, tone, aesthetic, plot sequence, characters and segments). At this juncture, the researchers should carefully think how they record their observations. Because relying on memory can be unreliable, it may be better to transcribe the broadcasts, or the narrative components or segments that are deemed to be important. Notes may also be taken, for example, on the style of the broadcast, shot sequence, presentational components, use of experts and camera angles used. Johnson et al.'s approach asks the researcher to identify the narrative (the bones of the text, the underlying deep structure) and the organisation of meaning (a contextual understanding of how the plot and story of a text are imbued with ideological dimension and indeed with how characters, situations and locations are often ordered through binary opposites, such as good and bad). Once these structural elements have been identified, Johnson et al. propose that the researcher ask questions about the relationship it may have to other texts. For example, a live televised sport broadcast would be understood in relation to the rather formulaic ways in which sport (the televised sport 'genre') is produced and indeed to previous encounters (the text is, thus, intertextual as it will refer to other texts) between two teams. Furthermore, the researcher should address the 'point of view' being conveyed. For example, a narrator in a film, or indeed a commentator or presenter of a sports broadcast, is often the authority and constructs the position from which we are meant to deduce meaning. Such conventions act to 'contain or manage what may be known about the world in important ways' (Johnson et al., 2004, p. 165).

To avoid a purely deterministic and structural approach, these textual reading practices also involve tracing the ways in which textual formations are linked to cultural formations. The researcher would need to locate the text politically, economically and historically, tracing the pathway between the text and cultural formations. In this way, such a reading of texts for dominance is not about privileging the text or its context (Johnson et al., 2004). Similar to Fairclough (1992), Johnson et al. propose that 'texts are always part of larger cultural processes and connected to social relations of power via the production context and the economic relations involved (those of the publisher, studio or television channel responsible for example) and the context of the text's appearance and reception by particular audiences at particular times and places' (Johnson et al., 2004, p. 165). Furthermore, texts should attend to 'explicitly political moments of power, including state policies and the machinery of government' (ibid, p. 171). As such, Johnson et al.'s approach is ground in asking the question: 'Why this text *now*?'. Similarly to CDA, this approach bridges the structural (e.g., properties of language, textually encoded meanings and conventions) and the contextual, historical, spatial and social.

With this argument in place, it is likely that the researcher would return to the text, looking again to see which passages, scenes and commentary stand out and may be used to elaborate, substantiate and extend the argument. Perhaps the text is silent on a specific issue. These reflections and elaborations will then aid the researcher to convince an audience that their dialogic reading has some form of validity. As we will discuss in Chapter 9, given the self-reflexive and dialogic nature of this approach, this would not be validity in a conventional sense. However, the researcher will have to consider what steps to take to ensure the reading appears as more than mere conjecture. They may allude to other examples, other texts, ground the work in certain academic literatures or adhere to different criteria to 'prove' validity (see Chapter 9). Finally, and as with all research, the researcher will need to consider the ways in which to represent their reading, a consideration we deal with in Chapter 8.

Following Johnson et al.'s approach, Silk and colleagues (2008; 2010) read the Disney film *Miracle* for dominance. Through **close reading** (step 1) and identification of the **narratives** (step 2) and structure, they were able to identify a simple dichotomy of good and evil in which the film paints a 'typical Disney picture of innocence' (Giroux, 2002) in which 'victory' could be achieved by an appeal to an untroubled white American masculinity. Focussing on the **organisation of meaning** (step 3), they followed the main characters, looked at the key locations and identified the key scenes. During this process, it became clear that Herb Brooks (the coach) and his players, who had struck such a symbolic blow against 'communism', were reconstructed in the film as de-politicized 'hockey-men', absent of political agenda. The focus was on masculine melodrama, played out in the aspirations of the US college kids picked for the Olympic dream; the trials, tribulations, traumas, fraternal bonding that these boys engage in; and, most importantly, in the efforts, willingness, hard work, sweat, guts and blood required to achieve victory. Focussing on the US players as good, white, family boys plucked by coach Herb Brooks from college hockey, who achieve against the odds, the reading suggested that the film settled on the myth of meritocracy, individualism and hard work in subservience to the higher national cause. Brooks, in turn, is represented as a tough, determined, uncompromising coach, yet also a family-oriented benevolent patriarch. At this juncture, rather than viewing the release in isolation, the researchers addressed **the relationship that the film had with other 'texts'** (step 4). It became clear that the film was part of a wider context that involved collusion between the Bush Administration and Hollywood executives; in the post-9/11 USA, Hollywood was asked to create a number of 'feel-good' patriotic movies. Given the film was released by Disney, and through reading about how Disney present complex issues (see Giardina, 2005) it became clear that complex Cold War issues would be painted relatively innocently. Further, at the same time the studio released *Miracle*, it became apparent they were dropping their release of Michael Moore's more controversial *Fahrenheit 9/11*. This moved the researchers to the next step, thinking about the **relationships between textual formations and cultural formations** (step 5) at the moment in history when the film was released. As with other cultural forms at the time, they were able to assert that the film offered a remembrance of what it means to be 'we' (the USA), taking 'us' back to time when things were apparently a lot simpler and when there was a common enemy to defeat. It does so through a historical amnesia that diminished who 'they' were – the Russians were not explicitly demonised; rather they were presented as a nebulous and vacuous enemy in *Miracle* – allowing for a reassertion of the spectres of the Cold War. In this sense, through the silences of the film, through representation of the 1980 Lake Placid Olympic games (almost devoid of real, menacing, realised Cold War rhetoric), the film provides viewers with a space in which a relatively bland and not especially threatening enemy (Soviets as represented in *Miracle*) were juxtaposed with 'freedom loving people'. This representation made it easier to slot 'terrorists' into the space previously reserved for 'communists' – a symbolic assertion of US power, a promise to defeat once again its enemies in the 'war on terror'. Following Johnson's analysis enabled the researchers to ask **Why this text now** (step 6), and to understand *Miracle* as part of the 'sanctioned' sporting texts that were mobilised in the affective substantiation of the geo-political trajectories of the Bush Administration (see Silk, Bracey & Schultz, 2008; Silk & Falcous, 2010).

Foucauldian discourse analysis

Michel Foucault (1972; 1978) is known as a poststructuralist analyst of the way language is connected to the use of power. Foucault himself identified as a historian of thought and often his own texts highlight how a particular discourse, or a way of knowing, evolved over time.

In this sense, Foucault's method would be directly useful to sport historians who aim to detect how sport or physical activity have come to be known over time. While most sport studies researchers do not engage in such a thorough historical analysis, Foucault's work can also serve as a meaningful way of analysing the ways knowledge is connected to power by focusing on texts. Foucault's own method is titled 'genealogy': 'an examination of the relations between history, discourse, bodies and power in an attempt to help to understand social practices or objects of knowledge that continue to have value in today's world' (Markula & Pringle, 2006, p. 32). Embarking on a genealogy thus requires an extensive historical analysis of knowledge development. However, Foucault's work can also be helpful in an analysis of how discourse and power are intertwined in a collection of texts from the contemporary world. Therefore, we offer a modified version of Foucault's method designed to be used with an analysis of a clearly specified sample of texts.

Both Fairclough and Foucault ground their methods on the concept of 'discourse'. As Fairclough actually borrows the term 'discourse' from Foucault, CDA and Foucault's method appear very similar in many ways. However, there is a profound difference in how they understand the impact of power and the role of language as part of power relations. It is therefore important to highlight how the concept of power informs Foucault's theoretical schema.

We discussed earlier how Fairclough draws from a theory of hegemony where ideologies are understood as systems of beliefs that the powerful groups use to maintain their position of dominance over the subordinate groups. Ideologies are thus transmitted through language and the task of CDA is to expose how ideologies maintain the hegemony of a certain group and oppress others. Foucault understands power quite differently: Instead of as a possession of a certain group, he sees power as relational. Foucault advocates that power 'exists only as exercised' within relationships with people (Foucault, 2000, p. 340). Power, therefore, is everywhere and anyone, who is not physically confined, is able to exercise it in relation to others (Foucault, 1978). This means that no one is outside power relations, but all are always necessarily involved in the use of power due to their relationships with other people. From Foucault's point of view individuals cannot be divided into those who 'possess' power (and thus oppress others) and those who are devoid of power and thus are innocent victims of the powerful (Foucault, 1978). Foucault asks 'how' power is exercised instead of 'who' has power and 'what' is power (Cole, Giardina & Andrews, 2004). He did not, however, assume that all individuals and groups are 'equal', but asserted very strongly that imbalances in power relations exist and devoted much of his research to examining how individuals were disciplined through discursive formations in society (Foucault, 1978).

Box 5.5 Major differences between critical discourse analysis and Foucauldian discourse analysis

* Different understanding of power;
* Difference between ideology and discourse;
* Different paradigmatic assumptions.

In a Foucauldian sense, discourses are ways of knowing and everyone using language participates in the circulation and creation of these knowledges (Foucault, 1978). Foucauldian discourse analysis aims to detect what knowledges dominate particular fields, where they come from and how they have become dominant. For example, everyone who talks or writes about sport participates in circulating how we know about this particular field. Foucauldian discourse analysis aims to detect what are the main ways of knowing about sport in, for example, newspaper texts, and how they have become so important. In other words, a Foucauldian would ask: Why do we consider certain ways of knowing about sport as important? It is crucial to note, however, that where ideologies are defined as tools for oppression, no discourse is good or bad on its own. Rather, what matters is how a discourse is used within the power relations. For example, sport media texts often prominently report on player transfer negotiations. These reports provide details about the money exchanged and thus the worth of each player in his sport. Thus, the media plays a part in how we know about sport as a wealthy entertainment industry with an ability to pay exorbitant salaries to its stars. However, for a Foucauldian researcher, the idea is not judge whether this way of knowing of sport is necessarily bad or 'oppressive', but how it is used to mould an understanding of contemporary sport. Again, no discourse is good or bad per se but its impact on the field depends on how it is used. In other words, a Foucauldian would be interested in what discourses define sport and how these discourses have become dominant within current power relations that structure elite sport. How, then, to know exactly what discourses define each field? What discourses are transmitted through texts?

Foucault does not develop a method for analysing language as clear as that of Fairclough. Nevertheless, he labels his early method as 'archaeology' (Foucault, 1972), which he later developed into what he titled 'genealogy' (Foucault, 1977; 1991). Following Foucault's methodology faithfully would require a detailed historical analysis. While some researchers of physical culture engage in this type of research, the principles of Foucault's work can also be used to analyse smaller samples of texts. In what follows, we present a version of Foucault's genealogical analysis modified for a textual analysis of physical culture. As Foucault asserted that discourses manifest in verbal performances, we can begin an analysis of texts based on Foucault's (1972) earlier analyses of scientific texts.

Box 5.6 Foucauldian discourse analysis

To detect discourses, identify:

- Objects: Specific topics about which we want to know;
- Enunciations: Where the objects are talked about;
- Concepts: How are the objects talked about;
- Individualised groups of statements: How concepts are organised into a coherent logic;
- Theories: How individual statements link with general domains of statements;
- Link to power relations.

The first step is to identify the **objects** of analysis. Objects are the specific topics to which the texts refer. Next the researcher needs to look for sources, or **enunciations**, where these issues are talked about. After identifying the enunciation, or the sample of one's study, the researcher needs to examine what **concepts** are developed in these 'texts' and how these concepts are organised. These concepts then form **individualisable groups of statements**. This stage of the analysis appears in many ways similar to CDA. However, a Foucauldian discourse analysis needs to expand from this stage by looking at how these concepts form meaningful theoretical formations. The **theoretical formations** are structured based on the statements identified before. However, at this stage, the researcher needs to connect these into themes that link the individual statements to the **general domain of statements** and further to discourses that structure the fields under investigation. This level of analysis is 'concerned with statements that coalesce within specific social contexts'

(Markula & Pringle, 2006, p. 29). Finally, these 'discourses', specific to the field, need to be connected to the power relations that define the field. The exploration of **operations of power** from transmissions and transformations of discourse constitutes the final phase of the analysis. It is important to note again that in Foucault's view power is relational and is, therefore, exercised to create certain practices. Consequently, the objective is to understand what effect or practice is produced through the discourses. In other words, the researcher asks: How are discourses and power relations linked? How have certain discourses become dominant in certain cultural and historical circumstances? In summary, Foucauldian discourse analysis aims to explore how certain discourses gain dominance and what effects these discourses have.

As Foucauldian analysis is based on analyses of how multiple concepts link into theoretical formations, it is more difficult to illustrate this type of analysis through displaying one text than to illustrate CDA. However, to demonstrate Foucauldian discourse analysis further, we offer an example of an analysis of the meaning(s) of 'healthy' fitness through contemporary fitness and exercise science text books. For further details regarding this analysis, see Markula and Pringle (2006). To illustrate the analysis process, we offer the following stages:

Step 1: Object of analysis: how do we know about 'healthy fitness' through textbooks?

Step 2: Enunciations:
- Sources where this 'object' is likely to be discussed are exercise textbooks.

Step 3: Concepts that emerge after an analysis of such texts and form individual statements:
- Health;
- Illness;
- Cardio-vascular fitness;
- Muscular strength and endurance;
- Flexibility;
- Body composition;
- Fitness;
- Exercise.

Step 4: Identification of individualised groups of statements: How were the different concepts linked together?
- Health = illness prevention;
- Cardio-vascular fitness, muscular strength and endurance, flexibility, body composition = physical fitness;

- Exercise = specific 'workouts' needed to improve each of the components of physical fitness.

Step 5: Identification of theories: How do these individualised statements link with a larger field of statements?

- Physical activity and health were linked as exercise was deemed to prevent illness. This statement was linked with a larger theory of 'health related fitness' designed to optimise illness prevention. These texts also identified practices (discursive practice) to promote health related fitness and titled it exercise prescription. The scholarly fields that support this connection between health (as absence illness) and physical activity (as exercise prescription) are medicine and exercise physiology.

Step 6: Connection to power relations:

- How are discourses and power linked? Certain understandings from medicine and exercise physiology have become the dominant meanings of health and physical activity.
- What relations of power have enabled this particular meaning of health to become dominant? Medicine and science are powerful, dominant sources of knowledge while other knowledges of health and physical activity are marginalised.
- Why do medicine and exercise physiology dominate the understandings of healthy physical activity? The type of knowledge these disciplines produce appeals to governmental policy makers.
- What are the effects of this dominance? Exercise prescription becomes the only acceptable understanding of healthy physical activity.

Validation for textual analysis research will be discussed in Chapter 9.

Summary

The various practices of textual analysis involve interpreting the meaning(s) of a variety of texts. Like all interpretations of empirical material, the exact analysis technique will depends on the researcher's paradigmatic stance and purpose. There are numerous approaches to all forms of text, but in this chapter we have detailed Fairclough's critical discourse analysis (CDA), Johnson's cultural studies approach and Foucauldian discourse analysis as approaches to reading sport media text. These approaches can, with care and consideration, be applied to the analysis of popular media texts, policy and internet or visual material. We discuss phenomenological analysis of (interview) texts in Chapter 4 and the interpretive approach to the analysis of narratives in Chapter 6.

While new types of 'texts' continually emerge with new information technologies, a successful and meaningful textual analysis is likely to have the following characteristics:

- It fulfils a clearly defined purpose;
- It has a clearly defined research logic. The selection of the analysis technique draws from a clearly defined theoretical and paradigmatic stance of the researcher. The research question is based on a thoroughly conducted literature review;
- The sampling of the texts is conducted purposefully;
- It is conducted by a well prepared, skilled and professional researcher who is aware of the multiple possibilities of conducting textual analyses;
- The appropriate analysis technique is clearly articulated.

Further reading

Critical discourse analysis:

Critical Discourse Analysis is a Routledge journal that specialises in different forms of CDA.

Johnson's cultural studies analysis:

Boyle, E. Millington, B. & Vertinsky, P. (2006). 'Representing the female pugilist: Narratives of race, gender, and dis-ability in Million Dollar Baby'. *Sociology of Sport Journal*, 23(2), 99–116.

Gruneau, R., Whitson, D. & Cantelon, H. (1988). 'Methods and media: Studying the sports television discourse'. *Loisir et Societe*, 11, 265–81.

Silk, M., Schultz, J. & Bracey, B. (2008). 'From mice to men: Miracle, mythology & the magic kingdom'. *Sport in Society*, 11, 279–97

Foucauldin discourse analysis:

Barker-Ruchti, N. (2009). 'The media as an authorising practice of femininity: Swiss newspaper coverage of Karin Thürig's bronze medal performance in road cycling'. In P. Markula (Ed.), *Olympic women and the media: International perspectives* (pp. 214–31). Basingstoke: Palgrave Macmillan.

6
Practice and the Politics of Interpretation: Narrative Analysis

In this chapter, we will

• Introduce the term narrative;
• Discuss personal narratives, life stories and life histories as narrative methods;
• Discuss different ways of analysing empirical material from these methods;
• Discuss memory work as a narrative method.

This chapter focuses on narrative inquiry as a way of practising research on physical culture. 'Narrative', as a term, has multiple meanings within qualitative research: some see it not as a method, but as an approach to qualitative research. Others connect narratives with so-called 'alternative ways of representation' or 'writing up' social science research. While we acknowledge all these possible uses for narrative, in this chapter we focus on narrative inquiry as one methodological practice of qualitative research. In addition, we introduce such methods as personal narrative, life history, oral history and memory work as part of narrative analysis. We discuss narratives as a way of representing research in Chapter 8.

What is narrative inquiry, narrative analysis or storied research?

With the proliferation of qualitative methods, so-called narrative methods have become more visible within sport studies. The term embodies multiple meanings and, as Smith and Sparkes note, 'to provide a definitive definition of narrative analysis is difficult' (2009b, p. 281). Markula and Denison (2005) observe that for many sport studies researchers the word narrative denotes critical readings of such 'narratives' as media texts, sporting events or celebrities' lives. The meanings of these 'narratives' are read through textual analysis (see Chapter 5) to determine the 'preferred reading' (McDonald & Birrell, 1999). We deal with this type of understanding of 'narrative' in Chapter 5, where we discuss textual analysis. However, 'narrative research' (Sparkes, 1999), 'narrative inquiry' (e.g., Chase, 2005; Clandinin & Connelly, 2000) or 'narrative analysis' (Smith & Sparkes, 2009b) in current qualitative research tend to refer to research that openly celebrates both the researchers' and the participants' voices. Therefore, in this book, analysis of media texts is understood as part of textual analysis whereas narrative analysis refers to qualitative research that includes both the researchers' and the participants' experiences of physical activity. Chase writes: 'Contemporary narrative inquiry can be characterised as an amalgam of interdisciplinary analytic lenses, diverse disciplinary approaches, and both traditional and innovative methods – all revolving around an interest in biographical particulars as narrated by the one who lives them' (2005, p. 651). Consequently, narrative research has two distinct features: it is concerned with life stories and it includes the researchers' voice implicitly or explicitly. For example, long-time advocates of this type of research, Clandinin and Connelly (2000) note that narrative research, in order to focus holistically on an individual's experience, begins with these experiences expressed in life stories. In addition, their version of narrative inquiry begins with the researcher's autobiographically oriented narrative that will highlight how the researcher became interested in the particular experiences. They visualise narrative inquiry within a 3-dimensional space that encompasses temporality (past – future), the inward, personal (internal feeling and hopes), the outward, social (the social environment where the experience takes place) and the physical space for the lived experience.

In addition to the generic components we suggested in Chapter 3, the method section for a narrative inquiry project should include the following sections:

Box 6.1 Content of a method section for narrative analysis

- Narrative inquiry as qualitative research:
  - Everyday life stories;
  - Researcher's self.
- Methods;

- Sampling;
- Ethics concerns (see Chapter 1);
- Analysis of empirical material;
- Issues of representation (see Chapter 8);
- Validation (see Chapter 9).

Sparkes equates narrative research to a type of story telling: 'Narrative is about the telling of stories. In the telling, listening, and reading of stories the opportunity arises to share experiences about our own lives and the lives of others' (1999, p. 19). However, in a later work, Smith and Sparkes distinguish between narrative and story. A story, they describe, refers to 'actual tales people tell' whereas narrative is a broader concept that includes general dimensions or properties of a story (e.g., tellability, consequences, sequences of speech act, structures, thematic/categorical content, rhetorical tropes, temporality) (2009a, p. 2). In this sense, the stories refer to the actual 'raw' material for narratives where the researcher, through an analysis, detects a structure for the story, its consequences for the teller (e.g., how an athlete construct a self-understanding based on a life story about himself) and the timeline for the events in the story. How does a researcher select stories to include in a narrative analysis?

Narrative methods and sampling

The most common way of collecting stories of every day life experiences is through different types of written or oral narratives. We have matched Chase's (2005) division of three different types of narratives – short topical story, extended story and entire life story – with a type of narrative method:

Box 6.2 Types of narrative methods

Type of story	Narrative method
A short topical story Oral or written	Personal narrative: Compelling topical narration
An extended story of a significant aspect of one's life Oral or written	Life story: A significant aspect of life

A narrative of one's entire life Oral or written	Life history: Extensive, oral or written, Autobiography
	Oral history: Interviews with focus on historical events for those who lived through them
	(adapted from Chase, 2005)

Chase understands a short topical story as a narrative 'about a particular event and specific characters' (p. 625) whereas life story refers to 'an extended story about a significant aspect of one's life' (p. 625) such as athletic career, an illness or participation in a social movement. While some researchers might use life story and life history interchangeably, according to Chase, life history can also refer to 'an extensive autobiographical narrative ... that covers all or most of a life' (p. 625). Oral history can be used by historians to 'describe interviews in which the focus is ... on the meanings that events hold for those who lived through them' (Chase, 2005, p. 625). While all the narratives can be written or oral, the oral data collection resembles qualitative interviewing. However, there are also distinct differences that give narrative research a quite separate 'flavour' from pure interview studies. We continue to rely on Chase (2005) to highlight these differences.

First, while the purpose of an interview can vary from asking participants' views about certain issues to seeking deep understanding of their experiences, narrative inquiry takes the self as its protagonist. This means that the meaning of collecting empirical material through narrative is to communicate the narrator's point of view of what happened and what emotions, thoughts and interpretations the events provoked in the narrator. In this sense, a narrative is retrospective meaning making: it aims to organise the life experience(s) into a meaningful whole.

Second, narrative is always understood as a verbal action that performs a version of the participant's self, experiences and reality. The main concern is to listen to the narrator's voice to understand how, where and in what way a particular experience took place.

Third, while the focus is on individual's self, the participant's narrative is always understood to be constrained by social circumstances. Therefore, a narrative is analysed as socially situated, interactive performances of the individual self.

Finally, the researcher is an integral part of the narrative data collection. As mentioned earlier, Clandinin and Connelly (2000) advocate that the researcher should include a personal narrative at the beginning of the narrative inquiry (even if the research focuses on narratives of 'others') to provide a better understanding of her/his interest in the particular experiences. However, not all narrative researchers include their stories as part of the work. In any case, narrative researchers always view themselves as the narrators of the final published research work that provides their interpretation of the participant's story. Consequently, these researchers tend to use the first person to present their work (Chase, 2005).

According to Smith and Sparkes (2009b), the special characteristics of narrative research can make it particularly relevant to sport studies, and thus by extension, research in physical culture. Using the metaphor of 'breathing' they argue that narrative research can breathe meaning and lived experience into sport research. Through these experiences, stories further highlight the personal and social fabric of people's lives, but also provide accounts of how real bodies are part of the complexity of human life. This way, they argue, personal narratives will aid in the development of further strategies for taking care of people and living 'differently'.

In summary, the primary methods for collecting empirical material for narrative inquiry are interviews, which enable the researcher to collect narratives orally. These interviews can be informal interviews for personal narratives, semi-structured interviews for life stories and oral history or semi-structured interviews for life or oral histories (see Chapter 4 for further description of these distinctions). The sampling for narrative inquiry interviews should follow the sampling techniques for qualitative interviewing (see Chapter 4). These interviews need to go through a similar ethical approval process to qualitative interviewing (see Chapter 2 for a discussion on ethics). The written narratives can be obtained directly from the participant(s), who can be asked to write about the specific event or a significant aspect of their lives. Alternatively, the researcher can use published autobiographies that are then analysed through narrative analysis (see data analysis below). While obtaining personal narratives specific to one's narrative project requires an ethical approval, using autobiographies already published in the public domain does not need to go through an ethics approval process. We also offer 'memory work' as a specific method that uses written narratives as its primary data (see below).

With the focus on personal narratives and the self, narrative research seems to appeal specifically for psychological research and the interpretive researcher interested in individual experiences. Some narrative researchers, like Clandinin and Connelly (2000), explicitly state that narratives focus on experience instead of how a person is constructed within formal structures: narrative accounts begin with experiences expressed in stories, not with theory. Their version of narrative excludes an analysis of the social, political and cultural context for the experience. Other narrative researchers, like Chase, point out that 'narrative research is embedded and shaped broad social and history currents' (2005, p. 669) which provides broader paradigmatic horizons for this type of enquiry. Consequently, narratives can be used by researchers from different paradigmatic orientations. What differs, however, is how the narratives are analysed: are the researchers interested purely in what was said and how it was said in the narratives or do they analyse, through social theory, how the individual self is constructed within larger social forces?

Narrative inquiry analysis

While there are several ways to analyse empirical material from narratives (e.g., Chase's analysis of narrative strategy (2005); Gubrium & Holstein's analysis of narrative practice (1998); Polkinghorne's paradigmatic analysis (1995); Smith & Sparkes's narrative analysis (2009b)), there are also shared understandings of certain basic characteristics (Smith & Sparkes, 2009b). Often narrative analysis techniques are classified based on whether they focus on the 'hows' and 'whats' of an individual story or, in addition to the content of the individual's story, aim to understand these experiences within a larger social context. We will discuss how to analyse the content (hows and whats) of a narrative and how the different techniques draw from the social context of the narrative.

Structural analysis: The 'whats' of the story

One of the most prominent proponents of structural analysis of narratives in sport studies is Andrew Sparkes. Through structural analysis, the researcher detects the key elements that hold the story together and the focus is therefore on the ways a particular story is structured or organised: 'the ways in which a story is put together' (Smith & Sparkes, 2009b, p. 283). Therefore, structural analysis focuses on the **'what'** of the story. To do this, the researcher first needs to identify the specific event that the story is depicting (Sparkes, 1999). This means understanding **the context and background** for the particular story: to locate a person within the story, it is important to provide some background for the main character. For example, Smith and Sparkes (2005) begin a structural analysis of a life story of a rugby player disabled by a spinal cord injury by providing details about his biography and the context for his sport and the resulting injury. Second, the researcher needs to focus on **the actual story**: what is the main plot, its setting and the actual structure of the story (Sparkes,

1999). The idea is to detect specific story lines: what is said and in what order. Based on this analysis, the researcher is able to identify the coherent, core narrative, even if the story itself proceeds in a 'messy' or disjointed manner. Smith and Sparkes (2009b) offer examples of the types of stories that might make a narrative: progressive, stable, regressive, heroic, tragic, sad, ironic, comic, risky, shameful, discovery, restitutive or chaotic. For example, their structural analysis of the disabled rugby player identified two types of stories in his narrative of disability: a restitution story where the player had clear belief of returning to his previous, 'non-injured' life and a chaos story when the player gave up this hope to realise that his disability is a permanent state of life (Smith & Sparkes, 2005). According to Smith and Sparkes (2009b) the goal of structural analysis – what types of stories people tell – is to identify what **cultural narratives** individuals draw on to shape their personal stories. For example, they detail how a disabled, former rugby player drew from the general narratives of what it means be disabled in society to construct an identity for himself (Smith & Sparkes, 2005). When the researchers know what type of story is guiding a person's life, they gain an ability to share different types of stories, but also, in the case of limiting personal stories, to develop ways for coping or create interventions that improve the teller's life conditions.

Performative analysis: The 'hows' of the story

While discourse analysis and conversational analysis (see interview analysis in Chapter 4) can also focus on the 'hows' of language use, Smith and Sparkes (2009b) offer performative analysis, or dialogic analysis, as a specific technique for narrative analysis. This type of analysis focuses on how the narrative is communicated and thus interactively produced and performed as narrative. It answers the question: How is *x* constructed in the telling? In addition, performative analysis views narratives, particularly if collected through interviews, as co-constructed by the participant and the researcher. Smith and Sparkes (2009b) acknowledge that examples of this type of analysis are rare in sport studies and as a technique it is therefore less developed and detailed than structural analysis. However, in addition to the content (what is said), performative analysis brings into focus the finer details of the experiences and story telling.

Analysis of narrative practice: The 'whats' and 'hows' of the story

The analysis of narrative practice, as advocated by Gubrium and Holstein (1998), aims to describe the production of the coherence of story telling under certain circumstances by accounting for an interplay between the actual action of story telling (the 'hows') and the circumstances surrounding the act of telling (the 'whats'). Therefore, the focus on both what is said and how it is said allows the researcher to 'see the storytelling process as both actively constructive and locally constrained' (Gubrium & Holstein, 1998, p. 164). Gubrium and Holstein offer several aspects for analysis in each storytelling process, but also rely on a technique they label 'analytic bracketing': the researcher can 'focus on one aspect of narrative practice while temporarily suspending analytic interest in another' (1998, p. 165). Consequently, it is possible to foreground the aspects presented below in order to return later to the others. The analytical aspects are organised in two larger headings: narrative composition and narrative control. We detail each aspect below.

Narrative composition

Narrative composition consists of two aspects: narrative linkage and narrative editing. Both refer to an analysis of the **'hows'** of the narrative.

1. Narrative linkage

   This aspect of analysis draws from how the story is authored. The meaning and coherence of each story is derived from its links to the context in which it is told, but at the same time stories told even in the same context differ. Therefore, the researcher focuses on how a coherent story is created through both shared and individual, unique linkages. This allows the researchers to look at the differences between individual accounts and culturally shared meanings. Gubrium and Holstein characterise these differences as **'narrative slippages'**. More formally, narrative slippage refers to 'the indeterminate interpretive circumstances and activities that exist at points of articulation among culture, lived experience, and storytelling, points at which there is considerable play or elasticity in the way shared understandings are circumstantially brought to bear on matters of interpretive concern' (Gubrium & Holstein, 1998, p. 167). For example, two injured rugby players, while drawing from the same culturally defined understandings of rugby union as a sport, will differ in their individual accounts of how to succeed in the professional game. However, each slippage still sustains the coherence of each story.

   The second aspect that provides linkages in the narratives is **'narrative footing'**. These provides clues about 'kinds of stories that could be told' from the narrator's point of view. For example, the two rugby players might provide difference stories based on the 'footing' for their sporting experiences. One might have had parents successful in the business world and a coach with a philosophy that supports the idea of success in similar terms. The other might have come from a rural background where rugby was considered traditionally a 'national' game. However, the 'footings' that the storyteller draws might also change during the story and as a result, the story shifts in direction and meaning. The shift in footing can also result in different linkages for the meaning of the story.

2. Narrative editing

   This aspect of narrative practice refers to the narrator's **self-reflexivity** as a storyteller: she/he actively decides the perspective of the story and also dictates how the listener should hear the story. Consequently, as the author of the narrative each storyteller constantly 'monitors, manages, modifies, and revises the emergent story' (Gubrium & Holstein, 1998, p. 170). Through editing, the narrator can establish a particular 'footing' and position the listeners/readers of the story. Therefore, the researcher, through following the modification and revisions as the story evolves, can further analyse multiple footings of the narrator and also how the narrator intends the story to come across to the 'audience'.

Narrative control

If the first two aspects refer to how the narrator composes or creates a coherent narrative while continually shifting between 'footings' to link the story with different contexts and different audiences, the aspects of narrative control refer to the control of the composition process: how do the **'whats'** of narrative constitute a coherent whole?

1. Substantive monitoring

   While narratives draw linkages between what the tellers say and the context of the story, they are also limited within what is locally relevant or acceptable: 'what good storytelling at this particular time and place should be' (Gubrium & Holstein, 1998, p. 173). Consequently, narrators actively monitor the local relevance of their story as there is 'local interest in what ... the story is about, not just active attention to how one tells it' (ibid., p. 174). In some instances or locations, an 'acceptable' story can assume quite a strict format following shared understandings of clear beginnings, middles and ends. For example, a researcher of successful rugby performances might listen to several stories to identify how the players monitor their narratives to create good storytelling in the context of professional rugby and whether a clear format of a 'good' success story emerges from these narratives.

2. Formal narrative control

Formal narrative control refers to the control by 'institutionalized storytelling circumstances or formal relations between interacting parties' (Gubrium & Holstein, 1998, p. 177) such as interviews. As one of the most common ways of obtaining narrative 'data' is through different types of interviews, formal control is a significant factor in the analysis of narrative practice. In these formal situations the research protocol dictates the topics and predetermines some of the storylines. Therefore, what is an appropriate story in such situations is dictated by the interaction between the interviewer and the interviewee. This means, however, that the listener, the interviewer, is an active co-participant in the production of the 'interview stories'. Nevertheless, the interviewer cannot, and should not, entirely control the conversation, but the formal nature of the interview situation should be counted as a part of the analysis of what is said in this particular context.

In their analysis of narrative practice, Gubrium and Holstein (1998) embrace not only the content of the narrative and how the teller controls the story in the situation of its telling, but also how the teller locates her/his story within a broader context. Therefore, their understanding of a narrative analysis is located within an interpretive paradigm within which a researcher reaches for individual experiences as structured in localised contexts. Their analysis does not link the stories with larger structures of power. We introduce memory work as one possible method for interrogating how larger social structures embedded in power shape individuals' stories.

Box 6.3 Analysis of narrative practice

Narrative Composition:

- Narrative linkage (authoring stories);
  - Slippage;
  - Narrative footing;
- Narrative editing (editing stories).
  Narrative Control (context for stories);
  - Substantive monitoring;
  - Formal narrative control.

(Gubrium & Holstein, 1998)

Memory-work

We provide 'memory-work' here as an example of how writing personal narratives can be used as a form of social science research, particularly to look at the social construction of identity. In brief, memory-work consists of writing individual memories and discussing them in a group setting. Memory-work, as a distinct method, was developed by a German researcher Frigga Haug to examine identity construction. Memory-work was then publicised in the 1980s by a women's collective of German feminists and socialists (Haug & Others, 1987) who originally came to together to work at an independent Marxist journal *Das Argument*. Haug and Others (1987) designed this method to reveal how they themselves played an active role in 1) the socialisation process by which 'practices of femininity' had become incorporated into their embodied selves, and 2) the social construction of their identities as 'women'. Memory-work assumes 'that we internalize social relations and practices in the process of self-formation', and that 'these social relations (e.g., between women and men, between parents and children) are characterized by power and hierarchies' (Willig, 2001, p. 137). Markula and Friend (2005) describe this methodological practice:

> Central to memory-work are discrete descriptive memories (i.e., detailed recollections of lived experiences without interpretation, explanation, or biography generated by a trigger or clue relevant to the research topic) through which the participants reflect the meanings of everyday life. These memories detail the 'rough edges' of experience – the contrasts and contradictions, ambiguities and inconsistencies, the gaps – that provide the grounding for understanding the construction of the self. They tell us how a situation was experienced – of 'being in' the situation – through an embodied subjectivity.
>
> (Markula & Friend, 2005, p. 446)

Unlike narrative research in general, memory-work originally assumed a very specific paradigmatic framework. It draws from critical theory to examine, through individual memories, the social construction of identity and its limitations. Furthermore, however, it draws from the interpretive paradigm to examine how social dominance is evident in individual experiences. It is assumed that the experiences are accessible through memories, because the understanding of the self is understood to arise, intersubjectively, through interaction with others. Consequently, the researcher, through the group discussions, is part of the interactive process of meaning making and the researcher's own memories are included in the research. Unlike the broader narrative research, memory-work as a research process follows very clearly developed phases. There are three general phases: writing memories, group discussion and theorisation. Therefore, data collection (the actual memories) and data analysis are combined into a coherent, joint progression of memory-work. We now detail each process.

Phase 1: Writing memories

In collaboration with the participants, the researcher compiles 'triggers' for each memory. The participants typically write one to two pages about a particular episode, action or event referred as a 'trigger' or cue. Ideally, memory-work begins with selecting, in consultation with the research group, a 'trigger' topic that is related to the research focus and objectives. Based on a trigger, each participant writes a pre-prepared memory for the group discussion. The length of the memory can vary, but it should be written in the third person with as much detail as possible, yet without interpretation or autobiography.

Phase 2: Group discussion of memories

The written memories are discussed in a group meeting. The meetings can be shaped based on the following order of events (see Figure 6.1):

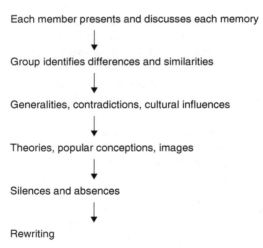

Figure 6.1   Order of the memory work group discussion

In the group discussion, each member presents her/his memory, which is then discussed by the entire group. When all the memories have been discussed, the group tries to identify differences and similarities between the different memories. As a third step the group, based on differences and similarities, aims to come up with generalities, contradictions and cultural influences and then connect them into popular conceptions, images or, if possible, theoretical perspectives. Finally, the group should identify any silences or absences in the memories to discuss their significance in the identity construction. Based on the discussion, some of the memories can be rewritten in the light of the further understanding of the individual identity construction process.

Phase 3: Theorisation

In this phase, the insights concerning the 'common sense' of each set of memories are related back to theoretical discussion within the wider academic literature. This part is usually done by one of the co-researchers as an individual (academic) exercise, yet drafts are subject to further discussion by other members of the collective (Onyx & Small, 2001).

In summary, memory-work draws from both an interpretive approach to individual experience and a critical approach to the ideological construction of identity. In this sense, it differs from other narrative inquiry approaches presented in this chapter. In addition, memory-work is based on participants' written accounts rather than interviews, which many other narrative approaches use to obtain empirical material. Finally, in memory-work the construction of narratives as an interactive process is emphasised in the discussions after which the memories are recreated. Memory-work also emphasises a connection to social theory more clearly than some other strands of narrative enquiry.

Issues of (re)presentation for narrative inquiry will be discussed in Chapter 8 and **validation** in Chapter 9.

Summary

While narrative methods are just entering studies of physical culture, they can offer further insights into the experiences of the researcher and the participants. Narrative enquiry differs from other qualitative methods by focusing on life stories and by including the researchers' stories, implicitly or explicitly, in the narrative. The empirical material for narrative inquiry can be oral or written stories. In this chapter, we discussed personal narrative, life story, life history and memory-work as methods for narrative inquiry. In addition, we outlined ways to analyse the 'hows' and 'whats' of narratives.

While narrative inquiry can draw from multiple paradigmatic per-spectives, currently, it is quite clearly located within the interpretive paradigm: most narrative approaches in this chapter focused on the 'whats' and 'hows' of the story itself without explicit discussion of the power relations through which the story is lived into existence. If the researcher aims to expand beyond an interpretive quest, it is important to locate the stories in a social context. We introduced memory-work as a possibility for critical examination of ideologically constructed writ-ten narratives. This method provided a tangible link between the rela-tions of power and individual understanding of identity.

Like any qualitative method, a successful narrative inquiry study has the following characteristics:

- It fulfils a clearly defined purpose.
- It has clearly defined research logic. The narratives need to be collected through actual methods. The methods draw from the research purpose, the research questions and the paradigmatic approach of the researcher.
- The sampling of the participants is conducted purposefully.
- It is conducted by a well-prepared, skilled and professional researcher who is well versed in the chosen narrative method (personal experi-ence, life story, life history, memory-work).
- The results are derived through a clearly articulated and appropriate narrative analysis technique.

Further reading

Allin, L. & Humberstone, B. (2006). 'Exploring careership in outdoor education and the lives of women outdoor educators'. *Sport, Education and Society*, 11, 135–53 (life history).

Carless, D. & Douglas, K. (2008). 'Narrative identity, and mental health: How men with severe mental illness restory life through sport and exercise'. *Psychology of Sport and Exercise*, 9, 576–94.

Clandinin J. (2007). *Handbook of narrative inquiry: Mapping a methodology*. Thousand Oaks, CA: Sage.

Dablaso, D. M. (2009). *Catching stories: A practical guide to oral history*. Athens, OH: Swallow.

Jones, R. L., Glintmeyer, N. & McKenzie, A. (2005). 'Slim bodies, eating disorders and the coach–athlete relationship: A tale of identity creation and disruption'. *International Review for the Sociology of Sport*, 40, 377–91.

Phoenix, C. & Sparkes, A. C. (2007). 'Sporting bodies, ageing, narrative mapping and young team athletes: An analysis of possible selves'. *Sport, Education and Society*, 12, 1–17.

7
Practice and the Politics of Interpretation: Field Methods

In this chapter, we will

- Discuss participatory action research as a field method;
- Discuss case study research as a field method;
- Discuss ethnography as a field method;
- Discuss visual ethnography as a field method.

In this chapter we focus on qualitative research that requires the researchers to attend a research 'field' (e.g., a physical education class, sport practice, sport club, exercise class, health club, a sport magazine office, mega-sporting event, sport organisation). This type of research generally uses multiple methods, usually a combination of participation, observation, interviewing and textual analysis, but narrative methods can also be used to understand individuals' experiences in a specific field. In this chapter we detail four qualitative field methods: participatory action research, case study research, ethnography and visual ethnography.

Participatory action research

Similar to several other methods introduced in this book, participatory action research (PAR) has several meanings. One interpretation is that the current PAR has evolved from two roots: 'classroom action research' – a qualitative, interpretive mode of research where empirical material is collected by the teacher (yet often together with the researcher) to improve teachers' own practice – and 'participatory research' – alternative social science research that draws from neo-Marxist approaches to community development and human rights activity often in the Third World (Kemmis & McTaggard, 2005). Our approach to PAR is closer to the latter but, as the research interests within physical culture are broad, we also draw from Kemmis and McTaggard's (2005) more recent understanding of what constitutes a PAR research project. It is, however, important to note that the way we discuss PAR here locates it strongly within the critical paradigm. As with the other practices we have introduced in this book, and along with the generic components of the methods section detailed in Chapter 3, a PAR methods chapter would likely include

Box 7.1 Content of a method section for participatory action research (PAR)

- Participatory action research as a qualitative research method;
- Research context;
- Research problem;
- Ethical procedures (see Chapter 1);
- Research design and collection of empirical material;
- Analysis of empirical material;
- Validation (see Chapter 9);
- Communication of results.

Participatory action research as a qualitative research method

Kemmis and McTaggard (2005) identify seven key features that characterise the diversity of PAR projects. First, PAR is a social process that explores the relationship between the individual and the social world. For example, they urge a PAR researcher to analyse how **social media and social structures** interact with the individual's participation in social practices and their ways of knowledge formation. For example, a PAR researcher would look at how media images and the social structures of power might influence on students' participation in physical education classes in low-income Hispanic neighbourhoods in Los Angeles. In this sense, PAR expands beyond the classroom action research that tends to focus on the individual actions within the narrow confines of teaching in a particular class. Second PAR, as the title indicates, has to be **participatory**. This means that PAR is not research done on 'others', but rather all individuals (including the researcher) will critically reflect on how their current knowledges and self-understandings inform their practices. Consequently, individuals can only research themselves. For example, the researcher, the physical education teacher and the students need to be part of the research team that examines physical education in low-income Hispanic areas in Los Angeles. Third, PAR is **practical** in that it examines existing social practices and collaborative in that the researchers, together with the participants, work to reconstruct social interactions by 'reconstructing the acts that constitute them' (Kemmis & McTaggard, 2005, p. 567). Therefore, a PAR project would aim to reconstruct the existing social interactions in the current PE classes for children and youth in low-income Hispanic areas in Los Angeles. Fourth, PAR is **emancipatory** as it aims, through the reconstruction of social practices, to help people recover and release themselves from limiting social structures. Fifth, PAR is **critical** as it aims to release people from the constraints of the social media (e.g., the unjust use of language, unsatisfying ways of interpreting and describing their world). Therefore, a PAR project would empower students and the teachers to recover the limitations for the PE participation and help them to describe their world in a new way. Sixth, PAR is **reflexive** as it aims to help people to investigate reality to change it. For example, the ultimate aim would be to offer better physical education classes that empower students to overcome the structural limitations of their low-income neighbourhood and the racial structures of US society. This change is embedded in a deliberate reflexive process of transforming social practices into 'a spiral of cycles of critical and self-critical social process' (Kemmis & McTaggard, 2005, p. 567). This cycle involves planning change, implementing change, observing the process and consequences for these actions, reflection on these processes and consequences, replanning based on the reflections and starting the cycle again. Finally, PAR aims to **transform both theory and practice**, which it plans to articulate and develop in relation to each other. Therefore, theory does not stand alone or above practice, neither is practice devoid of theory. For example, the PAR researchers, based on their project on physical education in a low-income Hispanic neighbourhood, can further develop the insights of critical race theory in the US context. Kemmis and McTaggard's (2005) approach draws heavily from Habermas's (1984; 1987) theory of communicative action, which locates this type of PAR within the critical paradigm.

Context for PAR

While not all PAR researchers explicitly base their method on a theoretical premise, its general goals – a more just society; material well-being; socio-political entitlement – locate most PAR projects within the critical paradigm (e.g., Park, 1993; Reason & Bradbury, 2001). Therefore, it is logical that target groups for PAR are often the poor, underprivileged and powerless in the context of the developing or developed world such as low-income Hispanic physical education students in the USA. The goal is to increase self-determination through self-reflection and problem solving and, as stated earlier, to provide empowerment through examination or, if possible, elimination of social constraints. If this is not directly possible, then PAR aims to minimise the limitations for people's self-determinations and the shared structuring of their own social lives. Because of its diverse goals, PAR is designed to produce interactive and critical knowledges (Park, 1993). **Interactive knowledge** refers to the type of knowledge we obtain by living and interacting with other people. As Park defines it: 'This knowledge does not derive from analysis of data about other human beings but from sharing a life-world together – speaking with one another and exchanging actions against the background of common experience, tradition, history, and culture' (1993, p. 6). Critical knowledge refers to the type of knowledge that 'comes from reflection and action, which makes it possible to deliberate questions of what is right and just' (ibid.). Gathering this knowledge will help people to identify the problems surrounding them and then achieve self-reliance and self-determination within this reality. For example, instead of such outsiders as researchers or government officials, a PAR project in physical education should empower the Hispanic students, teachers and possibly the members of the community to identify the problems in their own neighbourhood and reach self-reliance this way.

Because PAR is collaborative and participatory, the researcher's role in these projects can differ somewhat from the other field methods. As PAR cannot 'be done on others', the researcher has to be an active participant in the problem solving in the target community. Often the researcher assumes a role of 'facilitator'. This role, however, should not be equated with a 'process consultant' who, as a neutral expert, is called to administer techniques of knowledge gathering within a community (see Kemmis & McTaggard, 2005). A PAR researcher is neither an outside advisor nor a distant collector of knowledge regarding the community, but a participant in solving the identified research problem. For example, a PAR researcher should not simply observe problems in physical education at schools in low-income areas and then provide expert advice on how to solve these, but should rather be an active part of the problem-solving process.

Research problem

As PAR is a problem-based research approach, the target community takes an active role in identifying a problem that needs investigating or solving.

In many cases, the community actually invites the researcher to participate in their process of solving the problem instead of the researcher entering the community with a pre-defined research question in mind. For example, ideally the schools in low-income Hispanic areas should contact the researcher (rather than the researcher having a research plan ready to embark in, for example, ethnography in these schools). The role of the researcher, therefore, is not necessarily to identify a research problem for PAR, but rather to activate the community to tackle the issues they have identified themselves. Therefore, it is common that the research approach and process are negotiated with the community together. Depending on the size of the community, often different types of community meetings or 'townhalls' are called at the start, during and at the end of the PAR process. For example, the PAR researchers of physical education should organise meetings where the teachers, students, school personnel and the community members meet together to identify the nature of the project. The idea is to create continuous dialogue between the different participants (including the researcher) during the conduct of PAR.

Research design and research methods

Because PAR is a participatory, practical and collaborative social process, ideally all the participants serve as researchers actively collecting empirical material. In this sense, the researcher also becomes a community member. For example, the students and the teachers can collect empirical material for a PAR project on PE in schools located in low-income Hispanic neighbourhoods. However, in many PAR projects the researchers actually collect the empirical material while the participants take part in designing the research projects. For example, the research methods can be chosen collectively. Any research methods (also quantitative surveys) can be used in a PAR project. However, in the case of interviews or surveys, the participants, if not conducting the research, typically agree upon the interview or survey questions collectively. The ethical procedure depends on the methods used, but also on the context of PAR research: many 'westernised' notions of ethical research conduct do not necessarily apply worldwide (e.g., Tilley & Gormley, 2007). Some researchers posit that the so-called 'communitarian' model, which stresses the benefits of the group is the most suitable ethical procedure for PAR (e.g., Christians, 2005, see Chapter 1 for discussion of qualitative research ethics). As Christians explains: 'In communitarianism, conceptions of the good are shared by the research subjects, and researchers collaborate in bringing these definitions into their own' (2005, p. 157). The participatory nature of PAR also creates unique ethical challenges. If everyone is acting as a researcher and collecting the empirical material, for example through interviews, everyone will also have access to all the empirical material. What rules of privacy, confidentiality and anonymity will apply to such situations?

Analysis of empirical material in PAR

In the ideal case, the community members who have collected the empirical material should also analyse it. However, in many cases the analysis requires advanced research knowledge and often the researchers do the actual analysis of the empirical material. Again, the type of analysis depends on the methods used. For example, in terms of analysing interview material, the analysis techniques presented in Chapter 4 can be used. Most importantly, however, the dialogue between different researchers or the researchers and community must be kept open so that everyone is informed about the process of analysis of empirical material. For example, the PAR researchers of physical education should keep the students, the teachers, the school and the local Hispanic community continually informed of the results that they have obtained from the project. These can be presented in 'townhall' meetings as the analysis progresses or presented individually to the participants. Often it is easier for the participants to receive the results verbally than read through written research reports. In any case, it is important to present the results in a manner that is comprehensible to all of the participants in the project.

Issues of **(re)presentation** and **validation** for participatory action research will be discussed in Chapters 8 and 9, respectively.

Communication of results

As the main premise of PAR is to provide emancipation for the community involved, the results should first and foremost be used to find practical solutions to the their problems. However, as the PAR aims to also transform theory through practical findings from the 'field', the researchers use the results to inform their scholarly practices. It is important to keep the community informed how their 'data' is used for research purposes and provide the community access to any possible research publications.

Summary: Participatory action research

Participatory action research is a qualitative research methodology that derives directly from the 'problems' identified by the research participants. Its philosophical premise is located within the critical paradigm. As the ethos of PAR is strongly emancipatory, the participants usually come from socio-economically marginalised groups. The researcher, rather than acting as a leader of a research project, acts as a 'participant in problem-solving' facilitating the participants to conduct the research. Ideally, the participants collectively provide the researcher with questions, decide on an appropriate method, collect the empirical material and analyse the results. Therefore, PAR is a research method with a clear aim for direct community action and change by the participants.

Case study research

While case study research has long been practised in such disciplines as law, medicine, psychiatry and management, it has often been viewed as a scientifically weak method compared to evidence-based quantitative research that utilises randomised, controlled sampling (Yin, 2003). While more common in sport management, case study research has not been widely employed by qualitative sport science researchers. Nevertheless, there is no reason why this field method could not be adapted to the multiple uses of qualitative researchers (see also Flyvbjerk, 2001). While some advocates (e.g., Yin, 2003) see case study as a separate methodology from 'qualitative research', others posit that case study 'is not a methodological choice but a choice of what is to be studied' (Stake, 2005, p. 443). VanWynsberhe and Khan (2007) further note that case study has been referred to as a method, strategy, research design or methodology. We introduce case study here as a field method that uses several qualitative methods to understand social world using an 'exemplary' case as a window.

Box 7.2 Content of a method section for qualitative case study research

- Case study as a qualitative method;
- Case selection;
- Choices of methods;
- Ethical concerns (see Chapter 1);
- Analysis of empirical material;
- Issues of representation (see Chapter 8);
- Validation (see Chapter 9).

Case selection

According to Stake (2005), the 'case' is the primary focus, but it can be studied through multiple methods. Yin adds that a case is an empirical inquiry that 'investigates a contemporary phenomenon within its real-life context' (2003, p. 13). A qualitative case study, Stake adds, 'concentrates on experiential knowledge of the case and close attention to the influence of its social, political, and other contexts' (Stake, 2005, p. 444). Nevertheless, the focus is always on an importance of a singular case and the sample size will always be small (VanWynsberghe & Khan, 2007). Therefore, a case can be an athlete, fitness participant, sport student, coach, physical education class, fitness centre, coaching session, fitness class, sport club, sport organisation, a special sport 'case' reported in the media (such as a doping scandal in Tour de France), sport program, sport policy, a specific Olympic Games – almost anything that is a specific case or a 'bounded system' (Stake, 2005). Consequently, Stake defines **'boundedness'** and a specific activity pattern as useful concepts of defining a case: most cases 'have working parts and purposes, many have a self' (2005, p. 444). Nevertheless, case study research often takes place in a 'natural setting', in a field (VanWynsberghe & Khan, 2007). Because of the flexible definition for 'a case', there are several types of case studies.

Stake (2005) distinguishes between three case study designs: intrinsic, instrumental and collective case study. **An intrinsic case study** is undertaken because a researcher wants, first and foremost, to understand a particular case: the case is of interest in itself, not because it represents other cases or because it illustrates a particular problem. For example, a researcher might study an athlete with eating disorders because of an interest in the lived experiences of this particular athlete. Therefore, the idea is to understand why this particular athlete suffers from an eating disorder and how she copes with her condition.

An instrumental case study provides insights to an issue and, therefore, the case itself is of secondary interest and facilitates an understanding of something else. For example, a researcher chooses to study an athlete with an eating disorder to understand how and what conditions, in general, might induce eating disordered behaviour in sport. The athlete, whose behaviour and the context for this behaviour are still analysed in-depth, serves as a 'typical case' for external purpose, the development of eating disorders in sport contexts. Stake also emphasises that often the line between intrinsic and instrumental case study is far from clear: the researcher often has an interest in both the particular case and the general context surrounding it.

Finally, a number of cases are studied jointly, constituting **a multiple or collective case study**. Individual cases are selected 'because it is believed that understanding them better will lead to better understanding ... about a still larger collection of cases' (Stake, 2005, p. 446). For example, a researcher might choose to study athletes with eating disorders from several different sports to understand better how women athletes become engaged in eating disordered behaviour. Other classifications of case studies are based on the purpose of the study such as explanatory versus descriptive case study (e.g., Stakes, 2005; Yin, 2003). Nevertheless, all case study researchers seek to understand both what is common and what is particular about the cases, but the priority between the two might differ in different projects. All types of case studies, thus, aim provide a high level of contextual detail. VanWynsberghe and Khan characterise a case study researcher as carefully delineating an 'instance': 'defining it in general terms and teasing out its particularities' (2007, p. 4).

It is important to note that case study research is not devoid of theory. On the contrary, for a qualitative case study to have a research purpose it needs to be based on theoretical assumptions. Even a descriptive, intrinsic case study is done for a purpose and, thus, the researcher cannot avoid articulation with a theoretical position and a paradigmatic inclination underpinning the research project. Case study research, however, can draw from any paradigmatic and theoretical approach, but again, care should be taken not to mix and match theoretical and/or paradigmatic assumptions arbitrarily. For example, while a case study uses several different methods, they need to be conducted through a clearly defined paradigmatic and theoretical logic. For example, VanWynsberghe and Khan explain that case study research within a post-positivist paradigm allows the researcher to 'discover and study cases and generate and test hypothesis about the real world with them' (2007, p. 8). Within an interpretive paradigm, they continue, case study can be used to provide knowledge that 'goes deep enough to provide analysis' (ibid.). Case studies within this paradigm focus on describing a particular reality and 'the story-like rendering of a problem' (ibid.) in everyday life is often emphasised (see also Chapter 6 narrative analysis). Researchers in the critical paradigm, they further suggest, can use case studies to 'detail a history of contradictions that has led to injustices' (VanWynsberghe & Khan, 2007, p. 8). The ultimate goal for case study research (see also PAR above) in this paradigm is transformation and 'the movement towards a better, more rational world' (ibid.). Consequently, it is important to stipulate one's research purpose openly, locate it within a paradigmatic logic and then design a case study that will best answer the research questions.

As in all qualitative research, a case is chosen for a reason and, therefore, a researcher needs to identify a research problem and purpose. For a case study to be a valuable research method, the researcher needs to ask: 'What can be learned here that the reader needs to know?' Stake (2005) advises thinking about either a topical issue or a current social problem, or the evaluation or verification of an issue as the basis for a research question. For example, it is important to consider what can be learned in a case study of sport women's eating disorders that readers need to know. Is it valuable enough to report the experiences of such an athlete? What exactly is the research problem in this case? For example, a researcher could identify eating disorders as problematic not only for the athletes' health, but also for the club and the sport in general because women's sport becomes identified with mistreatment of athletes and poor performance. To select the suitable cases, the researcher can use qualitative sampling techniques similar to those introduced in Chapter 4 for interviewing. Depending on the research question, the researcher can then identify through what methods the case can be understood in an in-depth manner.

Method selection and analysis of empirical material

While a qualitative case study design can use multiple methods, Yin (2003) identifies six 'evidence sources' for this type of research: documentation, archival records, interviews, direct observation, participant-observation and collecting physical artefacts. It is not necessary to employ all these methods in each case study, but Stake (2005) asserts that a case study researcher should use document analysis to understand the context for the case, interviews to seek the unseen of the case and observation to seek the ordinary for the case. For example, if a researcher plans to conduct an instrumental case study on eating disorders in women's long distance running, after selecting the case, for example, a university women's long distance running programme, she should think what methods will provide the best evidence to illuminate the research problem. She could seek documentary evidence such as training programs, nutrition logs, coaching plans and policy documents regarding athletes' health to identify the context for eating disordered behaviour in the particular program. She could then observe the actual training and the athletes' everyday lives to identify the 'ordinary' training, eating and living practices. Finally, she could, based on these methods, identify certain athletes for interviews to collect evidence on issues that were not identifiable through document analysis and observation. In this sense, a case study design can be understood as an 'open-ended' research project that can only be finalised through its conduct and events that unfold in the research process.

It important to document the conduct of each method (see Chapter 4 for conducting interviews, Chapter 5 for textual and document analysis, and the section on 'Ethnography' in this chapter for conducting observation and participant-observation). In addition, it is important that the researcher seeks ethical approval for conducting each method (see Chapter 1 for ethical issues in qualitative research).

The empirical material from each method can be analysed similarly to the analysis of any interview, observation or textual analysis study (see Chapters 4 and 5). In addition, as always with data analysis, it is important to align the analysis with one's theoretical/paradigmatic approach. For example, it is inappropriate to use a Foucauldian discourse analysis to analyse the documents, but then employ interpretive analysis for the interviews and the observations. Stake (1995), however, recommends the following generic way to analyse empirical material from a case study:

1. Categorical aggregation: Collection of instances from the empirical material through which issue-relevant meanings emerge. For example, collection of athletes with similar life patterns outside of sport that seem to be connected to eating disorders.
2. Direct interpretation: Focus on a single instance to draw meanings. This requires a process of reorganising the material in more meaningful ways. For example, a direct interpretation of one athlete whose lifestyle patterns seem to exemplify the other eating disorder cases.
3. Establishment of patterns: Looking for correspondences between several categories (established through step 1). For example, looking for correspondences between women athletes with eating disorders, body dissatisfaction (but no obvious eating disorder) and athletes without an eating disorder.
4. Development of naturalistic generalisation: Establishing what can be learnt from the case or applying the findings to a population of cases. For example, what can be learnt about women's sport, coaching and training by examining women athletes' eating disorders.

Issues of (re)presentation and **validation** for case study will be discussed in Chapters 8 and 9, respectively.

Summary: Case study research

A qualitative case study takes an examination of a singular case as its main focus. A case itself can be defined broadly as having boundaries within which the case has a clearly identifiable system. Therefore, a case study is not limited to a study of an individual, but can consist of a larger entity as long as it has activity patterns within a 'boundness'. Case study research employs multiple methods to understand the case but, like all qualitative research projects, has a clearly defined problem embedded in a theoretical framework.

Ethnography

Ethnography, originally associated with anthropological fieldwork with 'exotic others' or 'primitive cultures', is one of most established qualitative methods. Ethnography has also evolved through the critiques of early anthropology into other social science disciplines. In this process, it has also diversified into forms that focus on everyday cultural settings close to the researcher rather than distant cultures. Furthermore, as ethnography has become a method used by a variety of researchers with a variety of theoretical approaches, it has developed into such distinct forms as interpretive ethnography, critical ethnography or postmodern ethnography. Such new forms as visual ethnography have also gained popularity in recent years. Despite this diversity, ethnography as a method still consists of fieldwork during which the researcher engages in participant-observation, document analysis and different forms of interviewing. Similarly to other qualitative methods, however, the way researchers interpret the ethnographic findings depends on their paradigmatic and theoretical approach. Keeping this in mind, Hammersley and Atkinson's (1995) classic definition offers a concise understanding of ethnography as a method:

> In its most characteristic form it [ethnography] involves the ethnographer participating, overtly or covertly, in people's daily lives for an extended period of time, watching what happens, listening to what is said, asking questions – in fact, collecting whatever data are available to throw light on the issues that are the focus of the research.
>
> (Hammersley & Atkinson, 1995, p. 1)

We focus on detailing particularly the centrality of the 'field' in ethnographic work. We continue with a discussion of participant-observation.

The other ethnographic methods (interviewing and document/textual analysis) are discussed in Chapters 4 and 5. We also provide a separate discussion of visual ethnography.

Box 7.3 Content of a method section for qualitative ethnography

- Ethnography as a qualitative method;
- The field;
- The ethnographer;
- Methods used;
- Sampling;
- Ethical issues (see Chapter 1);
- Analysis of empirical material;
- Issues of representation (see Chapter 8);
- Validation (see Chapter 9).

The field

The selection of the 'field' where the ethnographer plans to participate in people's everyday lives depends, naturally, on the researcher's topic and research questions. While the stereotype of an anthropologist might be a heroic male figure engaged in an exotic, unknown, distant and dangerous field with previously unresearched 'natives' or dangerous criminals, probably most ethnographic work today takes place in more familiar, close, everyday settings in westernised countries. For example, ethnographers of physical culture have chosen such 'fields' as body-building (Bolin, 2003; Klein, 1993), fitness (Markula, 1995), snowboarding (Thorpe, 2008), media production (Silk, 2001; 2002; Lowes, 2002; MacNeill, 1996), NASCAR racing (Newman & Beissel, 2009) or windsurfing (Wheaton, 2000). Therefore, the field can be defined very broadly to encompass different physical culture settings from close to the researcher to more distant settings such as the Commonwealth Games in Malaysia (Silk, 2002) or baseball in Dominican Republic (Klein, 1997).

What characterises ethnography is the researcher's extended stay in the field. This allows the researcher to capture the cultural context more fully. This is, understandably, not possible within a couple of days or even weeks, but usually requires a stay of a minimum of 6 months or more. If a researcher is forced to spend less time, it is better to talk about participant-observation research than a complete ethnography.

One of the central aspects of ethnographic research is gaining access to the field one plans to research. Because the researcher is often an 'outsider' to the intended cultural field, it is important to develop clear strategies of how the researcher plans to gain an insider status. More is at stake here than being merely able physically to access the field: as the ethnographers need to be able to observe everyday life and talk to people, they need to gain a position of trust among the culture. To obtain an understanding of the culture, the ethnographer cannot remain merely as an objective, distant observer. Access to the field is typically gained through 'gatekeepers': individuals who are in one way or another central to the cultural field and/or well known by the people in the field. Once in the field, the ethnographer usually seeks out 'informants': particularly knowledgeable and insightful individuals willing to collaborate with the researcher.

It is also possible that the ethnographer is already an insider in the field (e.g., a snowboarder, exerciser, bodybuilder, baseball player) who has decided to conduct an ethnography within their own cultural setting. In this case, access to the field and identifying informants is remarkably easier. It is perfectly acceptable, some would say even preferable, to examine one's own cultural field. We now discuss the role of ethnographer in detail.

The ethnographer

As ethnographers physically enter the field they plan to investigate, they will always influence, in one way another, the events that take place during their stay. In addition, as they become more familiar with the culture and the people they create closer ties to their field. Early anthropologists, such as Bronislaw Malinowski and Claude Levi-Strauss, were very concerned that getting too close to people studied would have a negative impact on the research results which would no longer be objective. The phenomenon of getting 'too' close to one's field was called 'going native': the researchers became more and more like the people studied as they learned to understand them better. 'Going native' was considered very detrimental as the researchers became partial to their field and, thus, the results were contaminated by subjective remarks in 'favour' of the 'natives'. However, as qualitative research epistemology is subjective, it is now commonly accepted that fieldwork will always produce 'partial truths': all research observations are filtered through the researcher's personal beliefs and cultural background (Clifford & Marcus, 1986). Therefore, the ethnographic research process will always be inherently subjective.

With this acknowledgement, it is also common that ethnographers study a field in which they are 'natives' themselves. To a certain extent familiarity with the field is, of course, an advantage as gaining access and identifying gatekeepers is much easier. However, it is equally important that the ethnographer has prepared the research project well in advance to bring in the self-reflexivity required for the added role change from an insider/practitioner to a researcher/ethnographer. Consequently, while qualitative ethnographers should not consider themselves objective, distant observers (being 'there') outside the field, neither should they be mere insiders who 'practise' the culture (being 'here') without any critical reflection. Therefore, some suggest that the ethnographer is located, rather, 'in between' the research 'culture' and the culture of the 'field'. Naturally, the exact focus of the ethnographic research depends on the ethnographer's paradigmatic stance. For example, an interpretive ethnographer might focus on the similarities and differences between ski instructors' experiences in a commercial ski resort, whereas a critical ethnographer could focus on the marginalisation of certain types of instructors (e.g., men versus women, children's instructors versus adult's instructors) produced by the commercial management of the field. A poststructuralist ethnographer might map the discursive construction of the instruction and skiing practices in the power/discourse nexus of tourism, commercialism, outdoor leisure and health. Nevertheless, each one of the ethnographers would need to employ several methods to gain answers to the research problems.

The methods: Participant observation

Similarly to all field methods, ethnography refers to a set of methods. While the type of empirical material required depends on one's research questions, most ethnographers use the following main methods – participant observation, interviews and textual analysis – to collect whatever empirical material is available in the field. We have discussed interviewing in Chapter 4 and textual analysis in Chapter 5. An ethnographic use of these methods does not depart from our earlier discussion and, therefore, in this chapter we focus on participant observation.

While participant observation actually refers to two distinct 'methods', participation and observation that can be conducted simultaneously or separately, some literature considers participant observation a subcategory of a larger field of observational research. Observation, like interviewing or textual analysis, can be conducted quantitatively or qualitatively. For example, objective observations of physical education teaching through the use of a pre-validated 'check-list' represents a quantitative observational technique. Participation is often understood to introduce a subjective element to such distant, objective observation. For example, Gold (1958) divided observers of 'natural settings' (or fields) into 'complete observers', 'observers-as-participants', 'participants-as-observers' and 'complete participants' (Angrosino, 2005; see also Hammersley & Atkinson, 1995). In this scheme, the complete observer was considered the most objective and the complete participant the most subjective researcher (and also the least 'scientific', even 'questionable' researcher). As qualitative forms of observation now abound, there is no hierarchy between observation and participation, but rather both are used based on the empirical material required to answer the ethnographer's research questions.

Observational research, however, can continue to include unobtrusive or participant observation. **Unobtrusive observation** is 'conducted with people who are unaware of being studied' (Angrosino, 2005, p. 732). For example, an ethnographer can observe children playing in a playground from a distance without them knowing about the researcher. **Participant observation** refers to the long-term immersion of the researcher in a community under study and requires, as does all ethnographic work, a considerable rapport between researcher and hosts (Angrosino, 2005). In this research, the ethnographers are always 'overt' observers – people in the field are aware of their role as researcher – as opposed to 'covert' observers who hide their research intentions from the people observed. Ethnographic observation should always be **overt**, as the researchers should affirm a membership in the field or community they study. This does not have to mean an acceptance of all the views presented in the field or harmonising them with one's own perspectives, but rather an acceptance of diverse 'truths' arising from the research. The ethnographers often refer to a 'dialogue' between the researcher and the people in field to denote an acceptance that multiple, even contradictory, voices, including the researcher's own voice, construct an ethnographic work (e.g., Angrosino, 2005; Clifford & Marcus, 1986; James, Hockey & Dawson, 1997; Tedlock, 2000; 2005). What exact empirical material should the observation focus on?

The classical aim for ethnographic participant observation is to provide 'thick description' (Geertz, 1973): description by which an ethnographer – through an 'empathy' with the participants – includes the meanings specific to the participants (not to the researcher). While Geertz's view of 'thick description' is later accused of being devoid of the researcher's influence on the interpretation, thinking of the aim of participant observation as obtaining material that illustrates the multiple meanings (including the researcher's meanings) that characterise the field can be helpful. Some researchers divide observational research based on increasing levels of specificity (e.g., see Angrosino, 2005). An ethnographer can begin with **descriptive observation** during which the researcher aims to record all the possible details. For example, the ethnographer can first focus on describing the environment, landscape and the general structure of a ski field where the instructors operate and then further map the management structure, clientele and ski instructor workday to provide a general picture of a ski resort as a workplace. This type of observation will result in large quantities of empirical material, some of which might not be used. **Focused observation** refers to more specific observation that concentrates on more defined activity or location in the field. For example, an ethnographer might become more interested in the different requirements and perceptions of the instructors of adult skiers and children. To obtain a more complete idea of these differences, the ethnographer can decide to focus on observing several instructors and differences in their work environment and expectations. Finally, **selective observation** refers to further specified observation of a more specific aspect of an activity or location. For example, after observing that women and beginning instructors tend to teach children while male, more advanced instructors are expected to instruct adults, the ethnographer can observe more closely a couple of instructors that 'typify' each category to obtain more detailed material of their daily lives. While not all ethnographers follow such standardised observational hierarchy – they might be involved in all three simultaneously – it can be helpful for a beginning ethnographer to go from more general mapping of the field to more specified interests that might develop during the process of participant observation.

These observations are recorded in **field notes**. As it is often difficult to keep writing notes during the participation, particularly if it involves physical activity, ethnographers usually write these notes immediately after their observation. These should, of course, be as detailed as possible to provide enough empirical material for analysis. Some ethnographers keep separate observation notes from personal notes. Observation notes, in this case, include descriptions of the field, the participants and possible research notes connecting these observations to cultural context or to previous literature. The personal notes contain ethnographer's personal feelings, struggles, doubts or self-reflections – the researcher's voice. Current qualitative ethnographic approaches advocate that the researcher is an integral part of the research process and, while having a voice, it should be in dialogue with the participants' voices. Consequently, many ethnographers today combine these two types of notes into one set of field notes. In any case, it is important to remember that participant observation involves more than mere description of events. An ethnographer must always reflect the empirical material against the broader cultural context of the field.

Sampling

During most ethnographic fieldwork, it is impossible to observe or interview all the people in the field or obtain all possible textual material regarding the field. Therefore, like most qualitative researchers, ethnographers must 'sample' only some individuals or texts to be part of the research. However, the same qualitative sampling techniques that are discussed in Chapters 4 and 5 can be used in an ethnographic study. In addition, as ethnography uses human subjects, the researcher must adhere to the ethical guidelines presented in Chapter 1. One must note that as ethnography involves several methods for collection of empirical material, the ethics application must detail all the methods involving human subjects.

Analysis of empirical material

As ethnography, similar to other field methods, comprises multiple methods, empirical material collected through each method can be analysed by using a technique appropriate for each method. For example, interviews can be analysed following the data analyses we discussed in Chapter 4 and texts can be analysed as discussed in Chapter 5. The field notes from participant observation, however, are likely to result in 'messier' data than the other methods. Therefore, in this section we provide some guidance for how to analyse the empirical material collected in field notes.

Analysing field notes can follow the general pattern of analysis in which the researcher first identifies main themes from the notes. This preliminary analysis can also inform 'focused observation' following from the first 'descriptive observation'. The themes should then be linked to larger narratives and finally with theory. Wolcott (1994) offers more specific steps for the analysis of ethnographic material that can aid in an analysis beginning with descriptive observations:

- Description: Systematic description of the material, which can by done chronologically (e.g., describing each observed day chronologically) or by an order created by the researchers (or narrator). The idea is to describe, in detail, a 'day in the life' of an individual or group belonging to the field. An ethnographer can also focus on critical or key events to develop a 'story' from the field, show informants with different views or examine group interactions.

- Analysis:
  o Display findings through tables, charts, diagrams or figures and systematically comparing findings;
  o Search for patterned regularities in the displayed material.
- Interpretation of the culture-sharing group: During this phase the ethnographer asks: What is to be made of empirical material collected in the field? The ethnographer also aims to contextualise the findings within a theoretical framework.

From an interpretive perspective, Creswell (1998) advises thinking of the data analysis process as a continual spiral in which the researcher begins data managing by reading and 'memoing' and moves through describing and classifying the data to interpretation and representation of the data.

The data analysis spiral:

1. Data managing: Organisation of data into files and units;
2. Reading, memoing: Reflections, writing notes;
3. Describing, classifying, interpreting: Contextualising, creating categories and comparisons;
4. Representing, visualising: Creating matrix, 'trees', propositions;
5. Final account.

(Creswell, 1998)

During this analysis, the ethnographer moves from small units through a series of steps to create broader classification and finally an interpretation through which the ethnographer links the findings to previous theory. This technique does not openly address the researcher's role in the ethnographic process, nor locate the 'field' within historical, economical, social and/or political power relations. However, researchers from the critical paradigm could use Cresswell's 'spiral' by adding self-reflection in step 2, by contextualising the findings in their historical and political context in step 3 and connecting the findings with critical theory and an examination of power in step 4.

Issues of (re)presentation and **validation** for ethnography will be discussed in Chapters 8 and 9, respectively.

Summary: Ethnography

Ethnography as a method is characterised by a researcher's extended stay within the 'field'. During this fieldwork, the ethnographer aims to collect any type of empirical material that highlights the culture and the experiences and meanings of the people within it. Participant observation and material collected in field notes are an integral aspect of ethnography, but an ethnographer can use other methods such as interviews and textual analysis to understand the culture. When the ethnographers enter the field, they become a part of the events unfolding during the ethnography. Therefore, they are always part of the ethnographic research process, which is often understood as a dialogue between the researchers and the people in the field. Where ethnography as a method has become a more popular method across the social sciences, different forms of it have began to evolve. One type of ethnography that has gained recent popularity is visual ethnography. We will now discuss this particular type of ethnography.

Visual ethnography

Visual ethnography refers to the use of photographs, film or visual images as a part of ethnographic research. This type of research can also be referred to as visual sociology or visual anthropology (Harper, 2005). In this research visuals or imagery are used to study specific questions or issues in the social sciences, including social investigations of physical culture. Wagner (2004) argues that visual research is important because, first, it can provide empirically credible images of culture in addition to the researcher's written text. Second, it can frame empirical observations to highlight new knowledge. Finally, visual research can challenge social theory by providing visual evidence for the researcher's argument. An ethnographer can, however, use the visuals in several ways to press a point or support an argument. Many visual researchers separate using visual material as empirical material from using visuals as part of the research representation. We will discuss both of these ways of including visual material in one's ethnography.

Visuals as empirical ethnography material

Ethnographers can create visual materials – photographs or film – during their fieldwork. These materials are then analysed similarly to any other empirical material from the field. However, pictorial data can be argued to go beyond the surface of everyday life to capture emotions and lived experiences in a deeper manner than other types of empirical material. Pictures, it is said, go beyond the written or spoken word to illustrate aspects of culture not captured through other research methods. Anthropologists have used visual material to achieve a multidimensional understanding, often focusing on a specific aspect of a culture (Pink, 2001). In addition, visual methods can be understood as multilayered methods using photography, writing and narratives regarding the particular images to understand a specific research question. The participants are an active part of the meaning making because these methods 'might present the fullest picture of a cultural phenomenon, in the worlds and from the perspective of participants' (Keller et al., 2008, p. 428).

A specific visual approach to collecting empirical material is **photo elicitation**. This method is often traced to Collier's (1967) work on visual anthropology. Photo elicitation involves the researcher using photographs or images to elicit memories or discussion of specific issues, experiences or meanings by the participants. This takes place in the context of semi-structured interviews and thus, photo elicitation commonly takes a form of an interview where the researcher shows certain pictures to elicit discussion with the interviewee (Banks, 2001; Keller et al., 2008). The photos are most often taken or obtained by the researcher. The photographs should, nevertheless, be selected because they are, in one way or another, significant for the participants (Prosser, 1998). These discussions are then audio-recorded and transcribed similarly to interviews. For example, an ethnographer can show pictures of different types of skiers or different types of slopes to aid ski instructors to talk about their experiences of dealing with different types of clients. As Harper explains, in photo elicitation studies 'photographs proved to be able to stimulate memories that word-based interviewing did not' (2005, p. 757). As a result the discussion can go beyond 'what happened and when' to the meanings of participants' life experiences. Therefore, photo-elicitation allows participants to reveal aspects of their lives beyond narratives or interview discussion.

Photo-elicitation is commonly based on pictures taken and/or chosen by the researcher. In **reflexive photography, hermeneutic photography, autodriving photography** and **photovoice** the process is driven by participants who have also taken the photos (Epstein et al., 2006; Keller et al., 2008; Pink, 2001; Wang & Redwood-Jones, 2001). Reflexive, autodriving and hermeneutic photography can be used by interpretive researchers. Akin to participatory action research, photovoice, inspired by Paulo Freire's research, emphasises the emancipatory impact of using visual images. This method uses photographs taken and analysed by the participants, in collaboration with the researcher, to make visible 'the aspects of the self in the environment and in social situations' (Keller et al., 2009, p. 430). Participants' choices for images reflect their perceptions and meanings of their social environment. These can be contextualised and analysed through discussions that then reveal the social, ideological construction of participants' assumptions and challenge taken-for-granted truths (Keller et al., 2008). Once revealed, oppressive ideological constructions can be challenged and possibly changed. Photovoice, thus, is a particularly appropriate method for researchers in the critical paradigm.

Visuals as research representation

A second and overlapping way of utilising visuals places them as a part of the final research article or thesis. When used in this way, the researchers debate whether visuals should occupy a role as illustrations for a theoretical discussion of the findings or should stand alone as records of cultural and social life.

Harper (2005) distinguishes between three types of use for visual illustrations. In the first, which he titles an **illustrated research article**, the visuals contextualise and connect the reader to the argument of the article, but remain secondary. In such articles, the visual are not integrated as a part of the research project and might not even illustrate the actual context of the research. For example, an article on ski instructors' experiences can be accompanied by popular pictures from any ski field with any ski instructors or skiers. Harper titles the second type of articles using visuals as '**photo essays**, where sociological thinking emerges directly from images rather reinforcing and elaboration on word-based thinking' (p. 749). In these essays, the visuals stand alone as the results, with minimal verbal or no explanation. For example, the ethnographer can decide to send to publication an article with only pictures of different phases of ski instruction with different clients. These visuals are then meant to stand alone as illustrations of what ski instruction might mean in a commercial ski field. Finally, Harper detects photo essays that focus specifically on **social change**: 'images that show the same social scene at an earlier time and a more contemporary time' (p. 749). Here an ethnographer might collect visuals from when a ski field first opened and contrast these to the contemporary operation of a commercial ski field.

As Harper's (2005) discussion illustrates, visuals are not always meant to replace text. While an 'illustrated research article' also uses visuals, most visual ethnographers insist that the visuals are meant to serve as equally meaningful elements of research to words, not merely as something to entertain or capture the reader. Simply adding pictures or using visuals as a background does not, by itself, constitute a visual ethnography. While photographs might have long dominated as visuals in social science research, new technology has provided visual ethnographers with a multitude of ways to use visuals through CD-ROMs, the Web, video and film. Harper (2005), Leeuwen and Jewitt (2001) and Pink (2001) provide further details and possibilities for visual ethnography.

One of the central issues currently facing visual ethnography is the ethical conduct of this type of method. The ethics for visual ethnography are complicated primarily because of the anonymity of persons pictured in photos, videos or films. Some of the current questions are: Should the ethnographer obtain written informed consent from all the possible people appearing in the photos? What type of harm can identifying 'subjects' in the visuals create? Is the visual portrayal in the final published ethnography 'accurate' for the participant? Is it used in a way preferred by the participant? How can any participant remain anonymous in a clearly pictured photograph or film? While there are no clear answers to these questions, visual ethnographers, together with their ethics boards, need to find workable solutions before embarking on this type of research.

Summary: Field methods

All field methods are characterised by a researcher attending a 'field'. While the time spend in the field varies depending on the researcher's purpose and questions, the researcher uses multiple methods to capture an understanding of the field in general. We have introduced four field methods: participatory action research, case study research, ethnography and visual ethnography. While participatory action research is clearly grounded on the assumptions of a critical paradigm, researchers from multiple theoretical perspectives can engage in case studies or different types of ethnographies. While the field methods discussed here differ in several ways, in general a good study using field methods should include the following characteristics:

- A clear purpose and connection to paradigmatic and theoretical framework;
- A clear explanation of the context, case, or the field;
- A clear explanation of all the methods used;
- A clear explanation of how ethical concerns regarding multiple methods were handled;

- An explanation of the analysis of the empirical material obtained through each method.

Further reading

Participatory action research:

Frisby, W., Reid, C. J., Millar, S. & Hoeber, L. (2005). 'Putting "participatory" into participatory forms of actions of research'. *Journal of Sport Management*, 19, 367–86.
McHugh, T.-L. & Kowalski, K. C., (in press) '"A new view of body image": A school-based participatory action research project with young Aboriginal women'. *Action Research*.
Reason, P. (2001). *Handbook of action research: Participative inquiry and practice.* Thousand Oaks, CA: Sage.
Winter, R. (2002). *A handbook for action research in health and social care.* London: Routledge.

Case study research:

Cousens, L. & Barnes, M. L. (2009). 'Sport delivery in a highly socialized environment: A case study of embeddedness'. *Journal of Sport Management*, 23(5), 547–90.
Henderson, K. A. (2006). *Dimensions of choice: Qualitative approaches to parks, recreation, tourism, sport, and leisure research.* State College, PA: Venture Publishing.
Lynn, S. K. & Mays Woods, A. (2010). 'Following the yellow brick road: A teacher's journey along the proverbial career path'. *Journal of Teaching Physical Education*, 29, 54–71.
Misener, K. & Doherty, A. (2009). 'A case study of organizational capacity in nonprofit community'. *Journal of Sport Management*, 23(4) 457–82.
Shaw, S. & Amis, J. (2001). 'Image and investment: Sponsorship and women's sport'. *Journal of Sport Management*, 15, 219–46.

Ethnography:

Giulianotti, R. & Armstrong, G. (2002). 'Avenues of contestation: Football hooligans running and ruling urban spaces'. *Social Anthropology*, 10(2), 211–38.
Hills, L. (2007). 'Friendship, physicality, and physical education: An exploration of the social and embodied dynamics of girls' physical education experiences'. *Sport, Education and Society*, 12, 317–36.
Howe, P. D. (2001). 'An ethnography of pain and injury in professional rugby union: The case of Pontypridd RFC'. *International Review for the Sociology of Sport*, 6, 289–303.
Klein, A. M. (1997). *Baseball and the border: A tale of two laredos.* Princeton, NJ: Princeton University Press.
MacNeill, M. (1996). 'Networks: Producing Olympic ice hockey for a national television audience'. *Sociology of Sport Journal*, 13, 103–24.
Madison, D. S. (2005). *Critical ethnography: Method, ethics, and performance.* Thousand Oaks, CA: Sage.

Markula, P. (1995). 'Firm but shapely, fit but sexy, strong but thin: The postmodern aerobicizing female bodies'. *Sociology of Sport Journal*, 12, 424–53.

Rinehart, R. & Grenfell, C. (2002). 'BMX Spaces: Children's grass roots' courses and corporate-sponsored tracks'. *Sociology of Sport Journal*, 19, 302–14.

Silk, M. (2001). 'The conditions of practice: Television production practices at Kuala Lumpur 98'. *Sociology of Sport Journal*, 18, 277–301.

Thorpe, H. (2008). 'Foucault, technologies of the self, and the media. Discourses of femininity in snowboarding culture'. *Journal of Sport and Social Issues*, 32, 199–229.

Wheaton, B. (2000). '"Just do it": Consumption, commitment, and identity in the windsurfing subculture'. *Sociology of Sport Journal*, 17, 254–74.

Visual ethnography:

Azzarito, L. (2009). 'The Panopticon of physical education: Pretty, active and ideally white'. *Physical Education and Sport Pedagogy*, 14, 19–39.

Makagen, D. & Neumann, M. (2009). *Recording culture: Audi-documentary and the ethnographic experience*. Thousand Oaks, CA: Sage.

Part III
Dissemination

Within this section we consider the sixth and seventh Ps of qualitative research, which are concerned with the various ways to **(re)present** research and **the promise** to qualitative work: how this work may be judged. *(Re)presenting qualitative research in physical culture* refers to the actual product of qualitative research. This is likely, although not necessarily, going to be a written text. We consider how existing academic conventions and the researcher's paradigmatic stance influence the final product. For example in certain paradigms, other (less traditional) ways of representing physical culture are beginning to challenge what has been held to count as 'academic' writing. We thus address a plurality of differential ways to present qualitative research, all of which we feel have legitimacy and offer exciting opportunities for researchers of physical culture to create meaningful (written) products to a variety of audiences.

The final P, *The Promise*, refers to the standards through which qualitative research is judged. Because the field of qualitative research includes multiple ways of approaching, understanding, conducting and representing research, there are also multiple criteria by which to judge the quality of such research. Those working within the positivist paradigms will, for example, be held to quite different criteria than researchers couched in the postmodern/poststructural paradigm who offer a poetic representation of their fieldwork experiences. Instead of providing one standard by which to judge all qualitative research, we celebrate the plurality of standards. These exist to ensure the quality of good physical culture research that fulfils its purpose through a clearly defined paradigmatic location. Thus, in the final chapter, *the promise*, we come full circle to consider the various standards, and judgement criteria, for qualitative research in physical culture. This discussion is only possible through recourse to the pathways that the researcher has taken throughout the project.

Part III
Dissertation

8
Presentation (and Representation)

In this chapter, we will discuss the different ways of 'writing up' qualitative research such as:

- Realist writing;
- Different forms of narrative writing;
- Autoethnography;
- Performance ethnography.

After collecting and analysing the empirical material, a qualitative researcher needs to write all these findings up into a dissertation, paper, book chapter or a report. This 'write up', our sixth P, is called the ***representation*** of the empirical material. Qualitative researchers have several choices regarding their research representation. The most common way of representing research has been so-called 'realist writing': an objective, third person account of the research findings. This way of representation has been considered so standard that a discussion of research writing tends to be absent from books of qualitative methods. In recent years, however, there has been a considerable shift as research writing has become an integral part of the qualitative research methodologies. In this chapter we first discuss the standard, realist style of research writing. We then trace the development of alternative research writing styles through the so-called 'narrative turn' that took place throughout the social sciences in the early 1980s and still continues. We will explain the meaning of the narrative turn in more detail later in this chapter, before introducing some examples of different ways of writing qualitative research.

Realist research writing

To read the leading journals in sports studies usually means reading articles where the researcher deploys a neutral voice written in the third person. This type of writing is called realist research writing (Sparkes, 2002). In these texts, the researcher's voice is largely absent. This type of writing thus characterises quantitative research in which the researcher is understood as an objective producer of knowledge whose influence on the research results is eliminated as carefully as possible. Realist writing assumes that the author is an invisible yet authoritative figure who provides a truthful account of reality. As Sparkes explains:

> The style of no style is the style of science. The stripped down, abstracted, detached form of language; the impersonal voice; and the statement of conclusions as propositions or formulae involves a realist or externalising technique that objectifies through depersonalisation. This technique allows the text to give the impression that its symbols are inert, neutral representations that exist quite independently of the interests and efforts of the researcher, who is presented as a neutral and disengaged analyst.
>
> (Sparkes, 1995, p. 161)

Realist writing is, then, characterised by objective, third person, impersonal interpretation, by the absent, authoritative author and by the passive voice.

Qualitative researchers acknowledge their subjective influence on the research process. Sometimes this is limited to implicitly assuming the principles of subjective epistemology. In these cases, qualitative research is also often represented through realist writing. As Krizek (1998, p. 93) has proposed, 'many of us do ethnography [qualitative research] but write in the conservative voice of science ... In short, we often render our research reports devoid of human emotion and self-reflection. As ethnographers [qualitative researchers] we experience life but write science'. Despite the inherent subjective epistemology, there is no mention of the researcher in the final text and, therefore, the researcher remains an absent, objective observer of social events, similarly as in quantitative research. For example, in the numerous qualitative studies concerning young people and physical activity one rarely sees the author reflecting on his or her own childhood experiences in sport. Qualitative studies around topics such as pain and injury, burnout, winning and losing, and body image tend to be characterised by an absent or anonymous narrator. Similarly, the gender studies or numerous investigations into issues of race and social class in sport seldom include a position statement from the authors where they openly discuss their own social categories. Thus, how the author has influenced the text and the conclusions drawn largely remains a secret.

While realist writing continues to be the most common style of research writing, it also has limitations for qualitative researchers. First, as qualitative research is considered openly subjective, it seems rather contradictory to assume an objective writing style to represent such research results. Second, this type of writing tends to provide a flat and unidimensional account of complex experiences in the world (Sparkes, 2002). While qualitative research attempts to provide deep, analytical accounts of how people understand physical culture, realist writing does not help to convey such complexity. These concerns were expressed more commonly across the social sciences when the so-called 'narrative turn' took place.

The narrative turn

In the 1980s qualitative social science researchers began to focus more intensely on the role of writing in the research process. The role of the author as an authoritative, objective presenter of facts had already been challenged by several poststructuralist philosophers such as Jacques Derrida, Michel Foucault and Francois Lyotard. Echoing these challenges Clifford and Marcus (1986) in anthropology and Denzin, Lincoln and Richardson in sociology spearheaded the recognition that qualitative research representations have fundamentally been the products of asymmetrical power relations. In their seminal texts, these scholars question writing as a transparent and taken-for-granted way of representing 'data' that is necessarily considered as some sort of 'raw' material for the researchers' analysis. Such unproblematised understanding of the role of research writing, they argue, assumes an 'immediacy of experience': providing an account of other people's experiences is only a matter of recording their words in the final research output. In such 'objective' accounts of the 'real' world, the researcher remains an invisible, but authoritative provider of 'truth'. As qualitative research fundamentally challenges this positivist logic, it is rather strange that realist research writing – which implied all these values – is left untouched. These observations resulted in the 'narrative turn' that led to a development of new forms of representations, which could include the multiple voices of those being represented including the researcher's voice (James, Hockey & Dawson, 1997). Denzin and Lincoln (2005) further observe that the narrative turn also resulted in *the crisis of representation*, during which qualitative researchers began widely to question the taken-for-granted role of research writing.

The narrative turn further cements the qualitative principles of 'partial truth', reflexivity and contextuality into the process of research writing. James Clifford and George Marcus (1986) emphasise that qualitative research always represents partial truths as the researcher is an active maker of the research. Thus, the results are necessarily filtered through the researcher's thought process, which is, in turn, influenced by each individual researcher's cultural and personal background. Consequently, objective research writing is logically impossible. Instead of an invisible authority, the researchers necessarily represent multiple voices: their own, the participants' voices, the voice of the research tradition and the cultures of the researcher and the participants. Each piece of written research is thus polyvocal and contextual. Because of these multiple voices, qualitative researchers need to be reflexive about the process of research writing: it is an active process through which the researchers partly structure the research findings. These observations started a wider shift in writing that has lead to several different ways of describing, inscribing, interpreting and (re)presenting qualitative research (Denzin, 1994).

As a result of the narrative turn, research writing is no longer a taken-for-granted aspect of the research process that qualitative research, to qualify as 'real' research, must follow. It is important, then, that qualitative researchers celebrate the unique access they have to people's (including their own) lived experiences and try to evoke those experiences with as much detail as possible. When writing qualitative texts researchers should consider a number of issues that surround the authors' place in the text such as: whose voice speaks, who is excluded and how the different voices are interpreted. As Sparkes elaborates:

> Whose voices are included, how they are given weight, along with questions of priority and juxtaposition, are not just textual strategies but are political concerns that have moral consequences. How we as researchers chose to write about others has profound implications, not just for how readable the text is but also for how the people the text portrays are 'read' and understood.
>
> (Sparkes, 1995, p. 159)

As a first response to the narrative turn, qualitative researchers, as well as those studying physical culture, began to reflect upon their subjective influence on the research process. For example, they included discussions how their own biases and values intersect with their research subjects' values, and thus became concerned with how their own experiences influence the research process. In addition to discussing such issues in a methodology section, many researchers now synthesise these values throughout the entire article or project. For this reason, many qualitative researchers insert their own selves into their research texts and include references to themselves by openly using the first person 'I' in the research text. In these accounts, the authors' presence is more clearly acknowledged alongside the participants' voices, which are included in extensive, verbatim quotations. Although the researchers' influence is more openly acknowledged this type of writing is, nevertheless, still considered realist writing because the writing style itself has not changed. To move further towards reflexivity, polyvocality and contextuality, some qualitative researchers prefer to move a step further towards more literary expressions of research writing.

Alternative ways of representing research

Research writing that differs from realist writing has been labelled in multiple ways: narrative writing, storied writing, evocative writing or alternative ways of representation. We have already discussed the multiple meanings of 'narrative' in Chapter 6. However, when referring to the ways to 'write up' research findings, we use the terms storied, evocative or alternative 'to signify texts that we as qualitative researchers have produced ourselves either through researching and writing up others' experiences or through studying our own lives' (Markula & Denison, 2005, p. 166). What unites these different writing formats is that they are 'produced through creative analytic practices' (Richardson & St. Pierre, 2005, p. 962). Richardson (2000a; 2000b); Richardson & St. Pierre (2005) labels such work where 'the author has moved outside conventional social scientific writing' as '**creative analytic processes**' (**CAP**) (Richardson & St. Pierre, 2005, p. 962). These works invite 'people in and open spaces for thinking about the social that elude us now' (ibid.) and is thus both analytical and creative. In CAP projects, the writing process and writing product are both privileged and, thus, deeply intertwined: 'the product cannot be separated from the producer, the mode of production, or the method of knowing' (ibid.). Consequently, the author's subjectivity, authority and reflexivity become tangled with the process of doing the research and its representational form.

We further define such terms as storied, evocative or alternative writing as indicative of CAP projects. These are characterised by a distinct writing style: 'a style that is more storied in nature and that attempts to employ certain literary devices to convey in a rounder more embodied manner how people's lives are lived into existence and experienced' (Markula & Denison, 2005, p. 167). This is a style of writing that is interesting, thought-provoking and evocative. It goes beyond cold-hearted description to create a more fleshed-out, visceral portrait of the 'real'. It is a style of writing that aims to move the reader to think and act critically and reflexively (Markula & Denison, 2005). Therefore, while there is significant overlap with narrative research, and narrative research can also be represented in an evocative manner, alternative ways of research representation refer to a writing style that employs literary devices to represent empirical material. In this sense, alternative research writing does not necessitate an engagement with narrative research or narrative research is not always represented through alternative, storied writing style. Most empirical qualitative material (e.g., interviews, participant-observation notes, participants' narratives, personal diaries, textual analyses, case study material) can be represented through alternative, evocative research stories. Most commonly, however, only part of a qualitative research text is written in a storied manner. For example, in a dissertation the research results can be written as a story or a research article can include a section on researcher's personal experience.

As we explained earlier, due to the narrative turn, qualitative researchers now acknowledge that they all tell partial truths or tales. They differ, however, in terms of how explicitly they acknowledge their roles in their stories. Consequently, there are multiple ways of creating research texts that convey the researcher's personal experience as an integral aspect of the qualitative research process. In addition, the researchers' experiences become interweaved with the empirical research material (the other people's experiences) into one colourful story in alternative research texts. There is, nevertheless, more than one way of creating evocative research texts. It is now possible to write up one's research results, for example, as recollections, personal experience narratives, confessional tales, research stories, writing stories, layered texts, polyvocal texts, ethnographic fiction, fiction, creative non-fiction, literary stories, poetry, drama, ethnodrama, narratives of the self, autobiography, autoethnography or autophenomenology. New terms continually emerge with the growing popularity of alternative ways of representation. When alternative ways of research writing advance, it becomes more complicated to assess what is the best way of representing one's qualitative research findings. It must also be emphasised that realist writing remains a very appropriate option for many qualitative research projects. We come back to this point later in this chapter. We will now discuss in more detail what types of writing have resulted from the acknowledgement of research as a creative analytic process to make sense of the differences between these possibilities.

Types of narrative alternative research representations

The goal of alternative ways of writing research is two fold: to include the researchers' voices in the text openly and to present polyvocal, visceral and contextualised accounts of others' experiences. As Richardson (2000b) describes these texts use imagination to show how individuals experience social context. Therefore, to make sense of the numerous ways of evocative, storied research writing we have, following Markula and Denison (2005) divided the alternative research representation into two broad categories: Personal experience narratives and research stories. We have further divided these categories into essayistic and literary. We will now discuss each category in more detail.

Box 8.1 Alternative ways of narrative research writing

---

* Personal experience narratives:
  – Essayistic;
  – Literary.
* Research stories:
  – Essayistic;
  – Literary.

(Markula & Denison, 2005)

Essayistic personal experience

Personal experience narratives focus on personal experiences of the author's/researcher's life. Richardson (2000b) defines these types of stories as highly personalised and revealing texts in which authors talk openly about their own lived experiences. The idea behind telling revealing personal stories is to enable the reader to share or to learn, from a researcher's personal experiences, about the social construction of a self in a specific context. Through personal stories such construction becomes more tangible and assumes a sense of 'reality'. Decontextualised personal confessions, dramatic personal experiences or emotional encounters per se are not qualitative research accounts and should not serve as techniques of alternative research writing.

Like all qualitative research, essayistic personal experiences should be based on empirical material. It is common that a researcher begins with moments that have in one way or another been influential in their choice of a research topic and the formation of a specific research question. The researcher then records them as personal **recollections**. Markula and Denison advise the researcher to:

> Keep a journal and start with an impression, feeling, or observation and see where you go with it. Notice who enters into your recollection and listen to what they say and how they say it. See what issues arise and become important because most likely those are the issues that matter to you. Write close to home, concerning subjects that really touch the heart of your own life.
>
> (Markula & Denison, 2005, p. 170)

They emphasise, however, that these recollection are raw empirical material for the researcher's personal experience narrative, not the final result. The recollections should begin to explain how events took place, where, when, why and how.

Several researchers of physical culture have used personal recollections as the basis of their research narratives (e.g., Denison, 1996; Duncan, 2000; Markula, 2003; Sparkes, 1996; Tsang, 2000). These recollections can then be written in a number of ways. Some researchers alternate between developed accounts of their personal experiences and theoretical discussions to explain the meaning of their experiences and how their 'stories' have been socially constructed. Other essayistic personal experiences are comprised of several, separate 'vignettes' where personal experiences or memories highlight meaningful events or developments that explain the social construction of a person's life experiences. Often, but not necessarily, the vignettes are organised chronologically.

Essayistic personal experience accounts are primarily characterised by the author recounting her/his personal experiences in the first person, 'truthfully', as they 'really happened' (Markula & Denison, 2005). Literary devices are used minimally in this type of writing as it aims to provide a faithful account of the events as the author remembers them. Some authors use such literary devices as time shifts, imagery and tension. Because of the minimal requirement of training in creative writing, essayistic personal experience narrative is a often good way for a beginning writer to start experimenting with alternative ways of research representation.

Literary personal experience narratives

To add to their evocativeness, personal experience narratives can also be written in a more literary style. While literary personal experience narratives, similar to essayistic personal experiences, are still based on events that really happened to the author, they call 'upon such fiction-writing techniques as dramatic recall, strong imagery, fleshed-out characters, unusual phrasings, puns, subtexts, allusion, flashback, flash-forward, tone shifts, synecdoche, dialogue, and interior monologue' (Richardson, 2000b, p. 11). In addition, they are based on empirically recorded recollections, but now these recollections are used differently to construct the final accounts. Using literary aesthetics allows the author/researcher to add sensuality, smell, sound, mood and intensity of feelings to provide nuanced and energetic writing full of vitality. As Markula and Denison observe '[i]nstead of recounting as 'truthfully' as possible what happened, researchers operating within this genre are concerned with time shifts, changing contexts, and the use of visual, olfactory, audio, and kinaesthetic imagery' (2005, p. 173). Because of the increased literary writing techniques, instead of **telling** about events in a clear cut manner like in essayistic personal experience accounts, the authors aim to **show** the meaning of their personal experiences. To demonstrate the social construction of identity, self and experience, 'literary personal experience writers hold "back the interpretation" (Richardson, 2000b, p. 11) inviting the reader to make multiple meanings out of the text' (Markula & Denison, 2005, p. 173). These stories thus aim to meet the coherence of good literary writing. Engagement in this type of research representation requires training in creative writing techniques and is thus more demanding than writing essayistic personal experiences. However, if the author/researcher has acquired the required skills, literary personal experience narratives can provide evocative accounts of the authors' highly emotional, significant experiences within physical culture or sensitive topics such as sexuality, abuse, harassment or discrimination, which are often left unsaid or cannot be said in more realist accounts.

Essayistic research stories

Because the idea behind alternative research writing is not only to explicitly include the researcher's voice, but also to provide contextual accounts of the polyvocality of experiences, evocative research writing should not be limited to the personal experiences of the researcher. All qualitative empirical material can provide meaningful raw empirical material for narrative research writing. For example, interviews, participant-observation notes, case study research or participants' narrative accounts can become more meaningful when represented evocatively. Researchers of physical culture have used empirical material from interviews, in particular, to produce essayistic research stories. Similar to essayistic personal experience accounts, these stories aim to be faithful for participants' voices by representing their words as was 'really' said in the interview transcripts. However, essayistic research stories aim to add evocativeness usually by organising the participants' words into a 'coherent' story rather than providing them in brief quotations as in realist accounts. By doing this, the stories can illustrate commonalities, shared experiences or the impact of a specific context more effectively than a realist account might allow.

For example, Bruce (1998) presents the voices of 22 women sport writers she interviewed through a single monologue to illustrate some the key experiences of these women interviewing male athletes. Denison (1996) represents 12 elite athletes' in-depth interviews through the voice of a few composite athletes recorded in three stories. These stories depict the athletes' experiences through their everyday language to reveal the world as they experience it. Markula (2011) compiles the voices of 14 contemporary dancers into a single narrative after observing remarkable similarities in how they experienced and described their injuries. Similar to Denison's stories, the dancers tell in their own words how the context of dance creates a culture where pain and injuries are ignored.

There are other forms of representing interviews in addition to providing a single story (e.g., see Bruce, 1998). Nevertheless, essayistic research stories, similar to essayistic personal experience accounts, use minimal literary devices. Therefore, in order to avoid descriptive, decontextualised accounts of the interviewees' experiences, these types of research stories need to be framed with theoretical analysis. The most constructive structure for essayistic research stories resembles the structure of a conventional research article with a literature review and theoretical framework to set up the essayistic research stories that then comprise the analysis/discussion section of the article. Therefore, essayistic research stories, while largely devoid of direct references to theory or previous research literature, are nevertheless framed by the researcher's theoretical perspective and thus answer particular research questions.

Literary research stories

Markula and Denison observe that literary research stories 'resemble, more than any of the other writing styles we have discussed up to this point, the qualities of fiction' (2005, p. 178). Similar to literary personal experience narratives, they **show**, rather than tell, how particular experiences are constructed within a certain context. Markula and Denison assert that

> They tend to avoid closure, enabling the reader to see that interpreta-
> tion is never finished, and that life continues on. They also attempt to
> provide a greater evocative depiction of others' lives through the
> heightened dramatization of real events using such literary devices as
> alternative points of view, strong characterization, unusual phrasings,
> and subtexts.
>
> (Markula & Denison, 2005, p. 178)

Literary research stories rely heavily on literary devices to create stories of the emotionally and physically 'moving' body and a sense of embodied experience. They also move between the worlds of social science and literature to contextualise such experiences. Furthermore, they offer the potential to open up the critical interrogation of the physical to a plethora of intimate and previously 'taboo' topics such as friendship, love, sexual-ity, physical violence, rape, body habitus, sexuality, ethnicity, physicality, misogyny, gender politics, (marginal) sub-identities, power, disempower-ment, diaspora, postcolonial narratives of race, nationalism and interna-tional politics, and exercise disorder behaviour, thus providing space for marginalised voices (Tedlock, 2000).

Recent trends

As evocative research writing evolves, new forms of research representa-tion also emerge. They build on the previous developments in the narra-tive turn, but aim to address further the complicated task of representing multiple voices from multiple contexts for multiple audiences. We discuss here two such recently popularised forms: autoethnography and per-formance ethnography.

Autoethnography

Autoethnography as a term has assumed multiple meanings. For exam-ple, in anthropology, some perceive it as a direct derivation from ethnog-raphy as a method. The autoethnographer nevertheless critically engages with and reflects on their participation in the research (e.g., Tedlock, 2005). This definition of autoethnography refers to a modified form of participant observation where the emphasis is on 'the observation of participation' (Tedlock, 2005, p. 467). There are, however, other more sophisticated uses of the same term. A recent special issue in *Journal of*

Contemporary Ethnography on analytic autoethnography further illustrates the multiple meanings attached to autoethnography. In this issue Anderson (2006) distinguishes between 'evocative autoethnography' and 'analytic autoethnography'. **Analytic autoethnography** recognises the researcher's presence in the text and in the research setting to contribute to the theoretical understanding of social phenomena. In this sense, analytic autoethnography aligns itself with modernist paradigms of qualitative research, which, while acknowledging the subjective epistemology, still aim to represent the real world truthfully. **Evocative autoethnography**, in turn, draws from the postmodern rejection of generalisable truths. The proponents of evocative autoethnography find in it a balance of self-narrative or the personal with a cultural and social context (e.g., Ellis, 2004; Spry, 2001) weaved together with artistic expression and a desire for social change (Denzin, 1997; Holman-Jones, 2005). Denzin, for example, explains that research writing is always political and pedagogical: 'it instructs our readers about this world and how we see it' (2006, p. 422). Through writing, the researchers can enact the worlds they study and thus impact the current ways of understanding these worlds. Literary aesthetics provide evocativeness, verisimilitude and emotional engagement for this type of writing. In this chapter, we follow the latter understanding of autoethnography as evocative writing.

Based on this definition, autoethnography could also be classified as personal experience narrative (as discussed above). We want, however, to devote a separate discussion to this genre to highlight some of most recent trends in alternative research representation. In our earlier discussion, it became evident that the essayistic personal narrative often separates theoretical research literature from the story part. On the other hand, literary personal narratives employ literary devices to contextualise the experience. This means that they are devoid of explicit theoretical discussion. While these attempts have expanded the ways of acknowledging the author's influence in the research, they have tended to separate theory from literature, realist writing from storied writing, research from art. More recently, researchers have begun to question whether such binary understanding is beneficial for qualitative research. In addition, should qualitative research writing entirely abandon theory in favour of fiction? What, then, makes research writing research? A number of further questions arise:

> What is a good story? Is just a good story enough? What must be added to story to make it scholarship? How do we derive concepts from stories and then use these concepts to understand people?

What – precisely – would have to be added to transform story material from the journalistic or literary to the academic?

(Josselson, 1993 in Sparkes, 1995, p. 183)

While some qualitative researchers support a complete shift to literary writing, others have started to experiment with ways of closing the gap between theory and literature. This does not mean abandoning theory, but rather integrating it more closely with the numerous alternative ways of research writing. One way of blending theory and literary writing style is to include theoretical discussion as footnotes to a narrative piece. One of the earliest attempts for this type of representation of physical culture is Kohn's and Syndor's (1998) piece, which is organised as 'a dialogue' between the two authors who, often full of self irony, reflect upon their multiple selves as academics. A separate theoretical narrative runs in footnotes to complement the authors' personal writing. More recently, Jones (2000) reflects what it means to be coach of a semi-professional football team with a speech impediment that constantly threatens his respectability, expertise and credibility. This autoethnography is located in the locker room before the game while the footnotes provide social context and theoretical grounding for the story.

While these research articles still place theory and literary narratives into parallel stories, Denison (2010) has attempted to seamlessly integrate theory, experience and literary aesthetics into one fluent story. In his article, Denison uses a Foucauldian theoretical perspective to problematise the role of 'evidence-based' research in coach education by presenting two different social contexts (one in the aftermath of an international track and field meet and another in a classroom). In this article, the politics of research permeate each section to weave with artistic expression into an evocative text of personal and public voices.

Performance ethnography

Another recent trend in alternative research representation is so-called performance ethnography. This type of representation involves not only writing that includes the researcher's voice and/or uses literary devices to express contextuality and polyvocality, but performance of the research text as well. Performance ethnography, however, is not whatever type of performance, but rather a specific representational technique advocated by Denzin (2003) to create social change.

In his book *Performance Ethnography*, Denzin envisions a social science that resembles a performance in order to become a socio-political act because 'performance-based human disciplines can contribute to radical social change, to economic justice, to a cultural politics' (2003, p. 3). Such political, performative social science 'puts culture into motion. It examines, narrates, and performs the complex ways in which persons experience themselves within the shifting ethnoscapes of today's global world economy' (p. 8). Similar to other forms of alternative research representation, performative social science necessitates the personal involvement of the researcher in the research act that produces and is a product of multiple voices. However, in performance ethnography, the researcher also 'acts' the research project – puts it into motion – and becomes a part of the pragmatics of changing the social reality. In these projects, text and performance exist in tension within one another: 'in a tension between doing, or performing, and the done, the text, the performance' (Denzin, 2003, p. 10). Therefore, the performance metaphor creates an 'oppositional' social science that moves research closer to 'the spaces of a progressive pragmatism' (Denzin, 2003, p. 4), but also further challenges the effectiveness of 'traditional' forms for research representation. As 'a form of kinesis, of motion, a decentring of agency and person through movement, disruption, action' (Denzin, 2003, p. 10) performing one's research questions the status quo within academia. Denzin summarises:

> Performance is an act of intervention, a method of resistance, a form of criticism, a way of revealing agency ... Performance becomes public pedagogy when it uses the aesthetic, the performative, to foreground the intersection of politics, institutional sites, and embodied experience.
>
> (Denzin, 2003, p. 9)

Nevertheless, this type of representation must combine artistic excellence with 'a moral responsibility ... to produce an active intervention' (p. 18). Performance ethnography requires, in addition to an ability to engage in alternative writing, that the researcher has education in the performing arts. Performance ethnography can nevertheless take multiple forms. Some find simply reading a narrative for an audience as sufficient for performance while others experiment with blending drama, music or dance with research texts into live performance ethnographies. Such performances as research presentations have great potential, and when they work the impact is quite tangible. Nevertheless, it is perhaps no wonder that attempts at performance ethnography among researchers of physical culture are rare when faced with the multiple requirements of research, artistic and performance merit.

Markula (2006a; 2006b; in press) has experimented with creating dance performance ethnography mainly to change the narrowly defined feminine (bodily) identity. She has struggled with similar issues to those facing autoethnographers: how to integrate dance and theory into a seamless performance that also has affect. Bringing dance into traditional research conferences also presents its own problems due to a lack of space, warm-up time or the usual technical requirements of dance performance (sound and lighting). In addition, as the bodily expression of dance is not as accessible to most research audiences as a written or read text, it is often a challenge to 'read'. While demanding and time consuming, dance performance ethnography can, nevertheless, be a rewarding and exciting way of representing qualitative research.

Challenges

Although alternative ways of writing qualitative research have gained huge popularity in the social sciences, they have not been visibly taken on by researchers of physical culture. It is necessary for all qualitative researchers, including those in physical culture, to consider writing as an essential part of their research act. But it can no longer be a taken-for-granted finish to one's research project. All qualitative researchers need to be aware of the different options available regarding the ways of representing their findings. While alternative ways of writing offer exciting possibilities, they are not necessarily suitable for all qualitative research projects. In addition, realist writing is by no means always a 'bad' way of presenting one's findings, but neither is it always the only option. Therefore, like in all other aspects of a qualitative research project, one needs to make an informed choice regarding the way of representing research. We offer a reminder of some of the most important aspects to consider when deciding upon a research writing style.

Writing skills

Because all alternative ways of writing use literary devices to some degree, they all require strong writing skills. Sparkes (1995), for example, warns against researchers rushing out to produce alternative forms of representation with which they might not be familiar. This is not to reject such representations outright, but to consider carefully the problems associated with their construction and with the integration of theory into these representations (Sparkes, 1995). Therefore, before embarking on alternative ways of research representation, undergraduate or perhaps graduate students should be asking whether they are 'experts' in the deployment of literary writing techniques or are they better versed in 'traditional writing'. For example, writing literary research narratives requires education in creative writing and thus one's ability to engage in this type of alternative research writing depends on previous training. Furthermore, the alternative ways of writing have now evolved over more than two decades and in this process, they have also developed into more complex and demanding undertakings. Therefore, the quality requirements have also increased. Alternative research representations no longer consist of personal confessions, accounts of personal injustices or complaints, diary entries, field notes or simple first person accounts. While some of these might act as the 'raw' data, they do not fulfil the requirements for any type of alternative research representation. It is, therefore, important to observe that alternative ways of research representation are not 'easy' options for those who find it difficult to express themselves through the logic of realist writing. On the contrary, one needs to be a strong 'realist' writer to expand beyond it with more literary expression.

Research topic

As noted earlier in this chapter, alternative research writing aims to present contextualised experiences through multiple voices. Naturally, research projects that explore experiences lend themselves well to this type of experimentation. The idea is not to abandon realist writing because it can also be the best suitable option, among others, for one's project. For example, if a qualitative researcher is interested in highlighting a clear theoretical point, a realist writing style is the best way to provide such a logical argument. It must also be remembered that realist writing does not necessarily exclude the author's voice. For example, it is possible to expresses one's theoretical argument through first person's accounts without using literary devices. Or it is possible to write about the results of a textual analysis and include the author's voice through the use of 'I'. Realist writing might still be the best option to represent the findings from these studies as they do not necessarily aim to provide multiple readings but present the researcher's clearly developed argument. Obviously, realist representation has not disappeared, but is gradually becoming only one form of expression *among* a number of visible forms of social description. Yet, adopting a different genre does not in and of itself ensure a better product.

Research output

Given that the alternative ways of representation have gained footing in qualitative research, there are also more journals that publish this type of research. For example, *Qualitative Inquiry* is one of the most prestigious of these types of journals. However, alternative research representations are just evolving within research on physical culture and, therefore, there are no journals specialising in evocative writing. As we highlighted, there have been special issues in the *Sociology of Sport Journal* and *Leisure Sciences* on alternative ways of writing. In addition, the *Journal of Qualitative Research in Sport and Exercise* has published research using alternative ways of writing. In any case, a qualitative researcher of physical culture needs carefully to consider the possible publishing outlets before deciding to engage with alternative ways of writing.

In terms of student work, the success of choosing an alternative research representation clearly depends on the supervisor's expertise and acceptance of this type of writing. There are, nevertheless, examples of undergraduate dissertations, master's theses and doctoral dissertations using alternatives styles of writing to represent their research findings. In these works, students are typically required to follow the traditional structure of a qualitative research process. It is unlikely or unadvisable that a poem, dialogue, short story, or fiction can comprise the entire work without theoretical framing, literature review and method section. A literary work by itself should be assessed as a creative writing project, not a qualitative research project. The results can, nevertheless, be represented through alternative ways of research writing, but have to naturally fulfil both the artistic and theoretical requirements of good qualitative research.

The dangers of 'navel gazing'

While alternative ways of representing research might not be suitable for every qualitative research project in physical culture, it is clear that the qualitative researchers' values should not be excluded as something messy and untidy but, rather, that there is a need consciously to acknowledge their various positions (Harrison, MacGibbon & Morton, 2001). At the same time, some scholars (e.g., Anderson, 1999; Sparkes, 1995) warn that situating the researchers' selves in the final output should not lead to exoteric or narcissistic naval-gazing scholarship or to subtler forms of what Fine (1992) terms 'ventriloquy'. Fine (1992) suggests ventriloquy occurs when the researchers appear to let the 'other' speak, yet all the while hide, unproblematically, under the covers of the marginal, now 'liberated', voices. Similarly, Johnson et al. (2004) point to the dangers of disguising the authors' power. Rather than camouflage themselves, qualitative researchers might position themselves as self-reflexive, critical and/or interpretive, participatory analysts. To consider research writing as an integral part of the research act is to question the hierarchies between the researched and the researcher (e.g., Fontana & Frey, 2005; Harrison, MacGibbon, & Morton, 2001). Socially meaningful qualitative texts are personal, yet political, and take the point of view of the historically and culturally situated individual. In such projects, the researchers persist in working outwards from their own biographies to the worlds of experience that surround them.

Qualitative research work can move beyond the detached, impersonal, depersonalised representation of the disengaged analyst. Alternative ways of writing can produce 'messier', uncertain, multivoiced texts that sit alongside the realist form of representation. Finally, we should heed Giroux's warning that these are not mere 'textual gestures' outside of the context of history, power and politics (Giroux, 2001, p. 10). Consequently, to seek to *articulate* those worlds with personal experiences with social context and theoretical rigour, requires writing that 'blurs genres' (Richardson & St. Pierre, 2005).

Summary

In this chapter, we have introduced several ways of 'writing up' qualitative research results. Realist writing refers to the most common way of research writing. It presents the research results in an objective, often third-person voice. Alternative ways of research writing refer to ways of writing that challenge the necessity of presenting research in a realist manner. In general, these include the researcher's voice in addition to some creative ways of writing. Richardson & St. Pierre (2005) characterises these writing practices with a general term 'creative analytic processes'. We provided more detailed accounts of a variety of creative analytic processes. We introduced alternative ways narrative research writing (which includes such sub-categories as essayistic personal experience narratives, literary personal experiences narratives, essayistic research stories and literary research stories), autoethnography and performance ethnography as alternatives to realist research writing. While these forms of writing can provide more evocative research accounts, they are not suitable for all research representation and thus should not always replace realist writing. Qualitative researchers need to consider carefully the audience they are addressing as well as their research purpose when choosing the best way of to represent their results.

Further reading

Special issue in *Leisure Sciences* 29, 119–30 2007, on Creative Analytic Practices

Essayistic personal experience narrative:

Tsang, T. (2000). 'Let me tell you a story: A narrative exploration of identity in high performance'. *Sociology of Sport Journal*, 17, 44–59.
Duncan, M. C. (2000). 'Reflex: Body as memory'. *Sociology of Sport Journal*, 17, 60–68.
Sparkes, A. C. (1996). 'The fatal flaw: A narrative of the fragile body-self'. *Qualitative Inquiry*, 2, 463–94.

Literary personal experience narrative:

Bruce, T. (2003). 'Pass'. In J. Denison & P. Markula (Eds), *Moving writing: Crafting movement in sport research*. New York: Peter Lang.
Tiihonen, A. (1994). 'Asthma'. *International Review for Sociology of Sport*, 29, 51–62.

Essayistic research story:

Silk, M. (2008). 'Mow my lawn'. *Cultural Studies ↔ Critical Methodologies*, 8, 477–8.

Literary research story:

Rinehart, R. (1998). 'Sk8ting: "Outsider" sports, at-risk youth, and physical education'. *Waikato Journal of Education*, 6, 55–63.
Rowe, D. (2000). 'Amour improper, or "fever" sans reflexivity'. *Sociology of Sport Journal*, 17, 95–7.

9
The Promise

In this chapter, we will

- Discuss how to assess the quality of a qualitative research article;
- How to assess the quality of a post-positivist research project;
- How to assess the quality of an interpretive research project;
- How to assess the quality of a critical research project;
- How to assess the quality of a postmodern/poststructuralist research project.

Within this chapter we address the seventh and final P, what we call *The Promise* – the criteria to which our qualitative work in physical culture is, or should be, judged. Thus, when we refer to 'judgement criteria', we refer to how to determine the quality of qualitative research: How do we know what is good qualitative research? This is a question that does not have one answer. Because of the multiplicity of qualitative research, there are several ways of defining what constitutes good quality research. As with other features of qualitative research, the manner qualitative work is judged depends on its paradigmatic assumptions. Therefore, there is no unified criterion for 'good' qualitative research. It is obviously important, however, that the authors clearly state their paradigmatic assumptions in order to provide a reader with the study's location within the broader field of qualitative research. The assessment of quality becomes a problem if qualitative research is judged based on the validation criteria from quantitative research. As these two research traditions have fundamentally different assumptions (as well as the many different assumptions within each), the appropriate selection of quality judgement criteria also has to reflect these differences. If there is no understanding of these differences, quality judgements will be unsuitable and thus, unfair. As Polkinghorne aptly notes:

> Typically, the issue of validity is approached by applying one's own community's protocol about what, in its view, is acceptable evidence and appropriate analysis to the other community's research. In these cases, the usual conclusion is that the other community's research is lacking in support for its knowledge claims.
>
> (Polkinghorne, 2007, pp. 473–4)

Validation of qualitative research articles

While it is generally agreed that qualitative research is theoretically sound, analytical, interpretive and provides deep knowledge, there is a continual debate regarding exactly what aspects of qualitative research should be focused on when judging its quality. A general framework that focuses on the logic of a particular qualitative work, but takes into account the specific requirements of each qualitative paradigm, can be used to assess qualitative research articles:

Introduction:
- Leads to the research topic in a logical and concise manner;
- Entices one to read the article;
- Provides a meaningful research purpose.

Literature review and theory:
- Relevant literature insightfully covered;
- Sound theoretical approach:
  - paradigmatic logic;
- Well formulated research question.

Research design:
- Links to theory and the research questions established:
  - paradigmatic logic;
- Sample and sampling technique provided;
- Methodological practices well described:
  - e.g., interviews, textual analysis, narrative analysis, field methods;
- Ethics:
  - anonymity, confidentiality, voluntary consent, right to withdraw;
- Analysis of empirical material and interpretation techniques clearly explained;

- Issues of representation (if needed):
  - Choices of representation;
  - Researcher's self-reflexivity;

Analysis/discussion:
- Theoretical rigour;
- Comparison and contrast to previous literature;
- Participants' voice;
- Researchers' voice;
- Resonance;
- Proceeds in clear and analytical manner;
- Allows participants' voices to speak.

Conclusion:
- Summary of the main findings;
- Contribution of the main findings to the field;
- Limitations of research;
- Future directions;
- Meaningfulness.

General:
- Clear, well edited writing;
- Appropriate referencing.

This type of evaluation of qualitative research can serve as a general guide for assessing quality. Nevertheless, several more specific criteria exist.

Paradigmatically based validation of qualitative research

These more precise ways of assessing the quality of qualitative research are particularly useful for student work such as undergraduate dissertations, masters theses and PhD dissertations where the authors have to demonstrate, in great detail, how they conducted the research process. These criteria in general aim to account for the differing levels of subjectivity in qualitative research.

While qualitative research is subjective in its epistemological assumptions, it is difficult to determine a 'proper amount' of subjectivity and its influence on the project. Despite these difficulties, there are several suggestions for different ways to validate the quality of qualitative research.

Morse et al. (2002), for example, divide the existing validation criteria into constructive and evaluative. **Constructive criteria** focus on ensuring that the qualitative research **process** is rigorous, whereas **evaluative criteria** aim to judge the post-research **impact** of the work by focusing on such aspects as the significance, relevance and 'impact utility of the completed' research. Morse et al. also observe a gradual shift from constructive criteria to evaluative judgement as a base from which to validate qualitative research. This shift can be linked with the general proliferation of the paradigmatic frameworks underpinning qualitative research. While post-positivist and interpretive researchers tend to validate their work through how well the research 'process' is constructed, critical researchers tend to evaluate their work more based on its impact on society. Sparkes' (2001) classification of ways of 'measuring validity' of qualitative research similarly aligns with the development of multiple paradigms in qualitative research.

Sparkes (2001) identifies four prominent 'perspectives' in the discussions related to the quality of qualitative research: Replication, parallel, diversification and letting-go perspectives. Researchers opting for the **replication** perspective believe that qualitative research should be judged by similar measures to quantitative research. Others believe that qualitative research should be judged based on entirely new criteria and, thus, there is a need for development for criteria that exist **parallel** to quantitative research. Other qualitative researchers go further to claim for the **diversification** of possible criteria for qualitative research. The entire notion of research, they argue, is socially constructed and so should be the ways by which we judge this type of research. Finally, Sparkes observes that some qualitative researchers adopt a **letting-go** perspective to validating qualitative research: they entirely abandon validity as a concept by which to judge their work.

Sparkes does not connect these perspectives clearly to the paradigmatic underpinnings of qualitative research. We want to emphasise that because qualitative research is subjective, there is no need for an evaluation of its validity and reliability as these are measures of objectivity. With this in mind, we will loosely follow Sparkes' four perspectives for judging qualitative research, but, in addition, will link these perspectives to the paradigmatic assumptions of different types of qualitative research. We first briefly discuss how quantitative research is judged to provide a basis for judgement criteria for post-positivist research that aims to replicate the validation process of quantitative research. We then discuss how interpretive researchers aim for a judgement criterion specific for the research process within their paradigm, whereas critical researchers focus on the impact of their research and thus call for a diversification of the judgement criteria for qualitative research. Finally, we discuss how poststructuralist/postmodern qualitative research might be validated. Therefore, although our main focus is on qualitative research we begin with how quantitative research is judged to show the incompatibility of its criteria with qualitative assumptions.

Foundationalism: Validation for quantitative and post-positivist research

We first consider the ways in which scholars engaged in quantitative research have attempted to demonstrate the quality of their work following positivist assumptions. This position is also termed 'foundationalism' (Guba & Lincoln, 2005; House, 2005).

As noted in Chapter 2, positivism as a paradigmatic stance assumes an objective epistemology to promote value-free research that, unencumbered by the researcher's influence, guarantees the best 'access' to truth. To be 'truthful' research also has to be generalisable. Thus, good quantitative research needs to demonstrate objectivity and the generalisability of its results. The level of **objectivity** is measured through **validity** and **reliability**. In general terms, validity refers to objectivity of the research instruments (they measure what they are meant to measure) and reliability refers to the objectivity of the researcher (how researcher's subjective influence has been minimised in the research project). Therefore, the quality of quantitative research is judged according to traditional criteria of objectivity (internal and external validity, reliability) and generalisability achieved through adhering to objectivity. The resulting analytical induction seeks to uncover causal explanations of phenomena that are sufficiently robust to allow for broad comparison and subsequent generalisation of findings (Ryan & Bernard, 2000). Such analyses are then positioned to define some aspect of an undeniable, independent relationship between knowable and operationalisable variables.

In summary, the foundational criterion serve to validate the objectivity of research. Thus, the quality of quantitative research is dependent upon the establishment of measures of reliability and validity. This allows quantitative researchers to position their work as adhering to established standards and provides readily recognisable metrics for determining what constitutes high – and low – quality work. Most qualitative research assumes subjective epistemology and, thus, the foundational criterion is unsuitable for the majority of qualitative research. However, post-positivist research adheres to objective epistemology while using qualitative methods and thus requires established validity and reliability measures that ensure objectivity and generalisability. Post-positivist research, in Sparkes' (2001) terms, assumes a replication perspective to its validation process.

Validation of post-positivist and grounded theory research

As we explained in Chapter 2, post-positivism engages in intraparadigmatic critique: they critique positivism, but do not challenge its underlying paradigmatic assumptions of objectivity and belief in one truth. Part of the critique involves using some qualitative methods. However, as the basic assumptions of positivism are adhered to, post-positivist research should be validated based on the quantitative standards of validity and reliability to ensure objectivity and generalisability of the results. One very commonly used way to increase reliability in this context is triangulation.

Triangulation

Triangulation refers to an attempt to use multiple methods, theories, researchers or data sources to decrease the researcher's bias or influence on the results. In addition, using several different methods ensures a more 'truthful' picture of the 'reality'. Patton (2002) distinguishes four different ways of triangulation: Method triangulation, triangulation of sources, analyst triangulation and theory/perspective triangulation. **Methods triangulation** involves using several methods to obtain data, but often post-positivist researchers like to compare and integrate data 'collected through some kind of qualitative methods with data collected through some of quantitative methods' (Patton, 2002, p. 556). A mixed methods approach helps answer different questions and thus enables a researcher to obtain 'a single, well-integrated picture of the situation' (Patton, 2002, p. 557). **Triangulation of sources** is used to check out 'consistency of different data sources within the same method' (Patton, 2002, p. 556). This involves only qualitative methods that are used at different times. For example, one can compare observations with interviews and then verify these results through an added textual analysis. Post-positivist case studies regularly bring together several methods to provide consistent information on one particular 'case'. Therefore, triangulation is often considered an important validation tool for case study research (e.g., Patton, 2002; Stakes, 2005; Yin, 2003). It must be remembered, however, that qualitative case study research can be informed by several different paradigms and triangulation will only help validate case study research that locates itself within post-positivism. **Analyst triangulation** uses multiple investigators to review the findings. For example, multiple interviewers using the same structured interview guide or multiple observers of the same situations help reduce 'researcher bias' and will thus increase the reliability and objectivity of post-positivist research. **Theory triangulation** involves using several theoretical perspectives to analyse the same data. It is important to remember that all these theories need to be grounded in positivist or post-positivist assumptions in order to increase validity and reliability. Theories from other paradigms do not assume objectivity and, thus, do not serve to validate research from a (post)positivist paradigm. For example, a post-positivist researcher can use stacking theory, Bem's sex role orientation theory and the theory of the female apologetic to understand why there are few women of colour playing soccer.

Grounded theory approach

While the grounded theory approach has diversified in several directions, we detail here how to validate a grounded theory project based on Corbin and Strauss' (2008) understanding of the methodology.

A grounded theory approach involves a researcher entering into a natural setting to obtain all the possible information, but without predetermined hypotheses to test a theory. Because such data is often 'messy' and, in the first place, unorganised, verification and validation are active parts of the entire research process for ensuring the objectivity of the collected data. In this sense, a grounded theory approach adopts constructive validation to ensure the rigour of the data collection process (Morse et al., 2002). Corbin and Strauss (2008) provide the following general criteria for judging grounded theory research:

Fit: How do the findings resonate with the experience of the participants?

Applicability: What insights from the findings can be used to develop policy or practice?

Concepts: How well are the findings organised around concepts derived from the research?

Contextualisation of concepts: How well do the concepts illustrate their context?

Logic: What is the flow of ideas? How clear are the methodological decisions?

Depth: How well detailed is the study to give depth beyond description?

Variation: How well is variation built into the findings?

Creativity: Do the findings say anything new?

Sensitivity: Did the researcher demonstrate sensitivity to the participants and the data?

Evidence of memos: How well do the memos grow in depth and degree of abstraction during the research?

To ensure further credibility for the findings or the theory arising from them, Corbin and Strauss developed the following criteria:

General research process: from open coding to categories:

- How was the original sample selected?
- What major categories emerged?
- What indicators pointed to these categories?
- On the basis of what categories did theoretical sampling proceed?
- Did the hypotheses pertain to conceptual relations and on what grounds were they formulated and tested?
- When did the hypotheses not hold up against what was actually seen?
- How and why was the core category selected?

Empirical grounding:

- Are concepts generated?
- Are concepts systematically related?
- Are there many conceptual linkages, and are the categories well developed?
- Is much variation built into the theory?
- Are the broader conditions built into its explanation?
- Has process (change) been taken into account?
- Do the theoretical findings seem significant and to what extent?
- Are the findings exchanged among the relevant social and professional groups?

A special challenge for grounded theory is to ensure objectivity of the 'messy' data collected in the natural setting as opposed to a controlled environment or through a validated questionnaire. Consequently, the process of validation for this type of research involves very detailed and numerous checks throughout the data collection process and following the completion of the research. For further discussion of these criteria see Corbin and Strauss (2008).

Summary

The foundational approach is only suitable for post-positivist qualitative research that assumes objective epistemology and a realist ontology of 'one truth'. Consequently, adopting traditional positivistic and post-positivistic standards means to 'measure' the quality through demonstrations of the reliability, validity and generalisability of one's work. Consequently, it is a way of judging that is not appropriate for most qualitative research, and it is important to be cautious of using this type of approach to judge qualitative research.

As we demonstrated in Chapter 2, there are also well-established critiques of the foundational, positivist and post-positivist research. For example, anti-positivists demonstrate the great difficulty of adequately capturing and subsequently expressing the external reality that foundationalists strive to uncover. As House surmises, 'we have huge gaps in our knowledge of social events – not only gaps we do not know about, but also gaps we do not even know we do not know about'(2005, p. 1072). As stated in Chapter 2, quantitative research has been further criticised for removing words from the contexts in which they occur, reducing data to fundamental meanings of specific words, emphasising the quantity of usage and offering cognitive simplifications of complex information and losing important subtle nuances (Ryan & Bernard, 2000). Given these shortcomings, qualitative researchers from interpretive and critical paradigms have developed their own criteria by which to judge qualitative research.

Quasi-foundationalism: Validation for interpretive research

Qualitative researchers from the interpretive paradigm assume that research is subjective but, nevertheless, the aim is to uncover the reality through fragments of a multitude of individual experiences. It is generally believed that despite the relativism of subjective experiences they reveal the essence of humanity. Each researcher's own subjective experiences is openly acknowledged to influence the production of knowledge. Because these researchers do not try to be objective, validity and reliability do not serve as good measures for the quality of this type of work. Rather, they have developed judgement criteria of their own that differ significantly from the foundationalist criteria. These so called quasi-foundationalist criteria are parallel to the foundationalist, quantitative criteria (Sparkes, 2001). In addition, these types of judgement criteria focus strongly on the process of conducting qualitative research and, according to Morse et al. (2002), could be characterised as constructive judgement criteria for qualitative research. Morse et al. acknowledge that it is impossible to adopt a neutral, unbiased research position from which to capture and portray the experience of the researched 'other'. The quality of qualitative research for quasi-foundationalists depends upon the application of appropriate methodological practices. This approach is seen as crucial both in uncovering an approximation of reality and in determining research quality (Smith & Hodkinson, 2005). As Denzin and Lincoln (2000) explain, such work is internally reflexive with the effects of the researcher and research strategy.

One of the earliest attempts for parallel judgement criteria for qualitative research is Lincoln and Guba (1985) set of criteria for 'operational naturalistic inquiry'. They argue that the foundationalist, positivist criteria of objectivity, which rely on internal and external validity and reliability, are not suitable for naturalistic enquiry. Consequently, they sought to develop parallel trustworthiness criteria for their qualitative research. To affirm trustworthiness, they call for credibility (parallel to internal validity), transferability (parallel to external validity), dependability (parallel to reliability) and conformability (parallel to objectivity). The researcher nevertheless addresses 'quality' with respect to the canons of 'validity' and 'reliability' during the research process. Within these criteria, **credibility** is established through prolonged engagement in the field and the triangulation of data sources, methods and investigators. **Transferability** refers to so-called 'thick description': Is sufficient detail provided to allow readers to appreciate the insights and can these be transferred to other settings? Dependability refers to creating an audit trail by documenting the methods used and the logic behind the results and conclusions. Finally, **confirmability** refers to providing a reflexive, self-critical account that exposes inherent biases in the work. In addition, researchers typically engage in 'peer debriefing'. This involves the researcher sharing the research project with 'disinterested peer in a manner paralleling an analytical session and for the purpose of exploring aspects of inquiry that might otherwise remain implicit within the inquirer's mind' (Lincoln & Guba, 1985, p. 308). Such a process allows another suitably qualified person – usually an informed colleague not involved in the research project – to explore the inquirer's biases, clarify interpretations and generally play 'devil's advocate' (Lincoln & Guba, 1985). Finally, transcripts, field notes and interpretations can be periodically returned to those in the field to allow participants to check facts and logic to see if the account 'rings true' (Lincoln & Guba, 1985).

Box 9.1 Qualitative & Quantitative trustworthiness

Qualitative trustworthiness	Quantitative trustworthiness
credibility	internal validity
transferability	external validity
dependability	parallel to reliability
conformability	objectivity
	(Lincoln & Guba, 1985)

Lincoln (1995) later revised their original criteria after criticism of emulating the quantitative criteria too closely by merely changing the terminology. In addition, she wanted to move away from the positivist concern of establishing trustworthiness primarily through assessing the method to evaluate larger concerns of qualitative research. Consequently, she revised their guidelines to assess that, first, the researcher adheres to the general guidelines observed by the qualitative community. Second, the researcher has to assume convincingly an authentic position within the research. Third, good qualitative research needs openly to acknowledge and privilege the participants' voices. Fourth, there must be reciprocity between the researchers and the participants to evidence established trust. Finally, the researcher must openly demonstrate self-awareness to provide critical subjectivity for the research process.

Box 9.2 Assessment of trustworthiness

- Guidelines: the qualitative community;
- Positionality: authenticity of the author's position;
- Acknowledgement of the participants' voice;
- Critical subjectivity: self-awareness;
- Reciprocity: trust.

(Lincoln, 1995)

Both of these criteria, although widely used, are now several decades old. Polkinghorne (2007) provides more recent criteria to address 'validity issues'. His work focuses particularly on narrative research (see Chapter 6), but can be used by other interpretive researchers as well. While Polkinghorne uses validity, he also refers to the validation of narrative research as a more appropriate term for qualitative research that makes no claims for objectivity. In general, he argues, narrative research – similarly to all research – involves engagement in two 'performances': the collection of evidence and the analysis/interpretation of that evidence. Consequently, narrative researchers also 'need to argue for the acceptance of the validity of evidence and the validity of offered interpretation' (p. 478). Validation of the collected evidence refers to how the researcher deals with **'validity threats'**: the disjunctions between the participants' experienced meanings and the 'languaged' text (spoken language used to express these experiences and written research language used to report the spoken language). Polkinghorne further details four 'validity threats' and offers ways to minimise them to provide good quality evidence:

- Validity threat 1:
  - The limits of language (to capture the complexity and depths of experienced meaning);
    - Solution: Encourage figurative expression instead of literal expressions.
- Validity threat 2:
  - The limits of reflection to bring notice to the layers of meaning that are present outside of awareness;
    - Solution: Encourage reflective exploration of meanings and focused listening.
- Validity threat 3:
  - Participants resistance to reveal their full experience;
    - Solution: conduct multiple interviews with the same person (3).
- Validity threat 4:
  - Co-creation of texts (interviewer's impact on the interviewee);
    - Solution: Account for interviewer's tone, body movements create responses.

Polkinghorne concludes that 'confidence in the texts can be induced by researchers' descriptions of how they dealt with the four sources of disjunction between participant's experiences and meanings and the languaged texts' (p. 482). To ensure this further, Polkinghorne, like Guba and Lincoln, suggests returning to the participants for further clarification or possible further questions. To attend to the validation of the second 'performance' in qualitative research, the analysis and interpretation of the evidence, Polkinghorne calls for a coherent argument to guide a viable interpretation of the collected empirical material. This means that a researcher's argument for the chosen interpretation is clearly evident in the research text. In addition, the steps for argumentation should be retraceable for the readers of the narrative. The interpretation in narrative research should uncover and clarify the meaning of the texts. Narrative research, therefore, 'extends the understanding of a story by contextualizing it' (p. 483). Consequently, a good interpretation should not be a mere summary of the storied text.

Other narrative researchers, particularly those engaged with alternative forms of writing, have entirely abandoned the use of validity in favour of other terms to assess the quality of qualitative research. Sparkes (2001) characterises this type of qualitative assessment as using 'let go' judgement criteria, because these researchers avoid using such conventional terms as 'validity' to reach to alternative terms to judge this type of work. In his work, Sparkes (2002) moves from conventional judgements of validity into the verisimilitude of qualitative research writing. Verisimilitude refers to how well the research story resonates with those who read it, even with those readers who do not share the experiences described in the story. Verisimilitude can be achieved by ensuring authenticity, believability, fidelity, literary aesthetics and contribution.

Box 9.3 Validating research stories

- Authenticity:
  - insightfulness;
  - expression of reality;
- Believability:
  - coherence;
  - impact;
- Fidelity:
  - author's aims and meanings;
  - author's ethical conduct;
  - self-reflexivity;
- Literary aesthetics
- Contribution.

(Sparkes, 2002)

Authenticity here refers to the insightfulness of the story: how well it expresses the reality experienced by the participants. **Believability** refers to how coherent and impactful research writing is, whereas **fidelity** refers to the author's ability to express her/his aims and meanings, demonstration of good qualitative research ethics and evidence of self-reflexivity. As the expression in the story can be enhanced by using **literary aesthetics**, it is important to assess how effectively these techniques are employed. Finally, it is important to assess the potential **contribution** of the story. Because Sparkes' criteria include judging the artistic quality of research writing they are not suitable for qualitative works written in a realist style. Therefore, they are limited to the assessment of a very specific type of narrative research writing and should only be recommended for literary representations of interpretive qualitative research.

Summary

All of the above approaches are intended to replace traditional, foundational quality criteria. Within the interpretive paradigm, the researchers are reflexive and acknowledge the impact that they may have had upon the world under investigation, perhaps through a role or rapport with the participants or the decisions made during observations. Within this approach, 'quality' becomes bound to credibility: convincing the audience that, despite some unavoidable bias, every effort has been made to represent the reality observed and recorded legitimately. These criteria seek to ensure as accurate a representation of reality as possible despite the researcher's subjective influence. Following Morse et al. (2002), the quality of interpretive research tends to be assessed based on the rigour of the qualitative research process.

Diversification of criteria: Non-foundationalist validation of critical paradigm and social constructionist research

As stated in Chapter 2, the interpretive paradigm has been critiqued for ignoring how individual meanings are constructed in relation to power in social contexts. Researchers within the critical paradigm are particularly concerned with issues of power: the ideological construction of individual meanings and experiences. The critical paradigm and social constructionism (see Chapter 2) reject the idea that qualitative research is, or can be, carried out in an autonomous realm that is insulated from the wider issues of power and from the particular biography, pathways, decisions and theoretical orientations of the researcher. In this way, social processes and personal characteristics will influence the empirical material and the write-up of the work (Hammersley & Atkinson, 1995). Following Sparkes (2001), researchers who approach qualitative research from this perspective believe that the entire notion of research, like other aspects of life, is socially constructed and so should be the ways we judge this type of research (see also Smith, 2009). In other words, they want to provide diverse ways, depending on the social context, by which to judge qualitative research. This is especially the case for those studies whose purpose claims to be to 'make a difference'. This type of research needs to be assessed on moral and ethical criteria in addition to 'academic' criteria and thus needs to be 'rigorous' – measured in more than one standard. Therefore, it is important to assess how well investigations are anchored within such research purposes as commitment to a civic agenda, enhancing moral life and the desire to promote social transformation and critical consciousness at every step of the way (Denzin, 2005). Criteria for judging such research embody the emancipatory notion of praxis: knowledge is about changing the world. Consequently, the evaluation criteria take into account the necessary political and moral nature of this research and thus require a debunking of the traditional criteria of validity, generalisability, credibility and believability to be assessed by the research community, other communities and the participants. This type research is judged based on how well it serves the interests of those who are researched: how much voice is given to research participants at all points of the project (Denzin, 2002; Harrison, MacGibbon & Morton, 2001; Madiz, 2000).

Under these conditions, questions of quality must be reframed and there is an obvious need for more diverse ways of judging qualitative research. Therefore, Sparkes (2001) characterises this type of understanding of qualitative research assessment as 'diversification'. Advocates of diversification also call for an increased shift from ensuring a rigorous process to **evaluative judgement**. Therefore, more emphasis is placed on the intended impact of qualitative research. In addition, criteria for evaluating the quality of qualitative research must be based on a holistic appreciation of the scholarship, particularly the decreased distinction between epistemology, aesthetics and ethics of qualitative research. Quality becomes *internalised* within the underlying research philosophy and orientation and researchers must consider the moral, social and political consequences for constructing research as a part of the criteria for its judgement. Judgements about the goodness or badness of research in this sense are moral or practical (Smith & Deemer, 2000). In this type of approach, researchers become increasingly answerable to their communities of origin and to their communities of interest (hooks, 1984). Quality thus becomes relational (Lincoln, 1995) emanating from an intense sharing, which in turn opens up all parties to all elements of the enquiry. Research comes to involve co-participation, bringing the audience into the text, creating shared emotional experiences, stressing political action, taking sides, moving people to reflect and even act, offering the presentational (alongside or as an alternative representational) form and building collaborative, reciprocal, trusting, friendly relations with those studied. In this sense, the research metaphors need to be adjusted from 'discovery and finding' to 'constructing and making' (Smith & Hodkinson, 2005). In this section we offer several examples of judgement criteria developed based on these basic assumptions that clearly divorce qualitative research from the premises of quantitative research. We begin with

Kvale and Brinkmann's (2007) proposition for judging qualitative interview research.

Box 9.4 Seven stages of validating the craftsmanship of a qualitative researcher

* Thematising;
* Designing;
* Interviewing;
* Transcribing;
* Analysing;
* Validating;
* Reporting.

(Kvale & Brinkmann, 2007)

Kvale and Brinkmann begin from the assumption that validity itself is socially constructed and, thus, diverse ways of validation of qualitative research are also needed. Like interpretive researchers they continue to acknowledge that validation needs to permeate the entire research process (constructivist criteria), but they want to move more clearly away from evaluating the level of objectivity of the research to assessing the credibility and craftsmanship of the researcher. Consequently, they redefine validity as quality of craftsmanship and offer a seven stage process for validating qualitative research with a focus on interview research.

Thematising refers to the demonstrated soundness of the theoretical presuppositions of the study and 'the logic of the derivations from theory to the research questions of the study' (Kvale & Brinkmann, 2007, p. 248). **Designing** refers to the adequacy of the design and methods for the purpose of the study. In addition, a well designed study should produce knowledge that is beneficial 'to the human situation while minimizing the harmful consequences' (p. 249). **Interviewing** as a method should be validated through 'careful questioning as to the meaning of what is said and a continual checking of the information obtained' (p. 249). The interviews should then be **transcribed** as accurately as possible from the oral language to the written language. A good analysis involves a sound **interpretation**. **Validation**, as a step, involves not only selecting the form of validation appropriate for the study and the community it addresses, but also tracing its concrete procedures. Finally, the study **report** should be validated based on whether it gives 'a valid' account of the main findings. This should also include the role of the readers in validations of the results.

In her approach, Manning (1997) advocates that researchers validate their work both through its thorough **construction** (the rigour of the research process) and its **evaluated impact** (judgement of research that is empowering and transforming). She uses the term 'trustworthiness' to refer to the constructive judgement and 'authenticity' to refer to the evaluative judgement of constructivist research. To assess **trustworthiness**, Manning recommends Lincoln and Guba (1985); Guba and Lincoln's (1989) judgement criteria of credibility, transferability, dependability and conformability. These were discussed earlier in this chapter and we present Manning's suggestion for judging the 'authenticity' of qualitative research. She sees **authenticity** as a concept entirely emerging from the nature of constructivist research without a parallel construct in positivist research. For her, authenticity involves five aspects – fairness, ontological authenticity, educative authenticity, catalytic authenticity and tactical authenticity – that commit the researcher to certain actions. Therefore, if these aspects are not attended to, the quality of the research (meaningfulness, usefulness, ability to enact social change) is compromised. Manning offers specific actions with which to check each of the five aspects of authentic constructivist research.

As a first aspect of judging the authenticity of research, **fairness** refers to giving voice to all of the participants in the research. This should be obtained through seeking **informed consent** from the participants (see Chapter 1 for discussion of ethical guidelines for qualitative research), member checking, prolonged engagement, persistent observation, reflexivity and peer debriefing. **Member checking** involves sharing field notes, interview transcripts, case study drafts or any other collected empirical material with the participants. **Prolonged engagement** refers to judgement as to 'whether the researcher has interacted closely with the participants for a sufficient period of time to build any understanding of their perspectives, ways of life, and culture' (p. 102) to add sufficient breadth to research. **Persistent observation** provides the study with depth and 'requires the researcher to expend the effort necessary to discover the important issues in the research context' (p. 103). **Reflexivity** refers to the researcher's beliefs and assumptions that impact the study. These should not be ignored. On the contrary, researchers need to engage in critical self-reflexivity in order to be able to address these explicitly in their study. Manning suggests keeping a 'reflexive methodological journal' during the research process to help with reflexivity. Finally, **peer debriefing** should be used to ensure fairness of research. This refers to the need for a dialogue with 'colleagues knowledgeable about the research methodology but not directly engaged in the study' (p. 104). Meaningful findings and interpretations are likely to emerge as a result of such sessions.

Box 9.5 Validation of trustworthy and authentic constructivist research

Constructive: Trustworthiness:
– Credibility, transferability, dependability, conformability (Guba & Lincoln, 1989).
Evaluative: Authenticity:
– Fairness:
  • Informed consent;
  • Member checking;
  • Prolonged engagement;
  • Persistent observation;
  • Reflexivity;
  • Peer debriefing.
– Ontological authenticity:
  • Dialogical conversations;
  • Openness of purpose;
  • Emic perspective: insider's point of view;
  • Caring trustful researcher–respondent relationship;
  • Respondents attributing to the growth of the research process.
– Educative authenticity:
  • Internal audit.
– Catalytic authenticity:
  • Joint construction;
  • Accessibility of findings;
  • Practical use.
– Tactical authenticity:
  • Negotiated use;
  • Confidentiality.

(Manning, 1997)

The second aspect of judging the authenticity of research, **ontological authenticity**, addresses the question: **'did the experience of the research process improve the respondents' conscious experiencing of the world?'** (Manning, 1997, p. 105). Similar to fairness, judging this aspect involves several parts: dialogical conversations, openness of purpose, an emic perspective, a caring trustful researcher–respondent relationship, and respondents contributing to the growth of the research process. Respondents' conscious experience can be engaged first through **dialogic conversation**. Manning argues that in this process, 'the respondent often comes to know his or her meanings in the process of saying it' (p. 105). To allow these meanings to emerge, the researcher needs to relinquish control of the process to realise that the participants are the experts in discovering their own meanings. To enable this process, trust and respect between the researcher and the participant are essential. **Openness of purpose** refers to the negotiation of goals by both the participant and the researcher. The researcher is required to provide a clear purpose for the ethical process of conducting qualitative research. An **emic perspective** further refers to gaining the insider's perspective, as the aim of constructivist research is to interpret meanings from the participants' rather from the researcher's perspective. This can be ensured by giving as much voice as possible to the participants through 'the use of direct quotations, shared authorship, and co-constructed findings' (Manning, 1997, p. 106). Caring and trustful **researcher–respondent relationships** will further deepen the focus on interpreting the participants' meanings through dialogic conversation. Finally, **respondents can contribute to the growth** of the research project by stating how it has provided them an ability to see new meanings. Manning suggests including any these types of statements as an appendix to the research report to provide further evidence of ontological authenticity.

The third aspect of judging the authenticity of research, **educative authenticity**, refers to the extent to which the research process broadened the respondent's understandings of other respondents' constructions and meanings. This can be achieved through member checking, explicit statement of research purpose (described earlier) and internal audits. An **internal audit** is conducted towards the end of the research process. This involves recruiting key respondents, gatekeepers or stakeholders to offer their insights into the researcher's findings. Manning suggests that the researcher prepares a set of questions for the auditors to prepare a response.

The fourth aspect of judging authenticity of research, **catalytic authenticity**, refers to ability to apply '[t]he insights and interpretations gleaned from the inquiry' to 'facilitate and stimulate action' (Manning, 1997, p. 108). Knowledge, according to Manning, 'should be applied in the context of practice and action' (p. 109). This can be ensured through jointly constructed interpretations, accessibility of findings and offering practical use for the findings. As established earlier, the interpretation of the findings should be **co-constructed** through member checking and dynamic dialogue between the researcher and the participants. Manning further asserts that each critical research project is dynamic and continually open to new interpretations. When meaning emerges from the co-constructed themes, 'the research project takes on a life of its own, diverging in ways unanticipated by researcher or respondent' (p. 110). To achieve this, research has to be **accessible** at the research site. Therefore, the researcher should disseminate the findings widely by providing copies to the key stakeholders, interested groups or practitioner-oriented journals. Finally, catalytic authenticity can be enhanced by actively putting the research findings into **practical use** by providing follow-up activities such as training sessions or further meetings between the researcher and the stakeholders at the research site.

The fifth aspect of judging the authenticity of research, **tactical authenticity**, refers to the extent to which the participants are 'empowered to act on the finding as a result of the research process' (Manning, 1997, p. 110–11). This can be enhanced by the researcher relinquishing some ownership and control of the research project to **negotiate** for the participants' needs. According to Manning, 'items to be negotiated include data use, interpretations, confidentiality, and respondent cooperation' (p. 111). To be just to the participants, 'the constructivist researcher must continually negotiate their authorship, create an audit trail to fairly attribute ideas to their sources, acknowledge the words of others, and discuss how the research process affected those involved' (p. 111). Inseparable from these concerns is the maintenance of **confidentiality** throughout the research process (see Chapter 1 for the ethical concerns of qualitative research).

Whittemore, Chase and Mandle (2001) can also be seen to offer both evaluative and constructionist judgement criteria for qualitative research. Addressing the multiplicity of qualitative research and the difficulty of incorporating rigour, subjectivity, creativity and a 'scientific' research process, they offer primary and secondary criteria for the evaluative assessment of validity and a focus on research techniques for the constructive assessment of validity.

Some of the aspects of Whittemore, Chase and Mandle's judgement criteria are similar to Manning's (1997) criteria. Thus, we provide details where their judgement criteria differ significantly. Whittemore et. al.'s **primary evaluative criteria** resemble Manning's quite closely as they are based on **credibility** (accurate, trustworthy interpretation of meanings), **authenticity** (adequate accounts of lived and perceived experiences), **criticality** (reflexivity of the researcher's assumptions) and **integrity** (interpretation clearly grounded within data). Their **secondary**

Box 9.6 Evaluative and constructive validation of constructivist research

Evaluative:

1. Primary criteria:
   - Credibility: accurate, trustworthy interpretation of meanings;
   - Authenticity: lived and perceived experiences;
   - Criticality: reflexivity of the researcher's assumptions;
   - Integrity: interpretation grounded within data.
2. Secondary criteria:
   - Explicitness: auditability;
   - Vividness: thick description;
   - Creativity: novel and imaginative designs;
   - Thoroughness (saturation): sampling, data collection, analysis;
   - Congruence: (of) research design and previous research;
   - Sensitivity: (to) human, cultural and social contexts.

Constructive:

- Research design;
  - Developing a self-conscious research design;
  - Sampling decisions (i.e., accuracy);
  - Employing triangulation;
  - Giving voice;
  - Sharing of privilege;
  - Expressing issues of oppressed group.
- Data generating:
  - Articulating data collecting decisions;
  - Demonstrating prolonged engagement;
  - Demonstrating persistent observation;
  - Verbatim transcription;
  - Demonstrating saturation.
- Analytic:
  - Articulating analysis decisions;
  - Member checking;
  - Expert checking;
  - Performing quasistatistics;
  - Testing hypotheses in data analysis;
  - Using computer programs;
  - Data reduction tables;
  - Exploring rival explanations;

- Performing a literature review;
- Analysing negative case analysis;
• Memoing;
  - Reflexive journaling;
  - Writing an interim report;
  - Bracketing.
• Presentation:
  - Providing an audit trail;
  - Evidence to support interpretation;
  - Acknowledging the researcher perspective;
  - Providing thick description.

(Whittemore, Chase & Mandle, 2001)

---

criteria focus on more narrowly defined aspects of qualitative research. **Explicitness** refers to the auditability (such as audit trail in Manning's criteria) of the research process. **Vividness** involves 'thick' or artful, imaginary, yet clear presentation of the research results, whereas creativity refers to the employment of novel research designs and imaginative ways of organising and analysing data. **Thoroughness** refers to the proficiency of sampling and data analysis. This means completeness, consistency or saturation of data collection, but also attention to 'connection between themes and full development of ideas' (p. 532). In addition, posed research questions should be clearly answered in a thoroughly conducted qualitative research study. **Congruence** refers to the compatibility of the previous research, the paradigmatic and theoretical assumptions of the researcher, research questions, the method and the findings. This means that the findings from the study should also be located within the contexts outside of the study situation. Finally, good qualitative research should be **sensitive** to 'the nature of human, cultural and social contexts' (p. 532). This also means that participants should benefit from good qualitative research one way or another. Whittemore, Chase & Mandle's constructive criteria refer to the actual ways in which qualitative research methods or techniques are employed in the process. They identify four major foci that demonstrate the validity of the techniques employed: **consideration of research design, data generation accounts, clarity of analytic techniques** and **presentation of the research**. A more detailed account of the ways of assuring the quality of each type of technique is provided in the box above.

218 Qualitative Research for Physical Culture

Echoing the other judgement criteria from a diversification perspective, Fine et al. (2000) identify **community connection** as a vital aspect of judging qualitative research. They ask the researcher to consider the promises they have made to themselves and the wider research community. More specifically they assess if the research project has:

- Connected the voices and stories of individuals back to the set of historic, structural, and economic relations in which they are situated (Is the physical empirical addressed in context?);
- Deployed multiple practices so that very different kinds of analysis have been constructed;
- Described the mundane (as opposed to just the unique or startling);
- Provided the opportunity for some informants/constituencies/participants to review the material and interpret, dissent to or challenge interpretations;
- Considered how such disagreements in perspective would be reported;
- Thought through how to theorise the words of informants;
- Considered how these data could be used for progressive, conservative, repressive social policies;
- Considered if the researcher has backed into the passive voice and decoupled responsibility for interpretations;
- Thought through who the researcher would be afraid to show these analyses and who is rendered vulnerable/responsible or exposed by these analyses;
- Considered the dreams the researcher is having about the material presented (in respect to the issues being pulled from the researcher's own biography and the degree of emphasis given these);
- Considered the extent to which analysis offers an alternative to the commonsense or dominant discourse and the challenges different audiences might pose (see also Silk, Andrews & Mason, 2005).

Summary

The advocates of these judgement criteria want to diversify the ways in which qualitative research is assessed and move clearly away from imitating the positivist criteria to use terms of judgement that derive from the unique nature of qualitative research. Therefore, judgement of critical and social constructionist qualitative research is based on negotiation (e.g., Guba & Lincoln, 2005) to assess whether it advances emancipatory action and empowers the researched (Harrison, MacGibbon & Morton, 2001). Consequently, trustworthiness of qualitative research is strongly bound with reciprocity and a concern with how research is perceived by the community and by research participants. Demand for credible and believable findings still exist, but alongside new requirements for research to serve the interests of those who are researched, and for the researched to have more of a say at as many points of the project as is possible (Frisby et al., 2005; Harrison, MacGibbon & Morton, 2001).

Within this paradigmatic position, meaningful and purposeful research on physical culture addresses the social ills of the world in a trustworthy and authentic manner. Its quality becomes bound to an ethic of personal and community responsibility that empowers those in disadvantaged positions. Quality is reframed and encompassed within social criticism, engendering resistance and helping persons imagine how things could be different (Denzin, 2002). Personally and socially situated, 'good quality' research becomes contextualised as a civic, participatory, collaborative project that joins the researcher with the researched in an ongoing moral dialogue (Christians, 2000; Denzin, 2002). This is research that 'takes sides' (Denzin, 2002) as researchers align themselves with particular groups, categories or actors to serve each groups' interests. For example, Denzin (2002) characterises this type of high quality research by its ability to decloak the seemingly race neutral and colour-blind ways of administrative policy, political discourse and organisational structures and experiences. Holman-Jones (2005) summarises the characteristics of judgement criteria for critical research by asking a series of questions that a critical researcher should be able to address:

- Is the relationship between authors and participants reciprocal?
- Have the researchers created a space for meaningful dialogue among different hearts and bodies?
- Have the researchers enacted their ethical obligation to critique subject positions, acts and received notions of expertise and justice?
- Have the researchers produced a self-referential tale that connects to other stories, discourses and contexts?
- Have the researchers offered a charged atmosphere as an incitement to act within and without the context of the work?

While emphasising the unique qualities for qualitative research (reflexivity, emancipatory action, dialogic nature of the research), several criteria for critical research tend to refer to 'validity' when addressing ways to judge this type of qualitative research. In fact, many of these researchers devote significant discussion to providing multiple definitions of the term validity in order to demonstrate its socially constructed nature. Regardless, they clearly see a need for establishing their assessment of qualitative research based on validity, albeit redefining it in several ways. For example, Whittemore, Chase & Mandle (2001) argue that exposing the 'paramount differences' between qualitative and quantitative research 'does not imply that all quantitative and qualitative validity approaches are incompatible ... but simply that an exacting translation is inappropriate and inadequate' (p. 524). In addition, many researchers express a need for common validity criteria in qualitative research despite the call for diversity to accommodate the 'uncertainty, fluidity, and emergent ideas' of qualitative research (e.g., Whittemore, Chase & Mandle, 2001, p. 528).

Problematisation of judgement: Validation of poststructuralist/postmodernist research

While the majority of judgement criteria for qualitative research use the term validity, it was originally assigned to ensure the objectivity of research and is thus an inappropriate measure for qualitative research that draws from a subjective epistemology. In the previous discussion, qualitative researchers have, indeed, argued for multiple meanings for the term, but have nevertheless retained the focus on assessing the quality of process of research and/or evaluation of its impact. Poststructuralist/postmodern work emphasises the theoretical contribution in addition to the process and the impact on the community. This departs from interpretive or critical research to place less significance on detailed, 'procedural' judgement criteria and call for a more in-depth, theoretically driven, yet practically applicable, socially situated knowledge production process. While choosing to use the term 'validity', Lather (1995) has provided judgement criteria that reflect the poststructuralist emphasis on the importance of theory in the overall research logic.

Based on her earlier work on 'simulacrum' or 'an impossible' chart, Lather intends to 'sketch ephemeral practices of validity after poststructuralism within the context of a particular inquiry to generate theory of situated methodology' (2005, p. 41). Consequently, the idea is to avoid a general recipe and understand 'what is at play in our practices of constructing a science "after truth"' (ibid.). While Lather provides four 'scandalous' categories of validity, each reflects the impossibility of providing a clear list of items that definitively assess the quality of the work in a complex world of experience, knowledge and power. The four categories are as follows:

- Ironic validity:
  - produces truth as a problem;
  - Foregrounds insufficiency of language;

- Resists the hold of the real;
- Disperses, circulates, proliferates forms;
- Creates doubled analytic practices.
- Paralogical validity:
  - questions limits;
  - Fosters differences;
  - Implodes controlling codes;
  - Anticipates justice;
  - Searches for the oppositional;
  - Is concerned with undecidables, limits, paradoxes, complexities.
- Rhizomatic validity:
  - Taps underground;
  - Generates new locally determined norms of understanding;
  - Supplements and exceeds the stable and the permanent;
  - Works against constraints of authority;
  - Puts conventional discursive procedures under erasure.
- Voluptuous validity:
  - Goes too far towards excess, leaky, risky practice;
  - Embodies a situated, partial, positioned, explicit tentativeness;
  - Constructs authority via practices of engagement and self-reflexivity;
  - Questions texts that are bounded and unbounded;
  - Brings ethics and epistemology together.

(Adapted from Lather, 1995)

Lather's highly conceptual and theory-based criteria are far from easily applied. They reflect the poststructuralist challenges for one 'truth', the representationality of the text, qualitative research as a part of power relations, the authority of the author and challenges to conventional ways of writing research. The idea is not to provide an easy checklist of how well one has followed set procedures, but rather to think what research practices can ignite in reading and writing – what is beyond the word – to tap into what is not yet known, elusive and unfinished.

Richardson's (2000b) postmodern judgement criteria for critical analytic practices (CAP ethnography) emphasise the social and theoretical impact of storied research writing. Richardson (2000b) proposes that alternative ways of research writing, instead of being 'easy options', need to be held to even more rigorous standards than other types of qualitative research. Like other postmodern research, CAP ethnography must make a **substantive contribution** to understanding social life and to advancing academic knowledge. In addition, Richardson (2000b; see also Richardson & St. Pierre, 2005) suggests holding this work to **aesthetic criteria** that open up the text, invite interpretive responses and consider how complex, artistically shaped and satisfying the text is. These are criteria focused on the embodiment of a sense of lived experience. Crucially, the onus is on the authors to demonstrate to the reader how they know what they claim to know through their research writing.

Box 9.7 Validation of CAP ethnography

- Substantive contribution to social science;
- Aesthetic merit: evocativeness;
- Reflexivity:
  - Epistemology of postmodernism;
  - Self-awareness, self-exposure;
- Impactfulness:
  - Emotionally moving;
  - Intellectually moving;
- Expresses a reality:
  - Lived experience;
  - Cultural, social, individual, communal sense of the 'real';
- The logic of the research process and its written account;
- Takes the paradigm into account.

(Richardson, 2000b)

Richardson focuses on the **impactfulness** and **expression** of reality. In addition, the story has to be intellectually moving to provide not only a sense of lived experience, but a cultural, social, individual and communal sense of the 'real'. In addition to the aesthetic merit of an evocative story, this type of research has to make a **substantive contribution** to social science and thus has to provide a clear **paradigmatic location** to support the logic of the research process and the written story. Richardson emphasises the researcher's **self-reflexivity**, which manifests in self-awareness and self-exposure in the story.

Summary

It is clear that there are no universal, uniform judgement criteria for qualitative research. This does not mean, however, that 'anything goes' in the name of qualitative research. On the contrary, to be able to assess the quality of each qualitative work requires knowledge of its paradigmatic underpinnings. Consequently, the clearer the researchers are about the paradigmatic assumptions the easier it is to provide an appropriate assessment of the work. On the other hand, relying on inappropriate judgement criteria is unfair to the merits of the work and demonstrates ignorance on the side of the one casting the judgement. In this chapter, we have provided several possible criteria for assessing post-positivist, interpretive, critical and poststructuralist/postmodern research.

In general, the further distanced the qualitative research paradigm is from positivism, the less validation relies on the process (or the methods) of constructing research. While positivists focus on assessing the validity and reliability of their methods, interpretive researchers seek to assess a quality construction of the subjective research process. Critical and social constructionist researchers have added the evaluation of the impact of the research to considerations of the quality of the research process. This adds to a different set of assessment that evaluates the impact of research on the participants, community and the researchers' self-development. Poststructuralists emphasise the theoretical rigor of the research in addition to process and impact. These differences underline the impossibility of relying on one criterion to assure the quality of qualitative research.

In thesis or dissertation work it is important for researchers to provide a detailed account of how they ensured that their work is of best possible quality. Consequently, it is necessary not only to list appropriate judgement criteria, but also to demonstrate how one has, in practice, produced good quality work. For example, it is not sufficient to state that an interpretive researcher followed Lincoln and Guba's (1985) criteria for qualitative trustworthiness. Instead, the researcher needs to detail how credibility, transferability, dependability and conformability were achieved in the study. Likewise, social constructionist researchers should not only state that they have used Kvale and Brinkmann's (2007) seven steps in their research, but demonstrate how each step was followed during the research process (e.g., how 'thematising' was ensured when developing the interview guide).

Assessing the quality of research in physical culture is more than just a technical or methodological exercise. It requires an understanding of the ontological and epistemological bases of the researcher and the research. This leads to quite different interpretations of the term 'quality' and how it is evidenced in qualitative research. Again, this pluralism is not problematic: quite the opposite, it speaks to the very vitality of qualitative research. As different approaches to research should coexist alongside each other, so should different ways of assessing the quality of that research. However, it is crucial to reflect continually on the form and need to assess quality by asking how qualitative researchers want to live their lives as social inquirers (Schwandt, 2000), how they grapple with issues of reciprocity, with textual pluralism, with interdisciplinarity, with self-reflexivity, with methodological plurality, theoretical rigour, with praxis, social change and the meaning of qualitative research.

Further reading

Validating post-positivist research:

Eisenhardt, K. M. (1989). 'Building theory from case study research'. *Academy of Management Review*, 14, 532–49.
Hammersley, M. (1990). *Reading ethnographic research: A critical guide*. London: Longman.
Seale, C. (1999). *The quality of qualitative research*. London: Sage.

Validating alternative ways writing:

Hopper, T. F., Medhill, L. E., Bratseth, D. D., Cameron, K. A., Coble, J. D. & Nimmon, L. E. (2008). 'Multiple voices in health, sport, recreation, and physical education research: Revealing unfamiliar spaces in a polyvocal review of qualitative research genres'. *Quest*, 60, 214–35.

Validating critical and social constructionist research:

Frisby, W., Reid, C., Millar, S. & Hoeber, L. (2005). 'Putting "participatory" into participatory forms of action research'. *Journal of Sport Management*, 19, 367–86.
Greenwood, D., Whyte, W. & Harkavy, I. (1993). 'Participatory action research as a process and as a goal'. *Human Relations*, 46, 175–92.
Reid, C. (2000). 'Seduction and enlightenment in feminist action research'. *Resources for Feminist Research*, 28, 169–88.
Ristock, J. & Pennell, J. (1996). *Community research as empowerment: Feminist links, postmodern interruptions*. Toronto, ON: Oxford University Press.

Conclusion

In this book, we have highlighted the process of conducting a qualitative research project in physical culture. It is clear that each research project needs a clear **design**, it has to be well **done** and well written to provide meaningful knowledge. We introduced the **7Ps** approach as a tool that can help in the process of conducting quality qualitative research. Following this approach, the researcher should first be able to identify a clear **purpose** that then helps to locate the project within an appropriate **paradigm**. The researcher can then embark on a **process** of selecting appropriate qualitative research **practices** (methods) and ways (**politics**) of interpreting the acquired empirical material. After an analysis, the researchers should choose the appropriate way of **(re)presenting** the results and be able to explain how they have ensured that the project is of the best quality it can be **(the promise)**. It is clear, however, that the researchers' paradigmatic stance determines the choices embedded in the many of the other Ps. Therefore, to summarise the main tenets of our book, we provide the following table (Table C1) that further clarifies each of Ps and their relationship to the researchers' choice of paradigm.

We also encourage qualitative researchers to think of practical applications for their projects: How qualitative research can be meaningful to wider society in addition to the academic research of physical culture. In essence, this involves thinking about what impact qualitative research that maps, critiques or enacts social change can have on people's lives (Denzin, 2002; Flaherty, 2002; Snow, 2002). Denzin (2005) suggests that qualitative methods are uniquely suited to 'impactful' research results, because qualitative methods give more freedom for researchers to construct meaningful projects than quantitative research, which requires strict objectivity of the researcher, the methods and the research setting. Consequently, there are numerous ways in which qualitative

Table C1 The seven Ps of qualitative research in physical culture

Concern / 2. Paradigm	Logical empiricism & positivism	Post-positivism	Humanism: Interpretive	Humanism: Critical theory	Poststructural / postmodern
	Ontology: one truth/reality Epistemology: objective	Ontology: one truth/reality Epistemology: objective	Ontology: one truth/reality Epistemology: subjective	Ontology: one truth/reality Epistemology: subjective	Ontology: multiple truths Epistemology: subjective
1. Purpose	Explanation: Prediction & control	Explanation: Prediction & control Mapping	Mapping: Understanding experiences	Critique: Transformation, emancipation	Mapping Critique Social change
3. Process	Deductive: Controlled Experimentation	Inductive: Theory grounded on data from natural settings. Mixed quantitative and qualitative methods.	Qualitative research logic to understand individual experiences and locate the researcher as self-reflexive.	Qualitative research logic to critique existing power, ideology and identity construction. Political, praxis oriented, self-reflexive researcher.	Qualitative logic to map power relations and the individual's, including the researcher's, role in them. Critique and negotiation of discursive construction. Search for multiple solutions for social change.

	Quantitative	Qualitative Quantitative	Qualitative: Interviews, interpretive textual analysis, narrative, field methods.	Qualitative: Interviews, textual analysis, narrative, field methods.	Qualitative: Interviews, textual analysis, narrative, field methods.
4. Practices					
5. Politics of interpretation	Statistical	Grounded theory analysis, statistical	Several techniques for analysing empirical material collected through different practices	Several techniques for analysing empirical material collected through different practices	Several techniques for analysing empirical material collected through different practices
6. (Re) Presentation	Detached, realist, 'third' person	Detached, realist, 'third' person	Realist, (often 'first person') narrative, autoethnographic	Realist, narrative, autoethnographic, performance ethnography	Realist, narrative, autoethnographic, performance ethnography
7. Promise: Judgement	Foundationalism Constructive focus on research process. Objectivity: Generalisability, internal, external validity, reliability.	Foundationalism Constructive focus on research process. Replication of quantitative criteria of objectivity: Generalisability, internal, external validity, reliability.	Quasi-Foundationalism Constructive focus on research process. Parallel criteria to Foundationalism: Trustworthiness, authenticity, credibility, self-awareness, participants' voices. Free-floating criteria: alternative ways of writing.	Non-foundationalism Constructive focus on research process and Evaluative focus on research impact. Diversification of criteria: Trustworthiness, Authenticity, Criticality, Reciprocity,	Non-foundationalism Theoretically and paradigmatically based focus on process and impact of research.

research can have a practical application, offer deeper understanding and critique existing ways of seeing and doing. For example, qualitative researchers have the potential to direct public policy (e.g., on physical activity and obesity), critique or expose instances of injustice (e.g., human rights at the Olympics, athlete abuse) and power imbalances (e.g., the media's trivialisation of the athletic women, or promotion of narrowly defined body ideal by glossy magazines), or directly intervene in key social issues of the time (e.g., targeting sweatshop labour or setting up groups for victims of domestic abuse). These impacts could occur at any point throughout the research process, not just at the conclusion. For example, a researcher may well have an impact on an individual who they meet as part of fieldwork or during an interview. Some researchers may make an impact by reproducing results in a more accessible or affective form. We offer the following list, which is by no means exhaustive, as a way of thinking through the various ways in which qualitative research can make a difference.

- Studying with/in a community and sharing question formulation, analysis, ideas, results.
- Writing in an accessible manner hoping that qualitative work will reach wide audiences.
- Working with the media (appearing in the media, writing blogs, writing columns).
- Giving public talks (e.g., at museums, schools, events).
- Work with a community such as coaching, instructing or teaching with an informed critical agenda.
- Changing the research community through qualitative methods (e.g., performance ethnography).
- Working with organisations to create policy change.

Some qualitative researchers in physical culture have managed to make a practical impact within a climate in which some universities and indeed some governments have started to favour scientific, evidence based quantitative research that *is perceived* to be of greater practical impact and offer greater 'proof' for policy makers (e.g., Denzin & Giardina, 2006; House, 2006; Lather, 2006; Morse, 2006; Silk, Bush & Andrews, 2010). Others have attempted to reach back to the public, including through public lectures or returning to an organisation where the empirical material was collected (e.g., Amis et al., 2008; Frisby et. al., 2005; Silk, 2005). These objectives will, of course, vary according to the purpose of the study and indeed the type of research being conducted. Not all qualitative researchers will be in a position to change the world with one research project. For example, the scope for an undergraduate research project might be beyond a practical application. Further, although well intentioned and well meaning, it might be beyond the beginning researcher who, at the first attempt, tries to understand the nuances of a community and also to seek to solve their problems. However, considering the potential impact of one's research project allows qualitative researchers further to think through the meaning of their work: How it might be useful, and to whom and how the research might make a difference.

References

Adams, M. L. (2005) '"Death to the Prancing Prince": Effeminacy, sport discourses and the salvation of men's dancing'. *Body & Society*, 11, 4, 63–86.

Allen Collinson, J. (2009). 'Sporting embodiment: Sport studies and the (continuing) promise of phenomenology'. *Qualitative Research in Sport and Exercise*, 1, 279–96.

Allin, L. & Humberstone, B. (2006). 'Exploring careership in outdoor education and the lives of women outdoor educators'. *Sport, Education and Society*, 11, 135–53.

Althusser, L. (1971). *Lenin and philosophy and other essays*. London: New Left.

Amis, J., Wright, P., Dyson, B., Vardaman, J. & Ferry, H. (2008). School physical education policy failure in Mississippi and Tennessee. Paper presented at the Society of Behavioural Medicine, San Diego, CA, 29th March.

Amis, J. & Silk, M. (2008). 'The philosophy and politics of quality in qualitative organizational research'. *Organizational Research Methods*, 11, 456–80.

An, J. & Goodwin, D. L. (2007). 'Physical education for students with Spina Bifida: Mothers' perspectives'. *Adaptive Physical Activity Quarterly*, 24, 38–58.

Anderson, L. (2006). 'Analytic autoethnography'. *Journal of Contemporary Ethnography*, 35, 373–95.

Anderson, L. (1999). 'The open road to ethnography's future'. *Journal of Contemporary Ethnography*, 28, 451–9.

Andrews, D. L. (2008). 'Kinesiology's "inconvenient truth" and the physical cultural studies imperative'. *Quest*, 60, 45–62.

Andrews, D. L. (2002). 'Coming to terms with cultural studies'. *Journal of Sport and Social Issues*, 26, 110–17.

Andrews, D. L. (2000). 'Posting up: French post-structuralism and the critical analysis of contemporary sporting culture'. In J. Coakley & E. Dunning (Eds), *Handbook of sport studies* (pp. 48–60). London: Sage.

Andrews, D., Mason, D. & Silk, M. (2005). *Qualitative research in sports studies*. Oxford: Berg.

Andrews, D. L. & Loy, J. (1993). 'British cultural studies and sport'. *Quest*, 45, 255–76.

Angrosino, M. (2005). 'Recontextualising observation: Ethnography, pedagogy, and the prospects for a progressive education'. In N. K. Denzin & Y. S. Lincoln (Eds), *The Sage handbook of qualitative research* (3rd edn) (pp. 729–46). Thousand Oaks, CA: Sage.

Atkinson, M. (2007). 'Playing with fire: Masculinity, health, and sports supplements'. *Sociology of Sport Journal*, 24, 165–86.

Atkinson, P. & Silverman, D. (1997). 'Kundera's "immortality": The interview society and the invention of the self'. *Qualitative Inquiry*, 3, 304–22.

Atkinson, J. M. & Heritage, J. (1984). *Structures of social action: Studies in conversation analysis*. Cambridge: Cambridge University Press.

Azzarito, L. (2009). 'The Panopticon of physical education: Pretty, active and ideally white'. *Physical Education and Sport Pedagogy*, 14, 19–39.

Banes, S. (1994). *Writing dancing in the age of postmodernism*. Hanover, NH: Wesleyan University Press.

Banks, M. (2001). *Visual method in social research*. Thousand Oaks, CA: Sage.

Barker-Ruchti, N. (2009). 'The media as an authorising practice of femininity: Swiss newspaper coverage of Karin Thürig's bronze medal performance in road cycling'. In P. Markula (Ed.), *Olympic women and the media: International perspectives* (pp. 214–31). Basingstoke: Palgrave Macmillan.

Baudrillard, J. (1983). *Simulations*. New York: Semiotext(s).

Berger, A. (1982). *Media analysis techniques*. Thousand Oaks: Sage.

Birrell, S. & Donnelly, P. (2004). 'Reclaiming Goffman: Erwin Goffman's influence on the sociology of sport'. In R. Giulianotti (Ed.), *Sport and modern social theorists* (pp. 49–64). Basingstoke: Palgrave Macmillan.

Birrell, S. & McDonald, M. G. (2000). *Reading sport: Critical essays on power and representation*. Boston, MA: Northeastern University Press.

Birrell, S. & Theberge, N. (1994). 'Ideological control of women in sport'. In D. M. Costa & S. R. Guthrie (Eds), *Women and sport: Interdisciplinary perspectives* (pp. 341–59). Champaign, IL: Human Kinetics.

Blommaert, J. (2005). *Discourse: A critical introduction*. Cambridge: Cambridge University Press.

Blommaert, J. & Bulcaen, C. (1997). *Political linguistics*. Amsterdam: John Benjamins.

Blumer, H. (1969). *Symbolic interactionism*. Englewood Cliffs, NJ: Prentice-Hall.

Bolin, A. (2003). 'Beauty of the beast: The subversive soma'. In A. Bolin & J. Granskog (Eds), *Athletic intruders: Ethnographic research on women, culture, and exercise* (pp. 107–30). Albany, NY: SUNY Press.

Borcila, A. (2000). 'Nationalizing the Olympics around the away from the "vulnerable" bodies of women: The NBC coverage of the 1996 Olympics and some moments after. *Journal of Sport & Social Issues*, 24, 118–47.

Boyle, E. Millington, B. & Vertinsky, P. (2006). 'Representing the female pugilist: Narratives of race, gender, and dis-ability in million dollar baby'. *Sociology of Sport Journal*, 23, 99–116.

Brohm, J.-M. (1978). *Sport: A prison of measured time*. London: Ink Links.

Brooks, S. (2009). 'Radio food disorder: The conversational constitution of eating disorders in radio phone-ins'. *Journal of Community and Applied Social Psychology*, 19, 360–73.

Bruce, T. (2003). 'Pass'. In J. Denison & P. Markula (Eds), *Moving writing: Crafting movement in sport research*. New York: Peter Lang.

Bruce, T. (1998). 'Postmodernism and the possibilities for writing "vital" sports texts'. In G. Rail (Ed.), *Sport and postmodern times* (pp. 3–20). Albany, NY: SUNY Press.

Bruce, T., Hovden, J. & Markula, P. (2010). *Women in the Olympic media: A global comparison of newspaper coverage*. Taipei, Taiwan: SENSE.

Burr, V. (1995). *Social constructionism*. Sussex: Routledge.

Burrell, G. & Morgan, G. (1979). *Sociological paradigms and organizational analysis*. London: Heinemann.

Carless, D. & Douglas, K. (2008). 'Narrative identity, and mental health: How men with severe mental illness restore life through sport and exercise'. *Psychology of Sport and Exercise*, 9, 576–94.

Carrington, B. & McDonald, I. (2009). *Marxism, cultural studies and sport*. London: Routledge.

Charmaz, K. (2005). 'Grounded theory in the 21st century: Applications for advancing social justice'. In N. K. Denzin & Y. S. Lincoln (Eds), *The Sage handbook of qualitative research* (3rd edn) (pp. 507–36). Thousand Oaks, CA: Sage.

Chase, S. (2005). 'Narrative inquiry: Multiple lenses, approaches, voices'. In N. K. Denzin & Y. S. Lincoln (Eds), *The Sage handbook of qualitative research* (3rd edn) (pp. 651–80). Thousand Oaks, CA: Sage.

Christians, C. (2005). 'Ethics and politics in qualitative research'. In N. K. Denzin & Y. S. Lincoln (Eds), *The Sage handbook of qualitative research* (3rd edn) (pp. 139–64). Thousand Oaks, CA: Sage.

Christians, C. (2000). 'Ethics and politics in qualitative research'. In N. K. Denzin & Y. S. Lincoln (Eds), *The Sage handbook of qualitative research* (2nd edn) (pp. 133–55). Thousand Oaks, CA: Sage.

Clandinin J. (2007). *Handbook of narrative inquiry: Mapping a methodology.* Thousand Oaks, CA: Sage.

Clandinin, J. & Connelly, M. (2000). *Narrative inquiry: Experience and story in qualitative research.* Thousand Oaks, CA: Sage.

Clifford, J. & Marcus, G. (1986). *Writing culture: The poetics and politics of ethnography.* Berkeley, CA: University of California Press.

Cole, C. L., Giardina, M. & Andrews, D. L. (2004). 'Michel Foucault: Studies of power and sport'. In R. Giulianotti (Ed.), *Sport and modern social theorists* (pp. 207–24). Basingstoke: Palgrave Macmillan.

Collier, J. Jr. (1967). *Visual anthropology: Photography as a research method.* New York: Holt, Rinehart & Winston.

Collins, P. H. (2004). *Black sexual politics: African American, gender, and the New Racism.* New York: Routledge.

Collins, P. H. (1990). *Black feminist thought: Knowledge, consciousness, and the politics of empowerment.* New York: Routledge.

Corbin, J. & Strauss, A. (2008). *Basics of qualitative research* (3rd edn). Thousand Oaks, CA: Sage.

Corbin, J. & Strauss, A. (1990). 'Grounded theory method: Procedures, canons, and evaluative procedures'. *Qualitative sociology*, 13, 1, 3–21.

Cote, J., Salmela, J. H. & Russell, S. (1995). 'The knowledge of high-performance gymnastics coaches: Methodological framework'. *The Sport Psychologists*, 9, 65–75.

Cousens, L. & Barnes, M. L. (2009). 'Sport delivery in a highly socialized environment: A case study of embeddedness'. *Journal of Sport Management*, 23, 547–90.

Creswell, J. W. (1998). *Qualitative inquiry and research design: Choosing among five traditions.* London: Sage.

Dablaso, D. M. (2009). *Catching stories: A practical guide to oral history.* Athens, OH: Swallow.

Davis, L. R. (1997). *The swimsuit issue and sport: Hegemonic masculinity in Sports Illustrated.* Albany, NY: SUNY Press.

Deacon, D., Pickering, M., Golding, P. & Murdoch, G. (1999). *Researching communications: A practical guide to methods in media and cultural analysis.* London: Arnold.

Deleuze, G. & Guattari, F. (1988). *A thousand plateaus: Capitalism & schizophrenia.* London: Athlone.

Denison, J. (2010), '"Messy texts", or the unexplainable performance: Reading bodies' evidence'. *International Review of Qualitative Research*, 3, 149–60.

Denison, J. (1996). 'Sport narratives'. *Qualitative Inquiry*, 2, 351–62.

Denison, J. & Markula, P. (2003). *Moving writing: Crafting movement in sport research.* New York: Peter Lang.

Denscombe, M. (2007). *The good research guide: For small scale social research projects*. Maidenhead, UK: Open University Press.

Denzin, N. K. (2006). 'Analytic autoethnography, or déjà vu all over again'. *Journal of Contemporary Ethnography*, 35, 419–28.

Denzin, N. K. (2005). 'Emancipatory discourses and the ethics and politics of interpretation'. In N. K. Denzin & Y. S. Lincoln (Eds), *The Sage handbook of qualitative research* (3rd edn) (pp. 933–58). Thousand Oaks, CA: Sage.

Denzin, N. K. (2003). *Performance ethnography: Critical pedagogy and the politics of culture*. Thousand Oaks, CA: Sage.

Denzin, N. K. (2002). 'Confronting ethnography's crisis of representation'. *Journal of Contemporary Ethnography*, 31, 482–90.

Denzin, N. K. (2000). 'The practices and politics of interpretation'. In N. K. Denzin & Y. S. Lincoln (Eds), *The Sage handbook of qualitative research* (2nd edn) (pp. 897–922). Thousand Oaks, CA: Sage.

Denzin, N. K. (1997). *Interpretive ethnography: Ethnographic practices for the 21st century*. Thousand Oaks, CA: Sage.

Denzin, N. K. (1994). 'The art and politics of interpretation'. In N. K. Denzin & Y. Lincoln (Eds), *Handbook of qualitative research* (pp. 500–15). Newbury Park, CA: Sage.

Denzin, N. K. & Giardina, M. (2006). *Qualitative inquiry and the conservative challenge*. Walnut Creek, CA: Left Coast Press.

Denzin, N. K. & Lincoln, Y. S. (2005). 'Introduction: The discipline and practice of qualitative research'. In N. K. Denzin & Y. S. Lincoln (Eds), *The Sage handbook of qualitative research* (3rd edn) (pp. 1–32). Thousand Oaks, CA: Sage.

Denzin, N. K. & Lincoln, Y. S. (2000). 'Introduction: The discipline and practice of qualitative research'. In N. K. Denzin & Y. S. Lincoln (Eds), *The Sage handbook of qualitative research* (2nd edn) (pp. 1–28). Thousand Oaks, CA: Sage.

Denzin, N. K. & Lincoln, Y. S. (1994). 'Introduction: Entering the field of qualitative research'. In N. K. Denzin & Y. S. Lincoln (Eds), *Handbook of Qualitative Research*. Thousand Oaks, CA: Sage.

Derrida, J. (1978). *Writing and difference*. Chicago: University of Chicago Press.

Derrida, J. (2004). *Positions*. London: Continuum.

Dickson, G. & Schofield, G. (2005). 'Globalization and globesity: The Impact of the 2008 Beijing Olympics in China'. *International Journal of Sport Management and Marketing*, 1, 1/2, 169–79.

Donnelly, P. (2000). 'Interpretive approaches to the sociology of sport'. In J. Coakley & E. Dunning (Eds), *Handbook of sport studies* (pp. 77–91). London: Sage.

Douglas, D. (2005). 'Venus, Serena and women's tennis association: When and where "race" enters'. *Sociology of Sport Journal*, 22, 256–82.

Duncan, M. C. (2000). 'Reflex: Body as memory'. *Sociology of Sport Journal*, 17, 60–8.

Edley, N. & Wetherell, M. (1995). *Men in perspective*. Hemel Hemstead: Harvester Wheatsheaf.

Edwards, D. & Potter, J. (1992). *Discursive psychology*. London: Sage.

Eisenhardt, K. M. (1989). 'Building theory from case study research'. *Academy of Management Review*, 14, 532–49.

Elling, A. & Luijt, R. (2009). 'Different shades of orange? Media representations of Dutch women medallists'. In P. Markula (Ed.), *Olympic women and the media: International perspectives* (pp. 132–49). Basingstoke: Palgrave MacMillan.

Ellis, C. (2004). *The ethnographic I: A methodological novel about teaching and doing autoethnography.* Walnut Creek, CA: AltaMira.

Epstein, I., Stevens, B., McKeever, P. & Baruchel, S. (2006). 'Photo elicitation interview (PEI): Using photos to elicit children's perspectives'. *International Journal of Qualitative Methods,* 5, 3, 1–9.

Fairclough, N. (2006). *Language and globalization.* London: Routledge.

Fairclough, N. (2002). *Methods of critical discourse analysis.* London: Sage.

Fairclough, N. (1995). *Critical discourse analysis: The critical study of language.* New York: Longman.

Fairclough, N. (1992). *Discourse and social change.* Cambridge: Polity Press.

Faulkner, G. & Finley, S. (2002). 'It's not what you say, its' the way you say it! Conversation analysis: A discursive methodology for sport, exercise, and physical education'. *Quest,* 54, 1, 49–66.

Featherstone, M. (1991). *Consumer culture & postmodernism.* London: Sage.

Ferguson, P. M., Ferguson, D. L. &Taylor, S. J. (1992). 'Conclusion: The future of interpretivism in disability studies'. In P. M. Ferguson, D. L. Ferguson & S. J. Taylor (Eds), *Interpreting disability: A qualitative reader.* New York: Teachers College Press.

Fine, M. (1994). 'Working the hyphens. Reinventing self and other in qualitative research'. In N. K. Denzin & Y. S. Lincoln (Eds), *Handbook of Qualitative Research* (pp. 70–82). Thousand Oaks: Sage.

Fine, M. (1992). 'Passions, politics and power: Feminist research possibilities'. In M. Fine (Ed.), *Disruptive voices: The possibilities of feminist research.* Ann Arbor: The University of Michigan Press.

Fine, M., Weis, L., Weseen, S. & Wong, L. (2000). 'For whom? Qualitative research, representations and social responsibilities'. In N. K. Denzin & Y. S Lincoln (Eds), *The Sage handbook of qualitative research* (2nd edn) (pp. 107–32). Thousand Oaks, CA: Sage.

Finley, S.-J. & Faukner, G. (2003). '"Actually I was the star": Managing attributions in conversation'. *Forum: Qualitative Social Research,* 4, 1, (no page number).

Flaherty, M. G. (2002). 'The "crisis" in representation: reflections and assessments'. *Journal of Contemporary Ethnography,* 31, 508–16.

Flyvbjerk, B. (2001). 'Five misunderstanding about case-study research'. *Qualitative Inquiry,* 12, 219–45.

Fontana, A. & Frey, J. (2005). 'The interview: From neutral stance to political involvement'. In N. K. Denzin & Y. S. Lincoln (Eds), *The Sage handbook of qualitative research* (3rd edn) (pp. 695–728). Thousand Oaks, CA: Sage

Fontana, A. & Frey, J. H. (2000). 'The interview: From structured questions to negotiated text'. In N. K. Denzin & Y. S. Lincoln (Eds), *The Sage handbook of qualitative research* (2nd edn) (pp. 645–72). Thousand Oaks, CA: Sage.

Foucault, M. (2000). 'The subject and power'. In J. D. Faubion (Ed.), *Essential works of Michel Foucault, Vol. 3: Power* (pp. 326–48). New York: New Press.

Foucault, M. (1991). *Discipline and punish: The birth of the prison.* London: Penguin Books.

Foucault, M. (1988). 'An aesthetics of existence'. In L. D. Kritzman (Ed.), *Michel Foucault: Politics, philosophy, culture: Interviews and other writing 1977–1984* (pp. 47–56). London: Routledge.

Foucault, M. (1983). 'The subject and power'. In H. L. Dreyfus & P. Rabinow (Eds), *Michel Foucault: Beyond structuralism and hermeneutics* (pp. 208–28) (2nd edn). Chicago, IL: University of Chicago Press.

Foucault, M. (1980a). 'Power and strategies'. In C. Gordon (Ed.), *Power/knowledge: Selected interviews and other writing 1972–1977* (pp. 134–45). Harlow, UK: Harvester.

Foucault, M. (1980b). 'Two lectures'. In C. Gordon (Ed.), *Power/knowledge: Selected interviews and other writing 1972–1977* (pp. 78–108). Harlow, UK: Harvester.

Foucault, M. (1978). *The history of sexuality, Volume 1: An introduction*. London: Penguin Books.

Foucault, M. (1977). 'Nietzsche, genealogy, history'. In D. F. Bouchard (Ed.), *Language, counter-memory, practice: Selected essays and interview by Michel Foucault* (pp. 139–64). Ithaca, NY: Cornell University Press.

Foucault, M. (1972). *The archaeology of knowledge and discourse in language*. New York: Pantheon Books.

Foucault, M. (1970). *The order of things: An archaeology of the human sciences*. London: Tavistock.

Fox, D. & Prilleltensky, I. (1997). *Critical psychology: An introduction*. London: Sage.

Frisby, W., Reid, C., Millar, S. & Hoeber, L. (2005). 'Putting "participatory" into participatory forms of action research'. *Journal of Sport Management*, 19, 367–86.

Frow, J. & Morris, M. (2000). 'Cultural studies'. In N. K. Denzin & Y. S. Lincoln (Eds), *The Sage handbook of qualitative research* (2nd edn) (pp. 315–46). Thousand Oaks, CA: Sage.

Fusco, C. (2006). 'Inscribing healthification: Governance, risk, surveillance and the subjects and spaces of fitness and health'. *Health & Place*, 12, 1, 65–78.

Gadamer, H.-G. (1975). *Truth and method*. London: Sheed & Ward.

Garfinkel, H. (1967). *Studies in ethnomethodology*. Englewood Cliffs, NJ: Prentice Hall.

Geertz, C. (1973). 'Thick description: Toward an interpretive theory of culture'. In C. Geertz (Ed.), *The interpretation of cultures* (pp. 3–33). New York: Basic Books.

Giardina, M. D. (2005). *Sporting pedagogies: Performing culture and identity in the global arena*. New York: Peter Lang.

Giorgi, A. (1985). *Phenomenology and psychological research*. Pittsburgh, PA: Duquesne University Press.

Giroux, H. (2002). *Breaking into the movies: Film and the culture of politics*. Oxford: Blackwell.

Giroux, H. (2001). 'Cultural studies as performative politics'. *Cultural Studies ↔ Critical Methodologies*, 1, 5–23.

Giulianotti, R. (2004). 'The fate of hyperreality: Jean Baudrillard and the sociology of sport'. In R. Giulianotti (Ed.), *Sport and modern social theorists* (pp. 225–40). Basingstoke: Palgrave Macmillan.

Giulianotti, R. & Armstrong, G. (2002). 'Avenues of contestation: Football hooligans running and ruling urban spaces'. *Social Anthropology*, 10, 2, 211–38.

Glaser, B. (1992). *Basics of grounded theory analysis*. Mill Valley, CA: Sociology Press.

Glaser, B. & Strauss, A. (1967). *The discovery of grounded theory*. Chicago: Aldine.

Goffman, E. (1959). *The presentation of self in everyday life*. New York: Anchor Books.

Goffman, E. (1961). *Encounters*. Indianapolis: Bobbs-Merrill.

Goffman, E. (1963). *Stigma*. Englewood Cliffs, NJ: Prentice Hall.

236 *References*

Goffman, E. (1967). *Interaction ritual*. New York: Anchor Books.
Goffman, E. (1969). *Strategic interaction*. Philadephia: University of Pennsylvania Press.
Gold, R. (1958). 'Roles in sociological field observations'. *Social Forces*, 36, 217–23.
Gough, B. & McFadden, M. (2001). *Critical social psychology: An introduction*. Basingstoke: Palgrave Macmillan.
Gramsci, A. (1971). *Selections from prison notebooks*. London: Lawrence & Wishart.
Gratton, C. & Jones, I. (2004). *Research methods for sport studies*. London: Routledge.
Greenwood, D., Whyte, W. & Harkavy, I. (1993). 'Participatory action research as a process and as a goal'. *Human Relations*, 46, 175–92.
Groenewald, T. (2004). 'A phenomenological research design illustrated'. *International Journal of Qualitative Methods*, 3 (1). Article 4 Retrieved 23 March 2010 from http://www.ualberta.ca/~iiqm.backissues/3_1/pdf.gronewald. pdf.
Grossberg, L. (1992). *We gotta get out of this place: Popular conservatism and post-modern culture*. London: Routledge.
Gruneau, R. (1983). *Class, sports, and social development*. Amherst, MA: University of Massachusetts.
Gruneau, R., Whitson, D. & Cantelon, H. (1988). 'Methods and media: Studying the sports television discourse'. *Loisir et Societe*, 11, 2, 265–81.
Guba, E. G. & Lincoln, Y. S. (2005). 'Paradigmatic controversies, contradictions, and emerging confluences'. In N. K. Denzin & Y. S. Lincoln (Eds), *The Sage handbook of qualitative research* (3rd edn) (pp. 191–215). Thousand Oaks, CA: Sage.
Guba, E. G. & Lincoln, Y. S. (1994). 'Competing paradigms in qualitative research'. In N. K. Denzin & Y. S. Lincoln (Eds), *Handbook of qualitative research*. Thousand Oaks, CA: Sage.
Guba, E. G. & Lincoln, Y. S. (1989). *Fourth generation evaluation*. Newbury Park, CA: Sage.
Gubrium, J. F. & Holstein, J. A. (1998). 'Narrative practice and the coherence of personal stories'. *The Sociological Quarterly*, 29, 163–87.
Habermas, J. (1987). *Theory of communicative action. Vol 2: Lifeworld and system: A critique of functionalist reason*. Boston: Beacon.
Habermas, J. (1984). *Theory of communicative action. Vol 1: Reason and the rationalization of society*. Boston: Beacon.
Habermas, J. (1972). *Knowledge and human interests*. London: Heinemann.
Hall. M. A. (1996). *Feminism and sporting bodies: Essays on theory and practice*. Champaign, IL: Human Kinetics.
Hall, S. (1992). 'The question of cultural identity'. In S. Hall, D. Held & T. McGrew (Eds), *Modernity and its futures* (pp. 273–326). Cambridge, MA: Polity Press.
Hall, S. ([1973] 1980). 'Encoding/decoding'. In Centre for Contemporary Cultural Studies (Ed.), *Culture, media, language: Working papers in cultural studies, 1972–79* (pp. 128–38). London: Hutchinson.
Hammersley, M. (1990). *Reading ethnographic research: A critical guide*. London: Longman.
Hammersley, M. (1989). *The dilemma of qualitative methods: Herbert Blumer and the Chicago tradition*. London: Routledge.
Hammersley, M. & Atkinson, P. (1995). *Ethnography: Principles in practice* (2nd edn). London: Routledge.
Hammersley, M. & Atkinson, P. (1983). *Ethnography: Principles in practice*. London: Routledge.

Hargreaves, J. (1987). 'The body, sport and power relations'. In J. Horne, D. Jary & A. Tomlinson (Eds), *Sport, leisure and social relations* (pp. 139–59). London: Routledge.

Hargreaves, J. A. & MacDonald, I. (2000). 'Cultural studies and the sociology of sport'. In J. Coakley & E. Dunning (Eds), *Handbook of sport studies* (pp. 48–60). London: Sage.

Harper, D. (2005). 'What's new visually?' In N. K. Denzin & Y. S. Lincoln (Eds), *The Sage handbook of qualitative research* (3rd edn) (pp. 747–62). Thousand Oaks: Sage Publications.

Harre, R. & Stearns, P. (1995). *Discursive psychology in practice*. London: Sage.

Harrison, J., MacGibbon, L. & Morton, M. (2001). 'Regimes of trustworthiness in qualitative research: The rigors of reciprocity'. *Qualitative Inquiry*, 7, 323–45.

Haug, F. and others (1987). *Female sexualisation: A collective work of memory*. London: Verso.

Heidegger, M. (1962). *Being and time*. New York: Harper & Row.

Henderson, K. A. (2006). *Dimensions of choice: Qualitative approaches to parks, recreation, tourism, sport, and leisure research*. State College, PA: Venture Publishing.

Hills, L. (2007). 'Friendship, physicality, and physical education: An exploration of the social and embodied dynamics of girls' physical education experiences'. *Sport, Education and Society*, 12, 317–36.

Hills, L. & Kennedy, E. (2009). 'Double trouble: Kelly Holmes, intersectionality and unstable narratives of Olympic heroism in the British media'. In P. Markula (Ed.), *Olympic women and the media: International perspectives* (pp. 112–31). Basingstoke: Palgrave Macmillan.

Hollands, R. (1985). *Working for the best ethnography*. Birmingham: Centre for Contemporary Cultural Studies.

Holman-Jones, S. (2005). 'Autoethnography: Making the personal political'. In N. K. Denzin & Y. S. Lincoln, Y. (Eds), *The Sage handbook of qualitative research* (3rd edn) (pp. 763–92). Thousand Oaks, CA: Sage

Holstein, J. A. & Gubrium, J. F. (2005). 'Interpretive practice and social action'. In N. K. Denzin & Y. S. Lincoln (Eds), *The Sage handbook of qualitative research* (3rd edn) (pp. 483–506). Thousand Oaks, CA: Sage.

Hopper, T. F., Medhill, L. E., Bratseth, D. D., Cameron, K. A., Coble, J. D. & Nimmon, L. E. (2008). 'Multiple voices in health, sport, recreation, and physical education research: Revealing unfamiliar spaces in a polyvocal review of qualitative research genres'. *Quest*, 60, 214–35.

House, E. (2006). 'Methodological fundamentalism and the quest for control(s)'. In N. K. Denzin & M. Giardina (Eds), *Qualitative Inquiry and the Conservative Challenge*. Walnut Creek, CA: Left Coast Press.

House, E. R. (2005). 'Qualitative evaluation and changing social policy'. In N. K. Denzin & Y. S. Lincoln (Eds), *The Sage handbook of qualitative research* (3rd edn) (pp. 1069–82). Thousand Oaks, CA: Sage.

Howe, P. D. (2001). 'An ethnography of pain and injury in professional rugby union: The case of Pontypridd RFC'. *International Review for the Sociology of Sport*, 6, 289–303.

Husserl, E. (1965). *Phenomenology and the crisis in philosophy*. New York: Harper & Row.

Husserl, E. (1931). *My ideas pertaining to a pure phenomenology and to a phenomenological philosophy*. New York: Collier Books.

Ingham, A. G. (1997). 'Toward a department of physical cultural studies and an end to tribal Warfare'. In J. Fernandez-Balboa (Ed.), *Critical postmodernism in human movement, physical education, and sport* (pp. 157–82). Albany: State University of New York Press.

Ingham, A. G. (2004). 'The sportification process: A biographical analysis framed by the work of Marx, Weber, Durkheim and Freud. In R. Giulianotti (Ed.), *Sport and modern social theorists* (p. 11–32). Basingstoke: Palgrave Macmillan.

Inglis, D. (2004). '*Theodor Adorno on sport: The jeu d'espirit of despair*'. In R. Giulianotti (Ed.), *Sport and modern social theorists* (pp. 81–96). Basingstoke: Palgrave Macmillan.

James, A., Hockey, J. & Dawson, A. (1997). *After writing culture: Epistemology and praxis in contemporary anthropology*. London, UK: Routledge.

Jameson, F. (1983). 'Postmodernism and consumer society'. In H. Foster (Ed.), *Antiaesthetic: Essays on postmodern culture* (pp. 111–25). Post Townsend, WA: Bay.

Johnson, R., Chambers, D., Raghuram, P. & Tincknell, E. (2004). *The practice of cultural studies*. London: Sage.

Jones, R. L., Glintmeyer, N. & McKenzie, A. (2005). 'Slim bodies, eating disorders and the coach-athlete relationship: A tale of identity creation and disruption'. *International Review for the Sociology of Sport*, 40, 377–91.

Jones, R. (2000). 'Dilemmas, maintaining "face", and paranoia: An average coaching life'. *Qualitative Inquiry*, 12, 1012–21.

Kamberlies, G. & Dimitriadis, G. (2005). 'Focus groups: Strategic articulations of pedagogy, politics and inquiry'. In N. K. Denzin & Y. S. Lincoln (Eds), *The Sage handbook of qualitative research* (3rd edn) (pp. 887–908). Thousand Oaks, CA: Sage.

Keller, C., Fleury, J., Perez, A., Ainsworth, B. & Vaughan, L. (2008). 'Using visual methods to uncover context'. *Qualitative Health Research*, 18, 428–36.

Kemmis, S. & McTaggart, R. (2005). 'Participatory action research: Communicative action and the public sphere'. In N. K. Denzin & Y. S. Lincoln (Eds), *The Sage handbook of qualitative research* (3rd edn) (pp. 559–604). Thousand Oaks CA: Sage.

Kerry, D. S. & Armour, K. M. (2000). 'Sports sciences and the promise of phenomenology: Philosophy, method, and insight'. *Quest*, 52, 1–17.

Kikl, L. A., Richardson, T. & Campisi, C. (2008). 'Toward a grounded theory of student-athlete suffering and dealing with academic corruption'. *Journal of Sport Management*, 22, 273–302.

Kihl, L. A. & Richardson, T. (2009). '"Fixing the mess": A grounded theory of a men's basketball coaching staff's suffering as a result of academic corruption'. *Journal of Sport Management*, 23, 278–304.

King, S. J. (2006). *Pink Ribbons, Inc.: Breast cancer and the politics of philanthropy*. University of Minnesota Press.

King, S. J. (2005). 'Methodological contingencies in sports studies'. In D. L. Andrews, D. S. Mason & M. L. Silk (Eds), *Qualitative methods in sports studies* (pp. 21–38). New York: Berg.

Kirk, D. (2006). 'Sport education, critical pedagogy, and learning theory: Toward an intrinsic justification for physical education and youth sport'. *Quest*, 58, 255–64.

Kohn, N. & Sydnor, S. (1998). 'How do you warm-up for a stretch class?' Sub/om/di/verting hegemonic shoves toward sport'. In G. Rail (Ed.), *Sport and postmodern times* (pp. 21–32). Albany, NY: SUNY Press.

Klein, A. M. (1997). *Baseball and the border: A tale of two laredos*. Princeton, NJ: Princeton University Press.

Klein, A. M. (1993). *Little big men: Bodybuilding subculture and gender construction*. Albany, NY: SUNY Press.

Krizek, R. (1998). 'Lessons: What the hell are we teaching the next generation anyway?' In A. Banks & S. Banks (Eds), *Fiction and social research* (pp 89–113). London: Altamira Press.

Kuhn, T. (1970). *The structure of scientific revolutions* (2nd edn). Chicago, Il: University of Chicago Press.

Kvale, S. (1996). *InterViews: An introduction to qualitative research interviewing*. London: Sage.

Kvale, S. (1992). 'Postmodern psychology: A contradiction in terms?' In S. Kvale (Ed.), *Psychology and postmodernism* (pp. 31–57). London: Sage.

Kvale, S. & Brinkmann, S. (2007). *Interviews: Learning the craft of qualitative research interviewing*. London: Sage.

Lather, P. (2006). 'This is your father's paradigm: Government intrusion and the case of qualitative research in education'. In N. K. Denzin & M. Giardina, M. (Eds), *Qualitative Inquiry and the Conservative Challenge*

Lather, P. A. (1995). 'The validity of angels: Interpretive and textual strategies in researching the lives of women with HIV/AIDS'. *Qualitative Inquiry*, 1, 41–68.

Lather, P. A. (1992). 'Postmodernism and the human sciences;. In S. Kvale (Ed.), *Psychology and postmodernism* (pp. 88–109). London: Sage.

Lee, L., Avis, M. & Arthur, A. (2007). 'The role of self-efficacy in older people's decisions to initiate and maintain regular walking as exercise: Results from a qualitative study'. *Preventative Medicine*, 45, 1, 62–5.

Leeuwen, T. & Jewitt, C. (2001). *Handbook of visual analysis*. Thousand Oaks, CA: Sage.

Lenskyj, H. J. (2000). *Inside the Olympic industry*. Albany, NY: SUNY Press.

Lewis, J. (1997). 'What counts in cultural studies'. *Media, Culture & Society*, 19, 83–97.

Liao, L. & Markula, P. (2009). 'Reading media texts in women's sport: Critical discourse analysis and Foucauldian discourse analysis'. In P. Markula (Ed.), *Olympic women and the media: International perspectives* (pp. 87–111). Basingstoke: Palgrave Macmillan

Lincoln, Y. S. (2005). 'Institutional review boards and methodological conservatism: The challenge to and from phenomenological paradigms'. In N. K. Denzin & Y. S. Lincoln (Eds), *The Sage handbook of qualitative research* (3rd edn) (pp. 165–82). Thousand Oaks, CA: Sage.

Lincoln, Y. S. (1995). 'Emerging criteria for quality in qualitative and interpretive research'. *Qualitative Inquiry*, 1, 275–89.

Lincoln, Y. S. & Denzin, N. K. (2005). 'Epilogue: The eighth and ninth moments – Qualitative research in/and the fractured future'. In N. K. Denzin & Y. S. Lincoln (Eds), *The Sage handbook of qualitative research* (3rd edn) (pp. 1115–26). Thousand Oaks, CA: Sage

Lincoln, Y. S. & Guba, E. G. (2000). 'Paradigmatic controversies, contradictions, and emerging confluences'. In N. K. Denzin & Y. S. Lincoln (Eds), *The Sage handbook of qualitative research* (2nd edn) (pp. 163–88). Thousand Oaks, CA: Sage.

Lincoln, Y. S. & Guba, E. G. (1985). *Naturalistic inquiry*. Beverly Hills, CA: Sage.

Lowes, R. (2002). *Indy dreams and urban nightmares: Speed merchants, spectacle, and the struggle over public space in the world-class city*. Toronto: University of Toronto Press.

Lynn, S. K. & Mays Woods, A. (2010). 'Following the yellow brick road: A teacher's journey along the proverbial career path'. *Journal of Teaching Physical Education*, 29, 54–71.

Lyotard, J.-F. (1989). 'Rules and paradoxes and svelte appendix'. *Cultural Critique*, 5, 209–19.

Madison, D. S. (2005). *Critical ethnography: Method, ethics, and performance*. Thousand Oaks, CA: Sage.

Madiz, M. (2000). 'Focus groups in feminist research'. In N. K. Denzin & Y. S. Lincoln (Eds), *The Sage Handbook of Qualitative Research* (2nd edn). Thousand Oaks, CA: Sage.

Makagen, D. & Neumann, M. (2009). *Recording culture: Audi-documentary and the ethnographic experience*. Thousand Oaks, CA: Sage.

Manning, K. (1997). 'Authenticity in constructivist inquiry: Methodological considerations without prescription'. *Qualitative Inquiry*, 3, 1, 93–115.

Markula, P. (2011). 'Dancing the "data": (Im)mobile bodies'. *International Review of Qualitative Research*, 4, 35–50.

Markula, P. (2009). '"Acceptable bodies": Deconstructing the Finnish media coverage of the 2004 Olympic Games'. In P. Markula (Ed.), *Olympic women and the media: International perspectives* (pp. 87–111). Basingstoke: Palgrave Macmillan.

Markula, P. (2006a). 'Deleuze and the body without organs: Disreading the fit feminine identity'. *Journal of Sport & Social Issues*, 30, 29–44.

Markula, P. (2006b). 'The dancing body without organs: Deleuze, femininity and performing research'. *Qualitative Inquiry*, 12, 3–27.

Markula, P. (2004). '"Tuning into one's self": Foucault's technologies of the self and mindful fitness'. *Sociology of Sport Journal*, 21, 302–21.

Markula, P. (2003). 'Postmodern aerobics: Contradictions and resistance'. In A. Bolin & J. Granskog (Eds), *Athletic intruders: Ethnographic research on women, culture, and exercise* (pp. 53–78) Newbury Park, CA: Sage.

Markula, P. (1995). 'Firm but shapely, fit but sexy, strong but thin: The postmodern aerobicizing female bodies'. *Sociology of Sport Journal*, 12, 424–53.

Markula, P. & Pringle, R. (2006). *Foucault, sport and exercise: power, knowledge and transforming the self*. London: Routledge.

Markula, P. & Denison, J. (2005). 'Sport and the personal narrative'. In D. L. Andrews, D. Mason & M. Silk (Eds), *Qualitative research in sports studies* (pp. 165–84). Oxford: Berg.

Markula, P. & Friend, L. A. (2005). 'Remember when … Memory-work as an interpretive methodology for sport management'. *Journal of Sport Management*, 19, 442–63.

Markula, P., Grant, B. C. & Denison, J. (2001). 'Qualitative research and aging and physical activity: Multiple ways of knowing'. *Journal of Aging and Physical Activity*, 9, 245–64.

Marx, K. (1967). *Capital (vol. 1)*. New York: International Publishers.

Maykut, P. & Moorehouse, R. (2000). *Beginning qualitative research: A philosophic and practical guide*. London: Routledge.

McDonald, M. G. (2008). 'Rethinking resistance: The queer play of the Women's National Basketball Association, visibility politics and late capitalism'. *Leisure Studies*, 27, 77–93.

McDonald, M. & Birrell, S. (1999). 'Reading sport critically: A method for interrogating power'. *Sociology of Sport Journal*, 16, 283–300.

McHugh, T.-L. & Kowalski, K. C., (in press). '"A new view of body image": A school-based participatory action research project with young Aboriginal women'. *Action Research*.

McNamee, M., Olivier, S. & Wainwright, P. (2007). *Research ethics in exercise, health and sport sciences*. London: Routledge.

MacNeill, M. (1996). 'Networks: Producing Olympic ice hockey for a national television audience'. *Sociology of Sport Journal*, 13, 103–24.

Merleau-Ponty, M. (1962). *Phenomenology of perception*. London: Routledge.

Miller, T. (2001). 'What it is and what it isn't: Introducing cultural studies'. In T. Miller (Ed.), *A Companion to Cultural Studies* (pp. 1–19). Oxford: Blackwell.

Mills, S. (2004). *Discourse*. London: Routledge.

Misener, K. & Doherty, A. (2009). 'A case study of organizational capacity in nonprofit community'. *Journal of Sport Management*, 23, 457–82.

Morgan, W. (2004). 'Habermas on sports: Social theory from a moral perspective'. In R. Giulianotti (Ed.), *Sport and modern social theorists* (pp. 173–86). Basingstoke: Palgrave Macmillan.

Morse, J. (2006). 'The politics of evidence'. In N. K. Denzin & M. Giardina (Eds), *Qualitative inquiry and the conservative challenge*.

Morse, J. M., Barrett, M., Mayan, M., Olson, K. & Spiers, J. (2002). 'Verification strategies for establishing reliability and validity in qualitative research'. *International Journal of Qualitative Methods*, 1(2), 1–19.

Newman, J. I. (In Press). '[Un]Comfortable in my own skin: On articulation, reflexivity, and the duality of the self'. *International Review for Qualitative Research*.

Newman, J. I. (2010). *Embodying Dixie: Studies in the performative pedagogies of Southern Whiteness*. New York: Common Ground Press.

Newman, J. L. & Beissel, A. S. (2009). 'The limits to "NASCAR nation": Sport and the "recovery movement" in disjunctural times'. *Sociology of Sport Journal*, 26, 517–39.

Newman, J. (2007). 'Army of whiteness: Colonel Reb and the sporting south's cultural and corporate symbolic'. *Journal of Sport & Social Issues*, 31, 315–39.

Nicholls, A., Holt, N. L. & Polman, R. C. J. (2005). 'A phenomenological analysis of coping effectiveness in golf'. *The Sport Psychologist*, 19, 111–30.

Onyx, J. & Small, J. (2001). 'Memory-work: The method'. *Qualitative Inquiry*, 7, 773–86.

Park, P. (1993). 'What is participatory research? A theoretical and methodological perspective'. In P. Park, M. Miller-Brydon, B. Hall & T. Jackson (Eds), *Voices of change: participatory research in the United States and Canada* (pp. 1–19). London: Bergin & Garvey.

Patton, M. Q. (2002). *Qualitative research & evaluative methods* (3rd edn). Thousand Oaks, CA: Sage.

Phillips, L. & Jørgensen, M. W. (2002). *Discourse analysis as theory and method*. London: Sage.

Phoenix, C. & Sparkes, A. C. (2007). 'Sporting bodies, ageing, narrative mapping and young team athletes: An analysis of possible selves'. *Sport, Education and Society*, 12, 1–17.

Pink, S. (2001). *Doing visual anthropology*. London: Sage.

Plummer, K. (2005). 'Critical humanism and queer theory: Living with tensions'. In N. K. Denzin & Y. S. Lincoln (Eds), *The Sage handbook of qualitative research* (3rd edn) (pp. 357–74). Thousand Oaks, CA: Sage.

Plymire, D. (2005). 'Qualitative methods in sport-media studies'. In D. L. Andrews, D. Mason, & M. Silk (Eds), *Qualitative methods in sports studies* (pp. 139–64). Oxford: Berg.

Polkinghorn, D. (1995). 'Narrative configuration in qualitative analysis'. In A. Hatch & R. Wisniewski (Eds), *Life history and narrative* (pp. 5–24). London: Falmer.

Polkinghorne, D. E. (2007). 'Validity issues in narrative research'. *Qualitative Inquiry*, 13, 471–86.

Potter, J. & Hepburn, A. (2005). 'Qualitative interviews in psychology: Problems and possibilities'. *Qualitative Research in Psychology*, 2, 281–307.

Pringle, R. & Markula, P. (2005). 'No pain is sane after all: A Foucauldian analysis of masculinities and men's experiences in rugby'. *Sociology of Sport Journal*, 22, 472–97.

Prosser, J. (1998). *Image-based research: A sourcebook for qualitative researchers*. Bristol, PA: Farmer.

Rail, G. (1998). *Sport and postmodern times*. Albany, NY: SUNY Press.

Reason, P. & Bradbury, H. (2001). *Handbook of action research: Participative inquiry and practice*. London: Sage.

Reid, C. (2000). 'Seduction and enlightenment in feminist action research'. *Resources for Feminist Research*, 28, 169–88.

Richards, T. & Richards, L. (1998). 'Using computers in qualitative research'. In N. K. Denzin & Y. S. Lincoln (Eds), *Collecting and interpreting qualitative materials*. Thousand Oaks, California: Sage.

Richardson, L. (2000a). 'Writing: A method of inquiry'. In N. K. Denzin & Y. S. Lincoln (Eds), *The Sage handbook of qualitative research* (2nd edn) (pp. 923–48). Thousand Oaks, CA: Sage.

Richardson, L. (2000b). 'New writing practices in qualitative research'. *Sociology of Sport Journal*, 17, 5–20.

Richardson, L. & St. Pierre (2005). 'Writing: A method of inquiry'. In N. K. Denzin & Y. S. Lincoln (Eds), *The Sage handbook of qualitative research* (3rd edn) (pp. 959–78). Thousand Oaks, CA: Sage.

Ricoeur, P. (1991). 'On interpretation'. In J. M. Edie (Ed.), *From text to action: Essays in hermeneutics* (pp. 1–20). Evanston, IL: Northwestern University Press.

Riffe, D., Lacy, S. & Fico, F. G. (1998). *Analyzing media messages: Using quantitative content analysis in research*. Mahwah, NJ: Lawrence Erlbaum Associates.

Rigauer, B. (2000). 'Marxist theories'. In J. Coakley & E. Dunning (Eds), *Handbook of sport studies* (pp. 27–47). London: Sage.

Riley, S., Burns, M., Frith, H., Wiggins, S. & Markula, P. (2008). *Critical bodies: Representations, identities and practices of weight and body management*. Basingstoke: Palgrave Macmillan.

Rinehart, R. (1998). 'Sk8ting: "Outsider" sports, at-risk youth, and physical education. *Waikato Journal of Education*, 6, 55–63.

Rinehart, R. & Grenfell, C. (2002). 'BMX Spaces: Children's grass roots' courses and corporate-sponsored tracks'. *Sociology of Sport Journal*, 19, 302–14.

Ristock, J. & Pennell, J. (1996). *Community research as empowerment: Feminist links, postmodern interruptions*. Toronto, ON: Oxford University Press.

Ritchie, J. & Spencer, E. (1994). 'Qualitative data analysis for applied policy research'. In A. Bryman & R. G. Burgess (Eds), *Analyzing qualitative data*. London: Routledge.

Rojek, C. (1995). *Decentring leisure: Rethinking leisure theory*. London: Sage.

Rowe, D. (2004). 'Antonio Gramsci: Sport, hegemony and the national-popular'. In R. Giulianotti (Ed.), *Sport and modern social theorists* (pp. 173–86). Basingstoke: Palgrave Macmillan.

Rowe, D. (2004). *Sport, culture and the media* (2nd edn). Berkshire, UK: Open University Press.

Rowe, D. (2000). 'Amour improper, or "fever" sans reflexivity'. *Sociology of Sport Journal*, 17, 95–7.

Ryan, G. & Bernard. R. (2000). 'Data management and analysis methods'. In N. K. Denzin & Y. S. Lincoln (Eds), *The Sage handbook of qualitative research* (2nd edn) (pp. 769–802). Thousand Oaks, CA: Sage.

Ryba, T. V. (2008). 'Researching children in sport: Methodological reflections'. *Journal of Applied Sport Psychology*, 20, 334–48.

Schutz, A. (1970). *On phenomenology and social relations*. Chicago: Chicago University Press.

Seale, C. (1999). *The quality of qualitative research*. London: Sage.

Shavelson, R. J., Hubner, J. J. & Stanton, G. C. (1976). 'Self-concept: Validation of construct interpretations'. *Review of Educational Research*, 46, 407–41.

Schwandt, T. (2000). 'Three epistemological stances for qualitative inquiry: Interpretivism, hermeneutics, and social constructionism'. In N. K. Denzin & Y. S. Lincoln (Eds), *The Sage handbook of qualitative research* (2nd edn) (pp. 189–214). Thousand Oaks, CA: Sage.

Shaw, S. & Amis, J. (2001). 'Image and investment: Sponsorship and women's sport. *Journal of Sport Management*, 15, 219–46

Silk, M. (2008). 'Mow my lawn'. *Cultural Studies* ↔ *Critical Methodologies*, 8, 477–8.

Silk, M. (2005). 'Sporting ethnography: Philosophy, methodology & reflection'. In D. L. Andrews, D. Mason & M. Silk (Eds), *Qualitative methods in sports studies* (pp. 65–103). Berg: Oxford.

Silk, M. (2002). 'Bangsa Malaysia: Global sport, the city & the refurbishment of local identities'. *Media, Culture & Society*, 24, 775–94.

Silk, M. (2001). 'The Conditions of practice: Television production practices at Kuala Lumpur 98'. *Sociology of Sport Journal*, 18, 277–301.

Silk, M., Bush, A. & Andrews, D. (2010). 'Contingent intellectual amateurism; or, what is wrong with evidence-based research'. *Journal of Sport & Social Issues*, 34, 105–28.

Silk, M. & Falcous, M. (2010). 'Sporting spectacle and the post 9-11 patriarchal body politic'. In M. Morgan (Ed.), *The day that changed everything*. New York: Palgrave MacMillan.

Silk, M., Schultz, J. & Bracey, B. (2008). 'From mice to men: Miracle, mythology & the magic kingdom'. *Sport in Society*, 11, 279–97.

Silk, M., Andrews, D. L. & Mason, D. (2005). 'Encountering the field: Sports studies and qualitative research'. In D. L. Andrews, D. Mason & M. Silk (Eds), *Qualitative research in sports studies* (pp. 1–20). Oxford: Berg.

Skille, E. (2010). 'Competitiveness and health: The work of sports clubs as seen by sports club representatives – A Norwegian case study. *International Review for the Sociology of Sport*, 45, 73–85.

Smishek, E. (2004). 'The body beautiful: Physical culture muscles its way into academic'. *UBC Reports*, 50, 9, Available at: http://www.publicaffairs.ubc.ca/ubcreports/2004/04oct07/body.html, accessed on 17 November 2005.

Smith, J. (2009). 'Judging research quality: From certainty to contingency'. *Qualitative Research in Sport and Exercise*, 1, 91–100.

Smith, J. K. & Deemer, D. K. (2000). 'The problem of criteria in the age of relativism'. In N. K. Denzin & Y. S. Lincoln (Eds), *The Sage handbook of qualitative research* (2nd edn) (pp. 877–96). Thousand Oaks, CA: Sage.

Smith, J. K. & Hodkinson, P. (2005). 'Relativism, criteria, and politics'. In N. K. Denzin & Y. S. Lincoln (Eds), *The Sage handbook of qualitative research* (3rd edn) (pp.915–32). Thousand Oaks, CA: Sage.

Smith, J. A. & Osborn, M. (2003). 'Interpretative phenomenological analysis'. In J. A. Smith (Ed.), *Qualitative psychology: A practical guide to research methods* (pp. 51–80). London: Sage.

Smith, L. (2000). 'Kaupapa Maori research'. In M. Battiste (Ed.), *Reclaiming indigenous voice and vision* (pp. 225–47). Vancouver: University of British Columbia Press.

Smith, B. & Sparkes, A. C. (2009a). 'Narrative inquiry in sport and exercise psychology: What can it mean, and why might we do it?' *Psychology of Sport and Exercise*, 10, 1–11.

Smith, B. & Sparkes, A. C. (2009b). 'Narrative analysis and sport and exercise psychology: Understanding lives in diverse ways'. *Psychology of Sport and Exercise*, 10, 279–88.

Smith, B. & Sparkes, A. C. (2005). 'Analyzing talk in qualitative inquiry: Exploring possibilities, problems, and tensions'. *Quest*, 37, 213–42.

Snow, D. (2002). 'On the presumed crisis in ethnographic representation: Observations from a sociological and interactionist standpoint'. *Journal of Contemporary Ethnography*, 31, 498–507.

Sparkes, A. C. (2002). *Telling tales in sport and physical activity: A qualitative journey*. Champaign, IL: Human Kinetics.

Sparkes, A. C. (2001). 'Myth 94: Qualitative health researchers will agree about validity'. *Qualitative Health Research*, 11, 538–52.

Sparkes, A. C. (1999). 'Exploring body narratives'. *Sport, Education and Society*, 4, 17–30.

Sparkes, A.C. (1996). 'The fatal flaw: A narrative of the fragile body-self'. *Qualitative Inquiry*, 2, 463–94.

Sparkes, A. C. (1995). 'Writing people: Reflections on the dual crises of representation & legitimation in qualitative inquiry'. *Quest*, 45, 188–95.

Spencer, N. E. (2004). 'Sister act IV: Venus and Serena Williams at Indian Wells: "Sincere fictions" and white racism'. *Journal of Sport and Social Issues*, 28, 115–35.

Spielvogel, L. (2003). *Working out in Japan: Shaping the female body in Tokyo fitness clubs*. Durham: Duke University Press.

Spry, T. (2001). 'Performing autoethnography: An embodied methodological praxis'. *Qualitative Inquiry*, 7, 706–32.

Stake, R. (2005). 'Qualitative case studies'. In N. K. Denzin & Y. S. Lincoln (Eds), *The Sage handbook of qualitative research* (3rd edn) (pp. 443–66). Thousand Oaks, CA: Sage.

Stake, R. (1995). *The art of case study research*. Thousand Oaks, CA: Sage.
Stevenson, D. (2002). 'Women, sport and globalization: Competing discourses of sexuality and nation'. *Journal of Sport and Social Issues*, 26, 209–25.
Stroh, M. (2000). 'Qualitative interviewing'. In D. Burton (Ed.), *Research training for social sciences: A handbook for postgraduate students*. London: Sage
Tedlock, B. (2005). 'The Observation of participation and the emergence of public ethnography'. In N. K. Denzin & Y. S. Lincoln (Eds), *The Sage handbook of qualitative research* (3rd edn) (pp. 467–82). Thousand Oaks, CA: Sage.
Tedlock, B. (2000). Ethnography and ethnographic representation. In N. K. Denzin, & Y. S. Lincoln (Eds), *The Sage handbook of qualitative research* (2nd edn) (pp. 455–86). Thousand Oaks, CA: Sage.
Thorpe, H. (2008). 'Foucault, technologies of the self, and the media. Discourses of femininity in snowboarding culture'. *Journal of Sport and Social Issues*, 32, 199–229.
Tiihonen, A. (1994). 'Asthma'. *International Review for Sociology of Sport*, 29, 51–62.
Tilley, S. & Gormley, L. (2007). 'Canadian university ethics review: Cultural complications translating principles into practice'. *Qualitative Inquiry*, 13, 368–87.
Tinning, R. (2004). 'Conclusion: Rumination son body knowledge and controls and the spaces of hope and happening'. In J. Evans, B. Davies & J. Wright (Eds), *Body knowledge and control: Studies in the sociology of physical education and health* (pp. 218–38). London: Routledge.
Tinning, R. (2002). 'Toward "modest pedagogy": Reflections or the problematics of critical pedagogy'. *Quest*, 54, 224–40.
Tsang, T. (2000). 'Let me tell you a story: A narrative exploration of identity in high performance'. *Sociology of Sport Journal*, 17, 44–59.
Van Manen, M. (1990). *Researching lived experience – Human science for an action sensitive pedagogy*. Ontario: The University of Western Ontario.
VanWynsberhe, R. & Khan, S. (2007). 'Redefining case study'. *International Journal of Qualitative Methods*, 6, 2, 1–10.
Wang, C. C. & Redwood-Jones, Y. A. (2001). 'Photovoice ethics: Perspectives from flint photovoice. *Health Education & Behavior*, 28, 560–72.
Wagner, J. (2004). 'Constructing credible images: Documentary studies, social research, and visual studies'. *The American Behavioral Scientist*, 47, 1477–506.
Warriner, K. & Lavallee, D. (2008). 'The retirement experiences of elite female gymnasts: Self -identity and the physical self'. *Journal of Applied Sport Psychology*, 20, 301–17.
Weber, M. (1968). *Economy and society: An outline of interpretive sociology*. New York: Bedminster Press.
Weedon, C. (1987). *Feminist practice and poststructuralist theory*. Oxford: Basin Blackwell.
Whannel, G. (2001). *Media sports stars: Moralities & masculinities*. London: Routledge.
Wheatley, L. (2005). 'Disciplining bodies at risk: Cardiac rehabilitation and the medicalization of fitness'. *Journal of Sport & Social Issues*, 29, 198–221.
Wheaton, B. (2000). '"Just do it": Consumption, commitment, and identity in the windsurfing subculture'. *Sociology of Sport Journal*, 17, 254–74.
Whittemore, R., Chase, S. K. & Mandle, C. L. (2001). 'Validity in qualitative research'. *Qualitative Heath Research*, 11, 522–37.

Wiggins, S. (2009). 'Managing blame in NHS weight management treatment: Psychologizing weight and "obesity"'. *Journal of Community and Applied Social Psychology*, 19, 374–87.

Willig, C. (2001). *Introducing qualitative research in psychology: Adventures in theory and method*. Philadephia, PA: Open University Press.

Wimmer, R. D. & Dominick, J. R. (2003). *Mass media research: An introduction* (7th edn). Belmont, CA: Wadsworth/Thomson Learning.

Winter, R. (2002). *A handbook for action research in health and social care*. London: Routledge.

Wolcott, H. F. (1994). *Transforming qualitative data: Description, analysis and interpretation*. Thousand Oaks, CA: Sage.

Woodward, K. (2004). 'Rumbles in the jungle: Boxing, racialization and the performance of masculinity'. *Journal of Leisure Studies*, 23, 5–17.

Wright, H. K. (2001). '"What's going on?" Larry Grossberg on the status quo of Cultural Studies: An interview'. *Cultural Values*, 5, 2, 133–62.

Yin, R. K. (2003). *Case study research: Design and methods* (3rd edn). Thousand Oaks, CA: Sage.

Young, I. M. (1980). 'Throwing like a girl: A phenomenology of feminine body comportment motility and spatiality', 3, 137–56.

Index

CPSIA information can be obtained
at www.ICGtesting.com
Printed in the USA
FFHW01n1302300818
48184227-51904FF

9 780230 230248